Malcolm X

Rhetoric and Public Affairs Series

Malcolm X

Inventing Radical Judgment

◇ ◇ ◇ ◇ ◇

Robert E. Terrill

Michigan State University Press
East Lansing

Copyright © 2004 by Robert E. Terrill
1st paperback printing 2007

∞ The paper used in this publication meets the minimum requirements of
ANSI/NISO Z39.48–1992 (R 1997) (Permanence of Paper).

Michigan State University Press
East Lansing, Michigan 48823-5245

Printed and bound in the United States of America.

13 12 11 10 09 08 07   1 2 3 4 5 6 7 8 9 10

LIBRARY OF CONGRESS CATALOGING-IN-PUBLICATION DATA

First Paperback Edition 978-0-87013-803-4 issued by MSU Press 2007.
The following cataloging data was provided for the original hardcover edition
0-87013-730-1.

Terrill, Robert.
    Malcolm X : inventing radical judgment / Robert E. Terrill.
        p. cm.—(Rhetoric and public affairs series)
    Includes bibliographical references and index.
    ISBN 0-87013-730-1 (alk. paper)
    1. X, Malcolm, 1925–1965. 2. African American Muslims--Biography.
I. Title. II. Series.
    BP223.Z8L5778 2004
    320.54′6′092—dc22   2004012334

Michigan State University Press is a member of the Green Press Initiative and is
committed to developing and encouraging ecologically responsible publishing
practices. For more information about the Green Press Initiative and the use of recycled paper in book publishing, please visit www.greenpressinitiative.org.

Book and cover design by Sans Serif, Inc.
Cover photo of Malcolm X: Library of Congress, Prints and Photographs Division,
[LC-U9–11695-frame #5].

Visit Michigan State University Press on the World Wide Web at:
www.msupress.msu.edu

Contents

Preface

Ifirst met Malcolm X as an undergraduate at San Jose State University. It was 1984, and I was a white kid from the suburbs. I did not know much about black culture in general, and I did not know anything about Malcolm in particular. I was an English major, preparing to become a high school teacher, and Nettye Goddard was guiding me patiently through an independent study course in African American literature. She suggested that I read *The Autobiography of Malcolm X*. Like so many readers before and since, I was awed by Malcolm's audacious honesty and captivated by the book's mythic sweep. Years later, as a first-year graduate student in Thomas Rosteck's rhetorical criticism course at the University of Arkansas, I was casting about for a topic, and across five years of teaching teenagers grammar and algebra I recalled my interest in Malcolm. I had never read any of his speeches; not knowing any better, I chose to analyze "The Ballot or the Bullet," perhaps his most complex oration.

I have been reading that speech for a decade now, and I feel I am only just beginning to understand it. But what I did begin to understand then was that Malcolm seemed to have an almost preternatural faith in the power of words. He understood that those who control the terms through which the world is known control the world, that those who control the language through which you describe yourself retain control over you, and that the best hope for empowerment is to learn to read this linguistic fashioning. My journey through graduate school, and much of my academic work since, was driven by following up leads suggested by reading and rereading Malcolm's speeches. In the developmental arc of his oratory, I can see an echo of the history of the development of rhetoric itself as the mythic world of ancient Greece was challenged by the rising need for public discourse to effect political judgment based on the analysis of contingency rather than certitude in precepts. Malcolm's discourse also echoes the age-old conflict between rhetoric and philosophy, between the need to make an immediate case to an audience required to act and the relatively detached quest for transcendent truth. But mostly I have come to see in Malcolm's best speeches a continuing effort to foster strategies of thinking and acting that might make his audiences better able to face the difficulties of life in modern times. This book is an attempt to make these strategies of thinking and acting available to others.

In the first chapter, I argue for the importance of the close study of Malcolm's speeches. He was many things—a leader, a visionary, a commanding and inventive intellect—but first and foremost he was an orator. While Malcolm X has been the focus of a good deal of academic attention, I argue that these assessments have missed what I take to be the most important aspect of his legacy: Malcolm's rhetoric demonstrates strategies of judgment and critique. I position myself within the ongoing discussion that constitutes what might be called "Malcolm studies," and argue that witnessing this species of rhetorical judgment requires attending carefully to Malcolm's medium, his oratory.

Malcolm often disavowed affiliation, especially during his tumultuous final year, after he left the Nation of Islam. But as a rhetorician, it was impossible for him to ignore the norms and expectations of his audience. These had been shaped by centuries of African American protest, and Chapter 2 establishes a continuum of this discourse through close readings of four representative texts. My intention is not to place Malcolm X within a historical tradition but rather to establish a rhetorical landscape against which both his discourse while he was a minister in the Nation of Islam and his discourse after he left the Nation can be brought into sharper relief. This chapter describes some of the norms and expectations of the rhetorical culture that Malcolm addressed, attending especially to the strategies of reading and interpretation that are associated with a discourse of prophecy.

In Chapter 3, I argue that these resources of prophetic speech become available to Malcolm X through two conduits: Marcus Garvey's Universal Negro Improvement Association and Noble Drew Ali's Moorish Science Temple movement. Garvey's influence on the Nation of Islam was the source for much of the Nation's "self-help" philosophy as well as, more importantly, the persistent quest of the Nation of Islam to locate an authentic black identity in the distant past. Noble Drew Ali brought into the Nation an embryonic form of esoteric Islam and a promise that someday America's race problem would be solved through divine intervention. I then turn to two speeches delivered by Malcolm while a minister in the Nation of Islam, one delivered to the faithful inside the mosque and the other delivered to the "devil" on a predominantly white college campus. In both cases, when Malcolm addressed audiences as a Black Muslim minister, he presented them with a codified set of revealed truths. Religion and history were fused into a fearful symmetry, and possibilities for human agency were severely limited. The modes of interpretation available within such a system were restricted to witnessing signs of Elijah Muhammad's eminent divinity and of Allah's inevitable intervention.

When Malcolm X left the Nation of Islam, the structuring worldview that had guided his discourse up to that time was unavailable, and he had to refashion his public self. In response, he invented the emancipatory rhetoric that is his most significant innovation. In Chapter 4, I illustrate some of the distinguishing features of this rhetoric through close analyses of key texts, including "The Ballot or the Bullet" and "Letter from Mecca." In stark contrast to Malcolm's Black Muslim discourse, this is a rhetoric of expanding horizons and outrageous possibilities. He does not ask his audiences to mine the distant past—neither a historical past nor a religious one—for stable and authentic identities, but instead encourages them to see themselves from multiple perspectives in the present. This interpretive stance is characterized by situational judgment and radical critique. Though I assemble my analyses in this chapter in chronological order, I argue that Malcolm's addresses should not be understood as merely marking out a development trajectory but instead as components within a dynamic rhetorical practice.

Chapter 5, my concluding chapter, is an assessment of this rhetorical practice. While presenting tremendous libratory potential, Malcolm's rhetoric also exhibits limitations. The histories of the two organizations that he founded in his last year, the Organization for Afro-American Unity (OAAU) and the Muslim Mosque, Inc. (MMI), illustrate in their anemic instability the most telling of these limitations—the shifting perspectives and emphasis on critique that characterize Malcolm's rhetoric make it unsuitable as the basis for robust collective groups. But the value of Malcolm's rhetoric is not in the organizations that it might sustain but in the models of interpretation and judgment that it presents. In assessing these models, I am careful not to attempt to do so from within the confines of a single, integrated theoretical schema. This would be anathema to Malcolm's rhetorical project and would attempt to inscribe upon his discourse a version of the controlling stability that he works to escape. Instead, I approach his rhetoric from three unrelated theoretical perspectives, each one acknowledged to offer only a partial account. These approaches do not cohere into a single analytical lens but instead emphasize different significant characteristics of the rhetorical practice in which Malcolm would have his audiences engage.

The structure of this book is partly chronological, in that I begin in the distant past with nineteenth-century texts, then discuss Marcus Garvey

and Noble Drew Ali from the early twentieth century, and finally follow
Malcolm X from his beginnings as a minister for the Nation of Islam and
through his remarkable final year. From this perspective, a coherent historical narrative undergirds the textual analyses, and the last four chapters of
the book exhibit a linear form: Chapters 2 and 3 provide background for
the emancipatory rhetoric described in Chapters 4 and 5. But my materials
and arguments also are arranged thematically, so that I discuss African
American prophetic rhetoric along an ahistorical continuum, often moving
forward and backward in time as I read Malcolm's speeches, and I finish by
arguing that a historical trajectory is not the most valuable framework
through which to understand the rhetoric of Malcolm's last year. From this
perspective, the book exhibits a symmetrical structure: Chapters 3 and 4
consist primarily of analyses of Malcolm's rhetoric before and after his split
with the Nation of Islam, and Chapters 2 and 5 supply the analytical categories that inform those analyses. Malcolm's rhetoric within the Nation of
Islam was largely controlled by historical norms, so I present those norms
before I analyze that discourse; Malcolm's rhetoric after the Nation of Islam
was an effort to resist those norms, so I present my analyses first and then
inductively round out some theoretical points implicit in those analyses. In
general, I use the past tense when describing historical events and the present tense when engaged in textual analysis. Some may dispute my reasoning, and some may find the tense shifts distracting, but I can think of no
other way to write about these texts that would be in agreement with my
central argument, that Malcolm X is addressing us.

Acknowledgments

My initial efforts to articulate many of the ideas in this book constituted a Ph.D. dissertation completed at Northwestern University under the direction of Michael Leff. I thank him for his patient faith that I would, eventually, come up with something interesting to say. The members of my dissertation committee, G. Thomas Goodnight and Thomas Farrell, offered a continuing willingness to ask hard questions and then help me to formulate adequate responses. Robert Ivie has been an invaluable source of advice and feedback, giving my revised manuscript a careful and insightful reading. Marty Medhurst was given every reason to pull the plug on this project after the first round of reviews, but he chose not to. The anonymous reviewers for Michigan State University Press challenged me to improve the book and provided a wealth of suggestions intended to show me how to do so. All of these scholars have contributed greatly to this work, and the finished product surely is as much theirs as it is mine—though I alone claim any of its shortcomings.

My most heartfelt gratitude, however, goes to my wife, Debbie. Without her support, wisdom, guidance, fortitude, and forbearance, this project could not have been completed. Nor could it have been begun.

1

Malcolm's Medium

◇ ◇ ◇ ◇ ◇

Malcolm X is among our most persistent cultural presences. He has inspired books, plays, raps, video documentaries, and a Spike Lee film. Posters, T-shirts, and jewelry bear his image. His autobiography is a standard entry in high school and college curriculums. And the Internet, perhaps the most reliable index of contemporary cultural consciousness, hosts thousands of pages dedicated to him.[1] Malcolm is cast forever as the threatening nightmare at the edges of Martin Luther King Jr.'s dream, so that no survey of late-twentieth-century American public culture would be complete without mentioning him. Reviled, feared, admired, and emulated both during his life and since his death, Malcolm X stands as a shining example of African American eloquence and as a resolutely insatiable call to our collective conscience.

But Malcolm X easily could be judged a failure. He never led his followers in large-scale collective political action, never organized a mass protest march, and never was associated with the passage of any piece of legislation designed to improve the condition of African Americans. None of his many admirers can point to a law that Malcolm changed, a sustainable movement that he established, or even a lunch counter that he desegregated. As Peter

Goldman puts it, Malcolm "left behind no concrete program for the deliverance of black Americans, no disciplined following to carry on for him, no organization sturdy enough to survive his death."[2] What Malcolm did do was talk, and this talk often was criticized as taking the place of real political action. The hundreds of speeches and statements and interviews and newspaper columns that Malcolm produced, a flood of words augmented by his radio and television appearances that has few rivals in either its vehemence or in its sheer volume, often was—and is—dismissed as mere verbal swagger. Charles Kenyatta, a close associate of Malcolm's, once said about him and the Nation of Islam that "they clean people up, don't drink, don't smoke, but they don't *do* anything. Don't even vote." Goldman reports that Whitney Young, head of the National Urban League, once complained that Malcolm "never got anybody a job or decent housing . . . but you could find his name in the *TV Guide* program listings more times than Johnny Carson's." And Thurgood Marshall simply dismissed Malcolm by saying, "All he did was talk."[3]

Such assessments stem from assumptions about the nature and power of rhetoric that must be modified before we can appreciate either Malcolm's eloquence or his potential contributions to contemporary public culture. If public address is considered merely a means to an end, then it is judged primarily according to its effects. When Malcolm X spoke, nothing much seemed to happen, so therefore he was a failure. But there are other standards of judgment, and these suggest other conceptions of rhetoric. As Michael Eric Dyson reminds us, "In African American cultures, acts of rhetorical resistance are often more than mere words."[4] Bayard Rustin, chief organizer of the 1963 March on Washington, has suggested that Malcolm "has to be seen over and above the pull and tug of struggle for concrete objectives. . . . King had to win victories in the real world. Malcolm's were the kind you can create yourself." Joe Wood, in his introduction to a provocative collection of essays on Malcolm X, writes that "Malcolm, in the end, gave us no coherent ideology, but he did leave us with a site for Black political discourse." And similarly, journalist A. Peter Bailey, who worked closely with Malcolm, puts it this way: "When someone asks, 'what did he leave, there are no buildings, no this, no that,' I say, 'Minds. He left minds.'"[5] These assessments do not dismiss Malcolm's words because he failed to produce quantifiable results. They point us, instead, toward an understanding of rhetoric that features its power to shape audiences and their perceptions; rhetoric, in this view, is appreciated not merely for its service to external ends but as being substantive and formative in its own right. This view understands rhetoric *as* action.

It may be useful, at times, to maintain a distinction between political actions, such as voting and marching, and rhetorical action, such as that enacted through and within Malcolm's oratory. But both should be understood as capable of effecting significant social change. Redefining the terms by which a people understand themselves and their situation and demonstrating for them the modes of judgment through which to invent emancipatory responses appropriate to those redefinitions are actions with far-reaching and radical potential. If, through his rhetoric, Malcolm X encouraged his audiences toward self-created victories, if he carved out sites where African Americans might become political actors, and if he left in his wake a new and liberated political consciousness—then he accomplished political action. But to witness action of this sort, we must attend carefully to his words.

Meeting Malcolm

The story of Malcolm's life is well known, in part because it is retold in almost every critical study. It is indeed a compelling tale, a trajectory of young promise followed by profligate waste and eventual redemption that, in its general outlines, is at least as familiar as Shakespeare's *Henry IV* or Augustine's *Confessions*. I shall retell it also, because its general outlines are essential to an understanding of Malcolm's rhetoric. My focus in this retelling, however, is not on the outline of Malcolm's life itself but rather on the common figures through which his life story is told.

Malcolm's life is most often presented, as Louis A. DeCaro Jr. puts it, as "a double-barreled conversion narrative," divided into thirds by two remarkable and parallel personal transformations.[6] In each of these, Malcolm casts off one set of beliefs or code of conduct and accepts another. The first of these transformations—Cornel West calls them "psychic conversions"—occurred in prison, when Malcolm became a member of the Nation of Islam and left behind his life of crime.[7] Rhetorical critics Celeste Condit and John Lucaites describe this as a shift in allegiance from a hustler code of behavior to a conservative and mythic one.[8] Eugene Victor Wolfenstein suggests, similarly, that in this transformation, Malcolm found "a comprehensive explanation of his situation and a transvaluation of values—an ethically rational interpretation of the world that was clearly superior to the simply rationalized nihilism of the hustling code."[9]

Malcolm was in jail when his brother Reginald first introduced him to the teachings of Elijah Muhammad; Malcolm writes in his autobiography that he was still thinking like a hustler so that his "automatic response was to think he [Reginald] had come upon some way I could work a hype on the penal authorities." Malcolm tells that his family, who had already converted, selected Reginald as their emissary because he "knew how my street-hustler mind operated," which is "why his approach was so effective." The conversion was difficult, and Malcolm explains how hard it was for him to "force" himself to bend his knees there in his jail cell and assume "the praying-to-Allah posture."[10] He persevered and, as Bruce Perry puts it, "the criminal Malcolm had become transformed into the religious Malcolm."[11] Before he found the Nation of Islam, the story goes, Malcolm X was a petty thief and Harlem hustler; after he joined the Nation of Islam, Malcolm was a minister who promised salvation for those who resembled his former self. Before the Nation of Islam, Malcolm was inarticulate and out of control; afterward, he was eloquent and almost preternaturally self-contained. Louis E. Lomax writes, "Malcolm X is the St. Paul of the Black Muslim movement. Not only was he knocked to the ground by the bright light of truth while on an evil journey, but he also rose from the dust stunned, with a new name and a burning zeal to travel in the opposite direction and carry America's twenty million Negroes with him."[12] As for Malcolm himself, he writes in his autobiography that "I do not now, and I did not then, liken myself to Paul. But I do understand his experience."[13]

The second of Malcolm's transformations, from Black Muslim to Sunni Islam, generally is set in parallel to the first.[14] This conversion is comprised of two closely related events during the last year of his life, his split from the Nation of Islam in March 1964 and his journey to Mecca in April. When Malcolm found himself being ousted from the Nation of Islam, he writes in the *Autobiography,* he "felt as though something in *nature* had failed, like the sun, or the stars."[15] But the loss of one structuring ideology was quickly repaired by adhering to another. Wolfenstein argues that when Malcolm visited Mecca, he experienced *Ihram,* the "ultimate form of Islamic group-experience" in which the "group's leader . . . is not a man but Allah himself," and "the individual is immediately identified with the abstract universal of the God-idea and the potentially concrete universal of unified humanity."[16] This may or may not be an accurate description of Malcolm's experience, but it does portray Malcolm as giving himself up to a larger truth. In the *Autobiography,* in an odd parallel to his initial suspicion that Islam was a prison-busting scam, Malcolm admits that throughout his pilgrimage he was "doing some American-type thinking" about how "with improved public relations methods the number of new converts turning to Allah could be turned into millions."[17] Before this second conversion, the story goes, Malcolm X was a fiery, racist demagogue; afterward, he was more reasoned and reasonable. Before Mecca, Malcolm X was a Black Muslim who issued a blanket condemnation of all whites and white institutions; when he returned, as El-Hajj Malik El-Shabazz, he was a Sunni Muslim who relented, somewhat, and offered whites almost a redemption. As Goldman puts it, Malcolm returned from Mecca "with his wispy beard and an astrakhan hat, both of which immediately became fashions in Harlem, and a slightly moderated view of white people, which did not."[18]

This is the tripartite narrative of the *Autobiography* and of Spike Lee's film. It fits a familiar sinner-redemption narrative structure and is partially responsible for Malcolm's continued resonance in American popular culture. It might stand as a sort of parable for the evolution and uplift of the race, which seems to have been at least partly Alex Haley's purpose in fashioning the *Autobiography*. Or it might serve as a structuring narrative to frame any number of personal challenges, as it serves Spike Lee in his story of the trials and tribulations of making his Malcolm X movie.[19] And I do not mean to suggest that this narrative is "wrong"—these things certainly happened to Malcolm, and in this order. But understanding Malcolm X only through this heroic narrative blunts an understanding of his rhetorical innovation in three ways. First, it domesticates him under various ideologies. He is portrayed as shifting his allegiances from one code to the next, inventing his own way only to the extent that he decided to which certainties to adhere. While he was a small-time hustler, Malcolm's thoughts were those of the black underworld of which he was a part; while he was a Nation of Islam minister, his ideas were those of Elijah Muhammad; when he became a Sunni Muslim, his ideas were guided by an ancient but new-found theology. This narrative, then, draws our attention away from the extent to which Malcolm, especially near the end of his life, was encouraging his audiences to resist coming under the spell of stable and collective modes of thought.

Second, this heroic narrative establishes a trajectory that shifts our attention from what Malcolm said to what Malcolm might have done. Even when the brief period between his return from Mecca and his assassination is considered as a time when Malcolm was his own man, free from the constraints of Nation of Islam doctrine, it generally is portrayed as an unfinished search for a new framework. Goldman, for example, suggests that

Malcolm was on a "quest" that "was still unfinished at his death."[20] Condit and Lucaites, also, refer to this period as a "search for a constructive rhetoric," characterized by Malcolm's efforts to find "a new path to achieving 'equality,' one that embraced neither King's nonviolent, humbling, identity-denying approach nor his own prior path toward a revised 'separate but equal' doctrine."[21] I discuss, in the final two chapters of this book, the importance of resisting this teleological urge with respect to Malcolm's rhetoric.

Finally, this heroic narrative overly isolates Malcolm X, so that his transformations and conversions seem motivated by personal matters and autonomous genius. A narrative of private evolution, in short, elides Malcolm's most fundamental identity—he was a public speaker faced with framing and responding to exigencies that transcended his personal life.

Malcolm's Words

Oratory was Malcolm's medium. He has been eulogized as "an eloquent orator and street-corner spell-binder" and "indisputably an orator of the first rank," and shortly before his death he was declared by the Oxford Union Society to be one of the greatest living orators.[22] But to say that oratory was Malcolm's medium is to say more than merely that he spoke well. For Malcolm X, the actual performance of public address was the primary process through which he made sense of the world. He did not sit down and write any systematic ideological tract, nor did he formulate any programmatic response to America's racial strife. He stood up and spoke. Even his autobiography was written by Alex Haley from extensive oral interviews.[23] As Goldman notes, Malcolm "did his cerebrating on his feet, in the heat of battle."[24] And the point can be made more forcefully yet; it is not merely that Malcolm X was eloquent or that public eloquence was his chosen instrument. Rather, for Malcolm X, public address *was* social change; his words *are* his deeds. It is through his public discourse that members of his audiences are made to see the limits imposed upon them by the dominant white culture and are shown attitudes and strategies that invite them to transgress against those limits. It is through public address that Malcolm models for his audience emancipatory modes of interpretation. It is through his discourse that he demonstrates radical judgment.

To perceive this action in Malcolm's discourse requires that we supplement a merely instrumental understanding of rhetoric. Malcolm's speeches do not encourage his listeners to engage in specific political actions. Rather, they demonstrate for his audiences ways of interpreting the world that do not *lead toward* liberation as much as they *are* a liberation; they supply a refurbished and decolonized mental attitude that frees its auditors and practitioners from the interpretive constraints of the dominant culture. When Malcolm X was a minister for the Nation of Islam, remembers Benjamin Karim, a close associate, he organized "public speaking" classes that "in fact had little to do with the techniques of preparing a speech or delivering a formal address" but instead were courses in critical reading. Malcolm's syllabi included history, geography, philosophy, and religious studies—he did not want his students merely to memorize what was there but to *re*read it, against the grain, simultaneously learning from and critiquing the materials. "Untruths had to be untold," Karim recalls Malcolm telling his students. "We had to be untaught before we could be taught, and once untaught, we ourselves could unteach others."[25] Malcolm's oratory functions similarly, schooling his audiences in potentially emancipatory strategies of critical interpretation and cultural production.

These interpretive strategies take form in Malcolm's speeches, enacted in their arrangement, their style, and sometimes in their sheer artful audacity. This is why attempts to abstract a formula or a procedure or a coherent ideology from Malcolm's rhetoric always will be frustrated; his words are not mere containers that might be emptied of their contents and then cast aside. Malcolm's message cannot be decoded by attending merely to the manifest content of his speeches and statements, for the same reason that his "success" or "failure" cannot be determined by measuring his political achievements or those of his followers. Malcolm's political action cannot be separated from his rhetoric, because the very shape of his discourse at the moment of its performance enacts the patterns of interpretation and judgment that he is encouraging in his audiences.

One way to conceptualize the process is to see that Malcolm X is schooling his audiences in a practice of *rhetorical invention*. Invention is the first of the five ancient canons of rhetoric, the others being arrangement, style, memory, and delivery. In simplest terms, of course, invention names the process through which speakers come up with things to say. There are differing theoretical approaches to this deceptively simple idea, but the most valuable with regards to Malcolm's rhetoric, and to the sort of action in which he would have his audiences engage, is an understanding of rhetorical invention as a process that weds interpretation with production. In this view, rhetoric is understood as a public art that finds its foundation in pre-Romantic notions of social knowledge rather than in modernist ideas of individual creative autonomy, so that invention always involves cultural interpretation. Producing discourse requires the critical analysis of existing discourse, for such analysis brings to light the patterns and logics through which further discourse may be produced. Rhetorical invention, by this account, is a two-sided and dynamic process in which the skills associated with interpretation and those associated with performance are recognized as insolubly interrelated, two components of a seamless process. Interpretation, developed in isolation from performance, may tack toward a closed encounter between critic and text and thus cripple invention as a social act. Performance, developed in isolation from interpretation, may tack toward an expression of autonomous creative genius and curb the potential of invention as a medium of political engagement. An understanding of rhetorical invention that brings both of these attitudes together as two elements in a single practice, however, situates invention as an essential skill for successfully negotiating public life. Malcolm's rhetoric models this sort of rhetorical invention: he would have his audiences reason and act in life as he has reasoned and acted in his speeches.[26]

Malcolm's Audience

Malcolm's audience most often is understood to consist of African Americans in search of a viable identity, and his discourse is understood as contributing to our understanding of race relations. Condit and Lucaites have noted, for example, that Malcolm "stretched both his own thoughts and the vision of Black America far beyond the social and political horizons that had been publicly articulated prior to his expression of them."[27] Bruce Perry concludes his biography of Malcolm X by writing that Malcolm "mobilized black America's dormant rage and put it to work politically. . . . By transforming black fear into white fear, he irrevocably altered America's political landscape."[28] Dyson notes that "Malcolm blessed our [black] rage by releasing it. His tall body was a vessel for our outrage at the way things were and always had been for most black people, especially those punished by poverty and forced to live in enclaves of urban terror."[29] And Cornel West writes that Malcolm's "profound commitment to affirm black humanity at any cost and his tremendous courage to accent the hypocrisy of American society made Malcolm X the prophet of black rage—then and now."[30] I am in no position to dispute these assessments, all of which are variations on Ossie Davis's famous eulogy of Malcolm as "our own shining black Prince."[31] But I do want to argue that Malcolm's influence should not be limited to one side of the color line and not even confined to the realm of race relations. Malcolm X enacts in and through his discourse *emancipatory strategies of radical judgment,* modes of interpretation and critique that invite his audiences to come to reasoned assessments without being constrained by the paradigms and formulas associated with the dominant culture. In this way, the rhetoric of Malcolm X potentially provides to a more general audience what Kenneth Burke calls "equipment for living."[32]

Part of the justification for the larger stage that I am claiming for Malcolm's rhetorical performances is based in Malcolm's own rhetorical practice. While he was alive, Malcolm spent so much time talking to white people that Karim recalls officials within the Nation of Islam complaining that "Malcolm was spending too much time outside the temple . . . speaking for the most part *to* the white devil."[33] Goldman suggests that Malcolm developed a "soft spot for white students," and Karim remembers that "throughout the early sixties Malcolm welcomed every opportunity to speak to college students."[34] Archie Epps reports that Malcolm X was, by 1964, "the second most sought-after speaker on college campuses"— behind Barry Goldwater.[35] Clearly, Malcolm believed his message was important to a broader audience. But at least as important as this circumstantial evidence regarding Malcolm's audience is the fact that his public career spans a period of sweeping change. Malcolm was responding to transformations within the civil rights movement, and these in turn were reflective (and, to some degree, causative) of changes in American political culture more generally. Malcolm's personal rhetorical development, in other words, is of interest because it parallels (and contributes to) the collective upheavals of the 1960s, which continue to reverberate through American culture.[36] The interpretive attitudes and strategies evident in Malcolm's later discourse, as a result, are well suited to contemporary life.

When he first was brought to national attention in July 1959, in a Mike Wallace television documentary titled *The Hate That Hate Produced,* Malcolm X was preaching an esoteric gospel that nonetheless resonated strongly with conservative American values. In the documentary, the Nation of Islam indictment of white society as inherently evil was balanced by images of neat and orderly African Americans attending meetings. In the wake of the 1954 Supreme Court decision in *Brown v. Board of Education,* outlawing segregated schools, the Nation of Islam's insistence on racial separation was interpreted by some as a reassertion of the status quo.[37] The Montgomery bus boycott, led by Martin Luther King Jr., signaled a resurgence in the fight for African American equality, but the relatively peaceful resolution of the boycott also suggested that the dominant culture could accommodate reform without revolutionary change. This was before the Greensboro, North Carolina, lunch-counter sit-ins in 1960, which, as Taylor Branch puts it, "helped define the new decade" of more aggressive civil rights challenges and resistance;[38] before the Mississippi Freedom Rides were interrupted by conflagration; and of course several years before brutal images of women and children being blasted by fire hoses in Birmingham, Alabama, prodded even the most recalcitrant toward a belated recognition that America did, indeed, have a race problem. The Bay of Pigs, the Cuban Missile Crisis, and the shooting down of U2 pilot Gary Francis Powers over Russia had not yet disrupted Cold War isolationism, and the rise of protest against the war in Vietnam was years in the future. At least within the white dominant culture, the unifying mythology of American exceptionalism, inclusiveness, and invincibility was, in 1959, still relatively unchallenged. Malcolm X and the Nation of Islam supplied to their followers a competing mythology, but one easily recognizable as a dark parallel to the stable oppositions that defined that dominant culture.

By the time Malcolm X was assassinated in 1965, however, this binding American mythology was being undermined. Both the necessity of the Civil Rights Act of 1960, guaranteeing African Americans the right to vote, and the high-profile difficulties that had accompanied efforts to enforce it had illustrated the recalcitrance of American racism. Four young African American girls had been killed when Birmingham's Sixteenth Street Baptist Church was bombed, and a president had been assassinated. The nonviolent civil rights movement had begun to fracture, as the supremacy of King's sermonic vision was being challenged by the younger and more radical members of the Student Nonviolent Coordinating Committee (SNCC) and the Congress of Racial Equality (CORE); and King himself, as John Cone argues, eventually began to move ideologically closer in some ways to Malcolm's own position.[39] The firm lines of demarcation between assimilation and separation that Malcolm had used to define his own position were breaking down, and this destabilization of African American protest was symptomatic of a fragmentation of American culture more generally. As Wilson Moses puts it, "The erosion of traditional black messianism is parallel, of course, to the disintegration of the myth of destiny that once flourished at the center of American consciousness."[40] Malcolm was faced with the need to refashion his position against a more complex and destabilized milieu; he had helped to usher in, and was forced to respond to, an era of increasing fragmentation and individualism. He eventually abandoned the collective mythology of the Nation of Islam, which taught people to read signs that foretold of coming crises and divine intervention, and fashioned instead a discourse that emphasized a more individualized practice of interpretation and judgment.

My primary aim in this book is to make Malcolm X's discourse available as an inventional resource. I read Malcolm's speeches, especially those near the end of his life, as providing rich models for a practice of rhetorical invention that is capable of enhancing social relations. The contribution that Malcolm X made to expanding and enlivening the cultural consciousness of his immediate black audiences is an essential part of Malcolm's story, but to see his contributions only within such a framework limits our understanding of Malcolm's rhetorical genius and robs us of the ameliorative and productive potential that his rhetoric offers a broader audience. Malcolm X challenges the status quo by widening the horizons of possibility for his audiences. He presents his audiences with multiple provisional personas rather than a single stable identity and with a process through which to perform judgment rather than an injunction to restate conclusions already fully worked out. Malcolm's discourse, in short, offers viable resources for making one's way in a volatile world.

Malcolm Studies

The growth of what might be called "Malcolm studies" burgeoned as soon as he and the Nation of Islam rose to national attention and has continued unabated into the present. I discuss in this section two broad categories of this work that are of particular importance in positioning this book within the ongoing conversation about Malcolm X: biographical studies and cultural studies. The most significant work in first category, of course, is *The Autobiography of Malcolm X*, published soon after Malcolm was assassinated. Having attained almost canonical status, it is the text through which many people first become acquainted with Malcolm, and it was the primary text from which the script for Spike Lee's movie was adapted. As effective as the *Autobiography* is as a portrait of the evolution of a revolutionary and as a literary achievement, it should not be confused for a transparent rendering of Malcolm X. Dyson notes that the success of the *Autobiography* "is as much a testament to Haley's ingenuity in shaping the manuscript as it is a record of Malcolm's own attempt to tell his story."[41] Similarly, Arnold Rampersad reminds us that even "Malcolm's Malcolm is in itself a fabrication; the 'truth'

about him is impossible to know."[42] We will never have access to an unmediated Malcolm. And more important, while Haley's book—especially
when supplemented by the reminiscences of those who knew him well,
such as Hakim Jamal and Benjamin Karim—can contribute to our understanding of Malcolm X the man and the world in which he lived, it does not
tell us about Malcolm the rhetor and the world he would have his audiences make.[43]

The same is true of the two most influential biographies of Malcolm X,
Perry's *Malcolm: The Life of a Man Who Changed Black America* and Wolfenstein's *The Victims of Democracy: Malcolm X and the Black Revolution*.[44] These
two books are, in many ways, mirror images of one another. Perry's biography is an effort to sheer away some of Malcolm's iconic sheen and show
him as a real, and flawed, human personality. His efforts have been criticized; Dyson, among the least vitriolic of Perry's critics, suggests that the
book "renders Malcolm smaller than life."[45] Much of this criticism seems
motivated either by a reluctance to relinquish the heroic and saintlike Malcolm of the *Autobiography* or by skepticism about some of Perry's claims.
But the critique that I wish to make is that Perry's work suffers from a sort
of developmental determinism. Perry conducted extensive interviews and
provides a richly detailed portrait of Malcolm's early years, but primarily he
is interested in a postmortem psychoanalysis through which the experiences of the young Malcolm determine and define his later politics. Among
Perry's most sensational set of claims, for example, is that Malcolm may
have firebombed his own home a week before his assassination; that Malcolm's father, Earl Little, may have burned down his family's home when
Malcolm was an infant; and that Malcolm's act was an unconscious imitation of his father's.[46] Perhaps this is an accurate portrayal of events; perhaps this even is an accurate portrayal of Malcolm's mental state; perhaps
much of Malcolm's discourse of violence was, indeed, motivated by a deep-
seated psychological urge to revenge his father's death or reenact his father's life. But such hypotheses, as intriguing as they may be, ignore
Malcolm's most central public persona—he was a rhetor. Malcolm X is portrayed as a scarred iconoclast working out personal issues rather than a
gifted critic and orator encouraging his audiences to alter the way they see
the political world.

Wolfenstein employs a Marxist-Freudian lens to frame Malcolm's life
story as an ideal manifestation of the black revolutionary mind. He provides a "psycho-biography" of Malcolm X as a "specific crystallization of
collective emotional experience."[47] Wolfenstein positions him as the

central and representative hero in the African American liberation struggle of the 1960s. Like Perry, Wolfenstein begins with a violent moment from Malcolm's childhood, a nighttime raid on his family's home by the local white supremacist group, the Black Legion. His treatment of this event is illustrative of the method of the book as a whole. Wolfenstein first situates this incident historically as a moment of intersection between the collective psychological trajectories of white racist anxiety and burgeoning African American race pride in the first decades of the twentieth century. Then, in the next chapter, he situates this same incident in the context of Malcolm's personal psychological development, especially as regards the troubled relationship between his parents: "In this sense," Wolfenstein argues, "the Legion attack was only the nightmare of everyday life in an intensified form." Malcolm's story, in Wolfenstein's analysis, becomes black America's story, so that "the project of his personal liberation was simultaneously the project of racial liberation."[48] Wolfenstein's book tells much the same story as Perry's, then, though with a more detailed attention to historical context and through a more explicitly theoretical lens.

Such studies are valuable explorations into Malcolm the man, hypothesizing explanations for some of his remarkable innovations of thought. And in the case of Wolfenstein, especially, they provide a rich contextualization of Malcolm's life in relation to the ongoing African American liberation struggle. They do not, however, provide significant insights into Malcolm the orator. Certainly Malcolm X was, like anyone, motivated by personal and psychological drives. But these were, and are, almost completely hidden from his audiences. As valuable as it is to recall that Malcolm X was both a troubled and a representative individual, framing his actions and innovations merely as responses to personal challenges or psychological drives makes them merely personal. Malcolm's speeches are not an invitation to live life as he lived it but to see the world as he saw it.

George Breitman's often-cited *The Last Year of Malcolm X: The Evolution of a Revolutionary* directs attention more specifically to Malcolm's oratory but does so in order to demonstrate that Malcolm's relationship with the American Socialist Party became "increasingly friendly" and culminated in his attempt to effect "a synthesis of black nationalism and Socialism that would be fitting for the American scene and acceptable to the masses in the black ghetto."[49] Breitman's claim is widely disputed; Goldman, for example, notes that Malcolm's socialism was never more than "a minor motif in his speeches," and John White notes that "Malcolm never moved beyond a vague critique of capitalism and never endorsed Marxism."[50]

Breitman himself acknowledges that Malcolm never formalized any association with any socialist organization and never called himself a socialist.

Certainly, it is true that Malcolm X laced his later speeches with socialist vocabulary, praised socialist presses, and often spoke on platforms sponsored by socialists. Malcolm was a complex man, and a great many things are true about him. But reading his public discourse, as Mark Bernard White points out, "demands something of the intellectual and analytical flexibility that Malcolm himself displayed."[51] Paradoxically, because of Malcolm's adamant refusal, especially in his later rhetoric, to remain comfortably in any single category, critics who are so motivated can select from his discourse passages that seem to place him into any number of categories. Malcolm never, in any of his recorded speeches or statements, urged his audience to become socialists. Indeed, the critical attitude that Malcolm X would foster in his audiences after his split with the Nation of Islam is one that would be as suspicious of socialism as it would be of any other codified, systematized set of precepts.

Some biographies, such as Perry's and Wolfenstein's, focus on Malcolm the iconic black man and thus miss that Malcolm also was a radical rhetorician. Other biographical studies, such as Breitman's, understand both the importance of Malcolm's oratory and its radical edge but insist on fitting Malcolm into a preexisting category of radicalness and thus miss the most truly radical characteristic of his rhetoric, which was its refusal to inhabit definitions. Dyson, in *Making Malcolm: The Myth and Meaning of Malcolm X,* provides an exemplary model for a different sort of study, one that has the potential to avoid these shortcomings. Dyson traces the relationship between Malcolm's resurgence into popular culture and the corresponding rebirth of black nationalist politics in the 1990s, noting that Malcolm's "heroic status hinges partially on the broad, if belated, appeal of his variety of black nationalism to Americans who, when he lived, either ignored or despised him." Dyson also argues that Malcolm X "is the rap revolution's rhetorician of choice"; that "without the sustained hero worship of Malcolm X, contemporary black cinema . . . is almost inconceivable"; and that the particular combination of Malcolm's indictment of liberalism, his articulation of black rage, his model of black spirituality, and his advocacy of racial identity may be especially attractive to young people.[52] Similarly, Cornel West argues that "the contemporary focus on Malcolm X, especially among black youth, can be understood as both the open articulation of black rage . . . and as a desperate attempt to channel this rage into something more than a marketable commodity for the culture industry."[53] That is, Malcolm X is adopted by young African Americans as a cultural container that gives shape and substance to their inevitable frustrations with a white-dominated culture. Adolph Reed Jr. takes this argument in a more cynical direction when he notes that "only a dead Malcolm X is available to young people today" and that a dead Malcolm is not expected to exhibit a "dynamic connection to the lived reality of the youth who invoke him." "A living leader is handicapped by having at some point to produce real outcomes," but the specter of Malcolm X can be conjured as a displacement of political action.[54]

Dyson, West, and Reed, to varying extents, are interested in the ways that Malcolm X reverberates through our culture as a symbol and icon. Their studies avoid the shortcomings of biography, for the most part, but at a price. Because they track the ways that Malcolm is read and used in American political and popular culture, they are more interested in what people have done with Malcolm than in what Malcolm did himself. These scholars lament the degree to which Malcolm X has become something of a caricature, that the image of an angry Malcolm X cultivated by the white-dominated media has become the totality of his legacy, and that his death has reduced him to a convenient cipher that displaces real political action. Yet by attending to the cultural uses of Malcolm X and ignoring the rhetorical action of his words, these scholars have contributed to the very problem of caricature that they decry. They call for a more substantive understanding of Malcolm X, but they draw their readers' attention away from the rhetoric through which such an understanding might be developed. Dyson, most tellingly, argues that it would be best if "the focus on Malcolm's last year would be shifted away from simply determining what he said and did to determining how we should use his example to respond to our current cultural and national crises."[55] Dyson would have us separate Malcolm's rhetorical performance from his cultural legacy, but that would reinscribe the split between critique and performance that Malcolm's own rhetorical performance rejected. In contrast, I argue that understanding the practices of interpretation and performance that Malcolm enacted in his rhetoric is essential for determining his potential influence upon our culture.

Studying Malcolm

Focusing on Malcolm's oratory requires addressing some issues regarding the state of his speech texts. Unlike the collected works of some African

American orators, such as Frederick Douglass, W. E. B. Du Bois, or Martin Luther King Jr., there has been no sustained or systematic attempt to edit and organize all of Malcolm's texts.[56] This is a by-product of the deflection of attention away from Malcolm's words. New and updated editions of his autobiography appear periodically, yet his public address lies in relative disarray, published rather haphazardly under the guidance of a great many editors and editorial agendas. As a result, the texts vary widely in quality and reliability.

For example, a speech delivered by Malcolm at the Harvard Law School Forum originally was included by Louis Lomax in his book on the Black Muslims, *When the Word Is Given*, and then five years later was reprinted by Archie Epps in *Malcolm X: Speeches at Harvard*. This is clearly the same speech, though Lomax identifies it has being delivered in 1960 and Epps in 1961. In a note to the text, Epps admits that he has "simply reorganized the paragraphs of this speech around seven sub-subjects which strike the eye right off," but a comparison of the two versions indicates that Epps has altered more than disposition.[57] A sample passage in Lomax's version reads: "This Christian government has failed to give 20 million ex-slaves justice for our 310 years of free slave labor."[58] In Epps's version, bracketed information has been added that significantly alters the meaning: "The [American] Christian government has failed to give her twenty million ex-slaves [just compensation] for three hundred ten years of free slave labor."[59] Is Malcolm X indicting Christianity, or the American government, or—as he often did—both? Is he asking for justice or just compensation, or are these terms synonymous? Lomax's version also contains numerous ellipses that may or may not indicate missing material, and these are entirely absent from Epps's version of the text.

Another of Malcolm's speeches, "The Black Revolution," was delivered April 8, 1964. It was published twice in 1965 by Pathfinder Press, both as part of the well-known anthology *Malcolm X Speaks* and also as part of a two-speech pamphlet.[60] Though both purport to be transcripts of the same speech, the version included in the anthology contains many ellipses and is approximately fifteen hundred words shorter than the version in the pamphlet, which itself clearly has been cut in places. Perhaps the audiotape from which this speech was transcribed was itself incomplete, or perhaps these two versions were transcribed from different tapes of the same performance, or perhaps these actually are two different speeches, delivered at different times, and merely mislabeled—it is impossible to tell.[61] Such deep and unexplained editing is especially problematic because of Pathfinder's socialist agenda and the insistence of Breitman, the editor of many of its publications, to read Malcolm X as something of a black Guevara. The fact that Malcolm X delivered varying versions, over weeks or even months, of some of his better-known speeches only adds to the potential confusion.

Though I draw from texts throughout Malcolm's published works, I concentrate my analyses on speeches that seem most representative, reliable, and complete. In his speeches, Malcolm was providing for his audiences coherence, order, and meaning as an antidote to the arbitrary brutality that they confronted every day. This rhetorical vision attains its form in the internal coherence of his speech texts, and this coherence is one of the most significant manifestations of the interpretive strategies he would inculcate in his audiences. Again, Malcolm makes his speeches in the way he would have his audiences make their world. Thus, to fragment those speech texts would be to limit his oratory's ameliorative potential and to negate its ability to demonstrate radical judgment for both his immediate audiences and the larger audience for which I have argued.

Most scholarship that focuses directly on Malcolm's discourse can be discussed under two headings. One group of essays, published in the years immediately after Malcolm's death, seeks primarily to explain his rhetoric. His discourse seems to confront these critics as something compelling and strange, a rhetoric that illustrates the limitations of some traditional precepts of rhetorical theory. A second group of essays, published decades later, after Malcolm's persistence in American culture was well established, seeks to trace his rhetorical influences upon that larger culture. Both groups of essays provide insights that resonate strongly with my own analyses, but my purpose differs: I do not wish only to explain his discourse or to account for its influence but instead to make Malcolm's discourse available as an interpretive resource. While these other studies attempt to account for Malcolm's rhetoric through the application of rhetorical theory, I gently invert that model in an attempt to read Malcolm's public discourse as itself presenting something like a "theory" of rhetorical action.

The earliest published essay that attends carefully to Malcolm's oratory is John Illo's "The Rhetoric of Malcolm X," which originally appeared in the *Colombia University Forum* in 1966. This eloquent and insightful essay has been cited so often and reprinted so widely that it has become something of a "classic" in the field of Malcolm studies. I want to linger over it because it is representative of many studies of radical rhetoric from the 1960s and 1970s in its dual and contradictory attitudes. On the one hand,

Illo clearly is impressed and intrigued by Malcolm's rhetorical skill. Malcolm, he suggests, supplies a "genuine" rhetoric in contrast both to "those within the establishment" who are committed to "the prudent justification of an absurd society" and thus "far from original reason, . . . committed to the apologetics of unreason," and to "those outside" the establishment, who "are conditioned by established styles, or are graceless, or are misdirected in eccentric contrariety." Malcolm's rhetoric, from Illo's perspective, offers something startling and even, perhaps, paradoxical—an eloquent dissent. "The achievement of Malcolm X," he continues, "seems marvelous."[62]

But the more interesting paradox is that Illo's rhetorical vocabulary seems to hobble his attempts to account for the peculiar power of Malcolm's rhetoric. "A Harlem rally is not the Senate of the Roman Republic," he acknowledges, and then goes on, "but Cicero would have approved Malcolm's discourses as *accommodatus, aptus, congruens,* suitable to his circumstances and subject." As I have suggested already, and as I will reiterate throughout this book, Malcolm's rhetoric does rely for a part of its suasory potential on a sort of fittingness or propriety. But this sense of appropriateness is not revealed in Illo's notations that Malcolm's "exordia were properly brief," that "he moved to his proposition within the first minute," that his "perorations were similarly succinct," and that his "narration and confirmation were densely analytical."[63] All of these things may be true about Malcolm's rhetoric, but none of them have very much to do with the power of his speech. Illo's comments are generated through the application of a set of standards at odds with Malcolm's rhetorical practice, and he therefore cannot account for Malcolm's eloquence. Cicero's approval, however flattering, is irrelevant to Malcolm's rhetorical purpose and to the needs of his audiences.

This is not to discount Illo's many insights. He acknowledges, for example, that Malcolm's cultural influence derives almost entirely from his rhetoric alone—the "charismatic strength of Father Divine, or of Elijah Muhammad," in contrast, "did not derive from rhetoric" but from the movements they led. Illo also sees that "instruction was the usual purpose of Malcolm's oratory; he was primarily a teacher, his oratory of the demonstrative kind, and his speeches filled with significant matter." And, most interesting, Illo notes that "in the rhetoric of Malcolm X, as in all genuine rhetoric, figures correspond to the critical imagination restoring the original idea and to the conscience protesting the desecration of the idea. Tropes and schemes of syntax are departures from literal meaning, *abusiones,* 'abuses' of a grammar and semantic that have themselves grown into abuses of original reason."[64] Illo acknowledges, in other words, that the *form* of Malcolm's rhetoric is responsible for much of its political work. He recognizes, in summary, that Malcolm's discourse falls outside the norms established for social movement leadership, that Malcolm's rhetoric was a mode of demonstration, and that Malcolm's most radically emancipatory strategies were effected in and through his manipulations of language. These insights form some of the fundamental assumptions from which my study begins.

But Illo's assertion that "in the full Aristotelean meaning," Malcolm X "was a rhetorician," sets up a number of contradictions. Illo declares, for example, that Malcolm's discourse was "as intelligible and obvious as a lynching," when even a casual perusal of Malcolm's rhetoric reveals much of it to be anything but simple and direct.[65] Rhetorical critic Thomas Benson, for example, notes that "Malcolm has an irritating propensity" for making a point that "may be inconsistent with another position" he also maintains, and Goldman agrees that Malcolm "could contradict himself from speech to speech, or sentence to sentence."[66] Illo's categorizing impulse further invites him to succumb to the temptation to extract codified ideology from Malcolm's discourse, reducing Malcolm's "central message" to the propositions that "colored people have been oppressed by white people whenever white people have been able to oppress them, that because immediate justice is not likely . . . the safest thing for all is to separate, that the liberty to 'sit down next to white folks—on the toilet' is not adequate recompense for the past 400 years."[67] This reduction closes off the demonstrative and substantive role that Illo himself argues is played by Malcolm's tropes, figures, and arrangement. Illo can describe Malcolm's rhetoric only by fitting him into preformed categories, and as Illo runs down the rhetorical canons—invention, disposition, style, and delivery— Malcolm can indeed be made to fit. But this compartmentalizing marginalizes some of Illo's own insights. Illo knows that "rhetoric, like revolution, is 'a way of redefining reality,'" but his instrumental assumptions about the power and reach of rhetorical discourse force him to renounce that knowledge at every turn.[68] Illo's allegiance to a stable set of categories hides from him his very object of study.

Illo's problem is not his fondness for classical rhetorical concepts but his calcified understanding of those concepts and his unwillingness to modify them in the face of innovative rhetorical practice.[69] In this sense, his essay marks out some central problems and strategies of reading radical black rhetoric. Two essays published in 1971, for example, are representative in their attempts to avoid the trappings of neo-Aristotelian methodologies while nonetheless remaining committed to some traditional assumptions about rhetoric.[70] Karlyn Kohrs Campbell, in "The Rhetoric of Radical Black Nationalism: A Case Study in Self-Conscious Criticism," argues that "traditional forms of rhetorical criticism emphasize the principles of democratic decision-making and tend to limit dissent to the arguments of the 'loyal opposition.'" The rhetoric of radical black nationalism cannot be accounted for through such assumptions because this discourse explicitly rejects such tactics as being "identified with White society as a trap for the Black man."[71] For example, Campbell points out, the traditional view of discourse as means to an end does not apply: the threat of violence in this rhetoric "is the whole rhetorical act, an end in itself, not the means by which the speaker is attempting to force the White community to the end of concessionary action." Here Campbell provides a productive insight that resonates strongly with my own analyses of the rhetoric of Malcolm X. However, this insight is undermined when Campbell also maintains an overarching instrumentalism through which black nationalist rhetoric becomes "an important means by which Black men can act to experience and achieve a sense of equality *from which to commence the struggle* over political, social and economic goals and policies."[72] Rhetoric, in this view, seems to be preparatory—once it is heard, then the struggle can begin. Despite her effort to avoid the traditional and instrumental separation of means and ends, the categories reemerge, and rhetoric again is understood primarily as a means through which some political action might be accomplished.

Richard B. Gregg's essay describing "the ego-function in the rhetoric of protest" bypasses this contradiction by more explicitly severing connections with traditional conceptions of rhetoric. He notes that the "usual view of rhetorical communication expects the entreaties, appeals, arguments, and exhortations of those asking for change to speak somehow to the basic reasoning and feeling capacities of those in authority." Protest rhetoric, however, may seek to avoid locating its legitimacy in the expectations of the dominant culture and thus may appeal primarily "to the protesters themselves, who feel the need for psychological refurbishing and affirmation." Such speakers, Gregg continues, can be understood as performing an "ego-function" by "*constituting* self-hood through expression; that is, with establishing, defining, and affirming one's self-hood as one engages in a rhetorical act."[73] This is a key insight into the rhetorical impact of protest rhetoric, and Gregg convincingly demonstrates that much of Malcolm's rhetoric is directed toward refurbishing damaged egos. But Gregg cannot describe the particular refurbishments being offered, because he does not attend to the internal textual dynamics where they are enacted.

Interest in the rhetoric of Malcolm X, and in radical black discourse in general, waned among rhetorical scholars beginning in the late 1970s, but Condit and Lucaites published two influential essays in 1990 and 1993 that helped to revive this line of research. These essays thoroughly reject the neo-Aristotelian assumptions that crippled some previous analyses but exhibit other limitations that this book attempts to address. In the first of these essays, for example, Lucaites and Condit place Malcolm X into dialogue with Martin Luther King Jr. to illustrate the ways that the rhetoric of these two martyred leaders together helped to shape American conceptions of "equality." This argument for the cultural impact of Malcolm's rhetoric outside of a narrowly defined black culture is an important advance in Malcolm studies, and my argument is indebted to theirs. Yet their labeling of Malcolm's rhetoric as "counter-cultural," in contrast to King's "culture-typal" discourse, continues to suggest a relatively narrow and marginalized audience. Malcolm's voice was the one "lacking legitimacy and maintaining a shadowy profile" in contrast to King's "legitimate and even popular" stance.[74] Further, in linking Malcolm's cultural influence to his role as the counterpart to King, the implication is that the broader potential impact of Malcolm's "counter-cultural" rhetoric is dependent upon King's "culture-typal" status. King and Malcolm both exerted considerable influence upon "equality" and as a result exerted considerable influence upon American rhetorical culture more broadly, but in this essay Malcolm's influence is portrayed primarily in counterpoint to King's. In this book, I concentrate on the rhetoric of Malcolm X, understanding it as substantive in its own right. This is not to say that Malcolm should be studied in isolation from his historical context but rather that his rhetorical innovations cannot be revealed if he is understood as locked into an ideological symbiosis with Martin Luther King Jr.

In their second essay on Malcolm X, Condit and Lucaites concentrate on his apparent lack of success as a revolutionary leader. Because a "rhetor takes up the burden to persuade an audience, no matter how difficult the task, not to beat it into submission," a revolutionary rhetor "must, therefore, finally abjure a true revolution, which calls for an unfettered and absolute rejection of all that is, in favor of a torturous path through the constructive visions of what might be."[75] In other words, because a rhetor must always draw upon existing ideological structures when addressing an audience, a radical who would effect change primarily through rhetoric cannot ultimately call for a full-scale revolution. If the existing culture suddenly were swept away, she or he would be bereft of rhetorical resources. This conclusion may seem in contradiction to Gregg's insight that protest speakers often ignore the dominant ideology altogether; but actually Gregg's insight, together with Condit and Lucaites's, helps to mark out the double bind that confronts radical rhetors: they may ignore the expectations of the dominant culture and thus turn their discourse inward toward their own damaged egos, or they may address the dominant culture in its own terms and thus "abjure a true revolution." I argue that Malcolm's escape from this double bind is a keynote of the emancipatory potential of his discourse. His rhetoric presents a mode of thinking and judgment that is revolutionary because of its ability to remain suspended between these twin cultural traps of solipsism and marginalization.

Illo, Campbell, Gregg, and Condit and Lucaites, like other scholars interested in the rhetoric of Malcolm X, fail to attend to its form and thus miss its essential constitutive component. By "form" I mean to refer to the tropes, arrangement, style, and other aspects of discourse that often are dismissed as mere ornament. It is in its form that a discourse displays the imprint of the culture it was designed to address, that it constructs a perspective through which to view itself and the world, and that it conveys this perspective to its audience. The form of a discourse, in this sense, is the habitation and textual enactment of what Kenneth Burke describes as an attitude.[76]

A Burkean sense of attitude does not name "a simple inclination to act; rather, it is an *approach*, something more like a *style*, which guides the action. . . . The manner is the way in which a thing is done, not the simple doing of it."[77] Burke provides this illustration: "To build something with a hammer would involve an instrument, or 'agency'; to build with diligence would involve an 'attitude,' a 'how.'"[78] Malcolm's rhetoric does not tell its audience what to do but shows them in what direction to think. He models, through the choices that he makes in his speeches, an attitude that he would pass on to his audience. This is an attitude of engagement; Malcolm's modeling of political judgment means that his rhetoric offers more than only Gregg's "ego-function." Malcolm certainly ministers to brutalized egos, but he does so by demonstrating attitudes of interpretation that, in turn, inform attitudes of speech and action. His rhetoric is, as Illo noted, "demonstrative," showing its audiences how to read and act, but it effects its demonstration through its shape or form.

Burke notes that "often we could with more accuracy speak of persuasion 'to attitude,' rather than persuasion to out-and-out action." Persuasion to action "is directed to a man only insofar as he is *free*"; when "a choice of *action* is restricted," Burke writes, "rhetoric seeks rather to have a formative effect upon *attitude*."[79] Malcolm's African American audiences were restricted, lacking the material resources required to take revolutionary action—and, indeed, even to participate in the dominant culture in any empowered way. C. Eric Lincoln, author of the first important book on the Nation of Islam, *The Black Muslims in America*, believes that Malcolm X probably was never under the illusion that blacks could mount a physical challenge: "But they could mount a psychological challenge, and if they were persistent, they might at least produce some erosion in the attitudes and the strategies by which the white man has always protected himself and his interests."[80] This psychological challenge is manifest in the attitudes that Malcolm X would induce in his audiences. His audiences *become* free when emulating Malcolm's attitudes because these are attitudes that invite his audiences to engage in acts of rhetorical invention beyond the terms and paradigms and formulas that the dominant culture has used to restrain them. This sense of attitude as an interpretive stance, a direction from which to confront an object of analysis, is foundational to the strategies of radical judgment that Malcolm models for his audiences.

Understanding discourse in this way is to make what Richard A. Lanham refers to as the "strong case for rhetoric," a case through which, as Michael Leff puts it, rhetoric "emerges not as ornamentation, nor as an instrument for disseminating truths gained through other means, but as the very medium in which social knowledge is generated."[81] To say that rhetoric was Malcolm's medium, then, is to suggest that his language constitutes an attitudinized practice of reading and critique through which his audiences might remake their world. To discern this form of social knowledge requires the critic to understand speech texts "in their full complexity, comprehending them both as linguistic constructions and as efforts to exercise influence, and it operates through paradigm cases rather than abstract principles."[82] This is an explicitly inductive approach to criticism in which theoretical insights are driven by the study of exemplars. My textual analyses are informed by these assumptions concerning the potential of public discourse and the role of the critic. Malcolm's legacy consists in his efforts to address particular audiences in particular settings; the processes of judgment through which Malcolm assembled his texts in these circumstances are the potentially emancipatory processes that he would have his audiences emulate when they must address other circumstances. Through my analyses of his speech texts, I aim to make these attitudes, strategies, and inventional resources available for this sort of emulation.

Conclusion

Malcolm X's most significant innovations and contributions are the strategies of interpretation and judgment that he enacts in his rhetorical performances. Through these performances, he is engaging in a practice of rhetorical invention that he would have his audiences emulate, one in which interpretation and production are fused into a dynamic whole. The particular variation of rhetorical invention that Malcolm demonstrates carries emancipatory potential because it fosters faculties of judgment that are quashed by the dominant culture. Because Malcolm's rhetoric demonstrates and enacts attitudes that are unauthorized by that culture, it encourages a radical judgment. Because this form of judgment was not otherwise available to his audiences, Malcolm had to invent it. These attitudes, strategies, and models of judgment attain coherence only within Malcolm's speeches; he demonstrates them through the choices he makes regarding style, tone, trope, and arrangement. Because they are enacted in his rhetoric, they cannot be abstracted into an instrumental set of methods or formulas. These rhetorical practices then can become inventional resources, of use when individuals or groups face analogous situations. The emancipatory potential of Malcolm's rhetoric can most profitably be assessed only through a sustained close textual analysis of his speeches.

Malcolm X was one of the most daring and original speakers of the twentieth century, but he did not exist in a historical vacuum. His rhetoric while he was a minister in the Nation of Islam was informed by the expectations shaped through hundreds of years of African American protest, and his rhetoric after he left the Nation was an explicit challenge to these expectations. One way to understand the norms of the rhetorical tradition within which Malcolm worked and against which he rebelled is to describe it as a discourse of prophecy. The analyses that occupy subsequent chapters require an efficient way to conceptualize some key elements of this rhetorical tradition, and referring to this tradition as a discourse of prophecy serves to emphasize its most relevant characteristics.

David Howard-Pitney notes that "messianic themes of coming social liberation and redemption have deep roots in black culture," and by the late twentieth century the norms of such discourse can be understood as constituting a part of the rhetorical situation faced by African American orators.[83] The resonant familiarity of such discourse, in fact, contributed substantially to the success of the Nation of Islam. Elijah Muhammad and his ministers, including Malcolm X, exploited masterfully the oratorical forms with which their audiences were familiar. After he split with the Nation of Islam, Malcolm X was charting new territory, and the compelling nature of his post-Nation of Islam rhetoric as well as some of its limitations can be attributed to his refusal to be confined by the expectations of his audience. Clearly, no very productive assessment of Malcolm's later rhetoric is possible without a grounding articulation of the norms that he was critiquing and transcending. In the next chapter, I provide such an articulation, concentrating on key historical examples of African American prophetic rhetoric and, through analyses of them, describing a rhetorical landscape against which Malcolm's rhetoric can be situated.

2

Prophetic Precedence

❖ ❖ ❖ ❖ ❖

This chapter develops an overview of African American prophetic protest. I work from textual examples to describe a range from rhetoric that exhibits a core faith in the underlying righteousness of American culture to that which denies that American culture can be reformed and insists instead upon cataclysmic revolution. My purpose is to develop a landscape of African American prophetic discourse in order to understand the multiple strands of prophecy that are interwoven in Malcolm X's public address. The articulation of this spectrum provides grounding for three arguments developed in the following chapters. First, part of the Nation of Islam's peculiar success and longevity was due to a prophetic discourse that allowed the organization to excite its membership to extraordinary labor while at the same time isolating this activity within fairly narrow boundaries. The Nation of Islam in this way avoided many of the pitfalls of previous African American separatist movements. Second, the prophetic concoction that characterized Nation of Islam discourse also contributed to Malcolm's split with the Nation in 1964. The tendency of Nation of Islam rhetoric to contain the membership within a hermetically sealed worldview rendered it ill-suited as a mode of address in the world outside the

mosque. As Malcolm began more frequently to address wider and more diverse audiences, he had to invent a more flexible and adaptive rhetoric—
but flexibility and adaptation were anathema to Nation of Islam doctrine.
Finally, understanding the range of previous African American political
prophecy and how Nation of Islam prophecy was an innovation only
within this range helps to underscore the radical nature of Malcolm's discourse after his break with the Nation of Islam. In that split Malcolm X rejected not merely the teachings of his mentor, Elijah Muhammad, but also
the entire range of prophetic discourse that had for centuries dominated
the African American response to American slavery and racism.

In this chapter, I analyze four well-known texts that were produced at
key historical moments in the history of African American rhetoric and
canonized because they so well exemplify particularly significant contributions to that history. As such, these texts offer the opportunity to understand the rhetorical norms familiar to Malcolm X and to his audiences.
These examples provide resources for comparison and contrast and enable
us to understand the ways that Malcolm's Nation of Islam rhetoric both recalls and refigures what others have said before. I do not mean to imply
that Malcolm X studied these historical texts or that he incorporated explicit references to them in his own discourse. The value, rather, of these
prior texts lies in the light they can shed on Malcolm's rhetorical practice.

I begin with an analysis of Frederick Douglass's speech "What to the
Slave Is the Fourth of July?," delivered on July 5, 1852. Douglass's rhetoric, as David Howard-Pitney notes, "provides a baseline for comparing later
responses" to the enduring American paradox between democratic promise and racial discrimination.[1] The Fifth of July speech, delivered to a white
audience, also shares in common some significant characteristics with the
prophetic rhetoric that Malcolm X delivered to white audiences. W. E. B.
Du Bois's "The Conservation of Races," delivered in 1897 to the American
Negro Academy and later published as a pamphlet, occupies a prominent
place in the lineages of both the National Association for the Advancement
of Colored People (NAACP) and the Harlem Renaissance. Its central feature is its call to resist assimilation and to "conserve" a separate black culture. Moving toward the more radical end of this spectrum of prophetic
protest, I draw upon the discourses of antebellum slave rebellion. David
Walker's *Appeal to the Coloured Citizens of the World,* published as a pamphlet
in 1829 and circulated widely throughout the South, was perhaps the most
incendiary document by an African American in the antebellum era. It offers protonationalist themes and a critique of white domination together

with threats of violent retribution from both divine and human hands. There is no evidence that it directly caused any rebellion, but certainly whites believed it could. And, finally, *The Confessions of Nat Turner*, published in 1831 immediately after Turner led the bloodiest of all slave uprisings, offers the most radical prophetic vision together with the most narrow range of possibilities for human agency.

All of these texts are prophetic, in that they assume that the trajectory of human history is influenced by a divine hand and that discourse is a means through which to transmit that influence. "Prophetic speech," James Darsey reminds us, "is incomprehensible except as the speech of a divine messenger; the prophet, properly understood, speaks for another."[2] But as this continuum of African American prophetic protest shades from those texts informed by an abiding faith in the ability of white American culture to amend its shortcomings, to those informed by a conviction that only a revolution can bring about the necessary changes, the prophetic tone also shifts. It is useful to understand this shift as analogous to a distinction that can be drawn between jeremiadic prophecy and apocalyptic prophecy. At one end of this continuum stand discourses that share a jeremiadic faith that in American exceptionalism and morality lie the potential to resolve issues of racism and inequity; at the other end are apocalyptic discourses that understand American culture to be so hopelessly corrupt that only a catastrophic cleansing guided by a divine hand can effect the necessary changes. Within this study, then, jeremiadic and apocalyptic rhetorics provide succinct vocabularies through which to describe the familiar forms sought out by African American rhetors in their efforts to address what they perceived to be critical exigencies. The importance of these vocabularies within this project is their presentation of themes, tropes, and forms essential to understanding the rhetoric of Malcolm X while he was a prophet for the Nation of Islam and during the last year of his life after he cast off the mantle of prophecy.

My central argument in this chapter is that these historical texts, once they are laid out along a continuum, provide a backdrop against which Malcolm's discourse is illuminated in productive ways. Specifically, as the argument is developed further in the next chapter: while Malcolm X was a Nation of Islam minister he delivered a rhetoric that was a curious blend of elements taken from different points along this continuum of African American prophetic protest; this blend proved highly successful for sustaining the Nation but markedly ill-suited as a means through which to foster emancipatory strategies of radical judgment.

Frederick Douglass: African American Jeremiah

Douglass's speech was delivered in Rochester, New York, at the invitation of the Rochester Ladies' Anti-Slavery Society. His audience was predominantly white, and Douglass was the most powerful black man in America—a well-known and gifted orator, an international celebrity, and a tireless abolitionist speaker and organizer. This speech may be, as Douglass biographer William S. McFeely puts it, "the greatest antislavery oration ever given."[3] Certainly it is Douglass's best-known oration. It addresses two central issues: the increasing sectional division in the 1850s over the future of slavery in the United States and Douglass's own recent public split with longtime paternal mentor William Lloyd Garrison.

Three historical legislative events marked the heightened sectional crisis in the years just prior to Douglass's address. The Wilmot Proviso, proposed in 1846 by Representative David Wilmot of Pennsylvania, would have negated the Missouri Compromise of 1820, which established latitude 36° 30'—Missouri's southernmost border—as the northernmost limit of slavery. Though eventually killed in the Senate, the voting revealed in startling relief the sectional tensions that now characterized national politics; instead of the expected split between Democrats and Whigs, the vote was split between Northerners and Southerners. The so-called Compromise of 1850 was built by Illinois senator Stephen A. Douglas from the shattered remnants of Henry Clay's bill to admit California as a free state and to organize New Mexico and Utah as territories. This bill threatened again to disrupt the delicate balance of power that had been working to keep both North and South in check because the ambiguity inherent in Douglas's doctrine of "popular sovereignty" was decoded sectionally—the North saw it as inviting the spread of slavery, while the South saw it as curtailing the spread of slavery. Perhaps the most insidious political development was a direct corollary of that compromise: the Fugitive Slave Act of 1850. This law established federal support in returning runaway slaves to the South. The runaways were not allowed to testify on their own behalf and were not permitted a trial by jury, and heavy fines were levied against individuals who aided them. Douglass vehemently denounced this act almost from the moment of its passage, declaring—as he would do in "What to the Slave Is the Fourth of July"—that it made the entire United States into a slave-holding territory.

This growing national tension over slavery was accompanied by growing tensions within the abolitionist movement. Throughout the 1840s,

Garrison was the leading abolitionist in America, and central among Garrisonian tenets was that the Constitution was a proslavery document. The only recourse was to dissolve the Union so that it might be rebuilt on more agreeable terms; as Garrison once put it, "he is no true abolitionist, who does not go against this Union."[4] Other abolitionist efforts were either ignored or openly attacked by Garrison in the pages of his newspaper—it was his way or no way.[5] Douglass was recruited by Garrison in 1841, and in accordance with the Garrison doctrine, he soon filled his speeches with attacks upon the Constitution and upon America in general. But Douglass began to eclipse Garrison as an oratorical star and also began to chafe under Garrison's inflexible formulae. In January 1851, just eighteen months before his Fifth of July oration, Douglass publicly broke with Garrison and declared the Constitution an antislavery document.

This accelerating political disintegration was well suited to jeremiadic appeal. In its most general outlines, this rhetorical form "accomplishes its goals rhetorically by a process leading readers to view themselves as a chosen people confronted with a timely if not urgent warning that unless a certain course of atoning action is followed, dire consequences will ensue."[6] It finds its origination with seventeenth-century New England Puritans as a sermonic mode that offered a ringing denunciation of a people fallen away from their covenant with God. As American exceptionalism became an integral component of the nation's secular political mythology, the jeremiad entered American rhetorical culture as a recognizable and familiar form. As the form became secularized, the declension from God's rules and the divine retribution that would follow unless those rules were reinstated was replaced by a declension from America's promise and the threat of political chaos that would ensue unless that promise was reinvigorated. As Sacvan Bercovitch summarizes this transition, the Yankee Jeremiahs had rung the following changes on the Puritan jeremiad: "they substituted a regional for a biblical past, consecrated the American present as a movement from promise to fulfillment, and translated fulfillment from its meaning within the closed system of sacred history into a metaphor for limitless secular improvement."[7] The American jeremiad, in its political form, casts the United States as a new Canaan and includes prophecies not only of the disasters to be visited upon a fallen people but also of America's unique and inherent future glory. As Perry Miller puts it, the present sins, travails, and embarrassments represent "a task" that "has been assigned" and "upon which the populace are in fact intensely engaged."[8] Douglass's jeremiad frames the growing sectional crisis as just such a task.[9]

Douglass could not have engaged in an abolitionist jeremiad as long as he was constrained by Garrisonian doctrine. Wilson Moses uses the term "black jeremiad" to refer to "the constant warnings issued by blacks to whites, concerning the judgment that was to come for the sin of slavery." These black Jeremiahs generally agreed that America is fundamentally good, that the current outrages are an aberration, and that a return to the values from which the culture temporarily had strayed would encourage emancipation, equality, and general fair-dealing. The jeremiads they delivered, Moses continues, revealed that African Americans had "a conception of themselves as a chosen people, but it also showed a clever ability to play on the belief that America as a whole was a chosen nation with a covenantal duty to deal justly with the blacks."[10] Garrison did not harbor any such faith—but Douglass had to, in order to deliver the speech that he did on the fifth of July, 1852.

The Fifth of July

There are any number of ways that Douglass's Fifth of July speech might be partitioned for analysis. Douglass himself offers six subheads.[11] Gerald Fulkerson has demonstrated that Douglass's speech can be mapped onto the divisions of classical disposition: an *exordium* in which Douglass establishes his humble character, a *narratio* in which he reviews the actions taken by the "Founding Fathers" to gain independence from Britain, a *confirmatio* in which a critique of the "internal slave trade" is presented, a brief *refutatio* articulating his critique of the Garrisonian interpretation of the Constitution as a proslavery document, and a peroration in which Douglass offers hope for the future.[12] For the purposes of this analysis, following Bernard W. Bell, I suggest as a heuristic the three-part division of the jeremiad.[13] "The complete rhetorical structure of the American jeremiad," David Howard-Pitney writes, "has three elements: citing the [exceptional American] *promise;* criticism of the present *declension,* or retrogression from the promise; and a resolving *prophecy* that society will shortly complete its mission and redeem the promise."[14] Though Douglass subtly subverts the jeremiadic form, he does begin with an extended encomium on the meaning of the Fourth of July; he follows with a cinematic catalog of the horrors of slavery; and he finishes with a reiteration of faith in American ideals.

The first third of Douglass's speech may not seem particularly remarkable, because it had long been expected that a Fourth of July oration should contain sustained praise for the Founding Fathers.[15] Douglass's praise is significant, however, for he locates the American promise in the *attitudes* of the Founding Fathers. The greatness of the Founding Fathers lies not merely in what they did but in their revolutionary refusal to follow the expectations of decorum and civility in their day. Douglass notes, for example, that it has become "exceedingly easy" to say that America was right and Britain was wrong. "Everybody can say it"; indeed, it "is fashionable to do so."[16] But the Founding Fathers did not follow the fashion of their own day, and it is for their indecorousness that they are to be praised: "To side with the right, against the wrong, with the weak against the strong, and with the oppressed against the oppressor! *here* lies the merit, and the one which, of all others," he concludes, "seems unfashionable in our day." Instead of prudent accommodation to cultural expectations, the Founding Fathers' "statesmanship looked beyond the passing moment, and stretched away in strength into the distant future" to seize upon "eternal principles." As a result, "[t]heir solid manhood stands out the more as we contrast it with these degenerate times" (365).[17]

Throughout this section of the speech, Douglass repeatedly differentiates himself from members of his audience by referring to them as "you." July 4th, Douglass tells his listeners, "is the birthday of *your* National Independence" (360); he reminds them that "you were under the British Crown" (361); "your fathers" did not subscribe to the "infallibility of government" (361); they sought redress, were rebuked, and the rebuke made "the cause of your fathers grow stronger" (362); ultimately, "they succeeded; and today you reap the fruits of their success" (363). By the end of this passage, by Fulkerson's count, Douglass has used pronouns in this way thirty-three times to divide himself from his audience.[18] To Neil Leroux, "the charge is clear: The principles of liberty, recognized and practiced by Washington (and the fathers), have been neglected by contemporary America."[19] But at the same time, Douglass repeatedly refers to his audience as "fellow-citizens": "I am glad, fellow-citizens, that your nation is so young" (360); "fellow-citizens, I shall not presume to dwell at length on the associations that cluster about this day" (361). There is a doubled movement, then, which Eric Sundquist describes: "Douglass places himself outside the American dream but within the circle of the post-Revolutionary generation's principle rhetoric."[20]

Three implications of this distancing are of particular importance to this study. First, as Kenneth Burke has reminded us, every division carries with it an incipient and compensatory identification.[21] As Douglass separates himself from his white listeners, he pushes them toward their own past. Those ideals that are celebrated on the Fourth of July, to which he admonishes his audience to cling to "with the grasp of a storm-tossed mariner to a spar at midnight" (364), are *theirs,* and Douglass is pressing them into contact with those ideals by repeatedly assuring them that they are not *his.* Second, and relatedly, Douglass places the onus on his audience. If these ideas are to be recovered, then it is his white audience who must do so; these are not his ideals, and as a result neither he nor the people he represents can recover them. And finally, Douglass has claimed for himself the archetypal prophetic position, in contact with his hearers but not identified with them. Darsey explains that prophetic discourse is "both of the audience and extreme to the audience. It might fairly be said that the prophet shares the ideals of his audience rather than the realities of its everyday life."[22] When Malcolm X addressed white audiences as a Nation of Islam minister, as we shall see, he regularly established himself in the marginal position of the prophet and repeatedly pointed out the ironic distance between American ideals and American racial reality; but while he often did place the responsibility for doing the hard work of cultural reformation with those white audiences, Malcolm also expressed no very great faith that the whites he was speaking to were capable of shouldering the burden.

In his speech, Douglass has thus far suggested that there is hope for America and that this hope consists in his white audience's willingness to revivify dormant revolutionary attitudes. But before portraying for his audience the horrors of the present day, Douglass silences himself. A prophet, of course, does not present her or his arguments as arguments but rather as revelations of truth; as Darsey points out, prophets are "confident that if the people could simply be made to feel the truth, reform would follow as a necessary consequence."[23] To effect this sort of transparency, the prophet must not appear actively to be shaping the discourse. Douglass accomplishes this by arguing against his own ability to argue. If the "great principles of political freedom and of natural justice, embodied in the Declaration of Independence," were extended to himself and to those for whom he is speaking, he declares, then he would find his present task "light" and his "burden easy and delightful." Indeed, if that were the case, even "the dumb might eloquently speak" (367). "But," Douglass reminds his listeners, "such is not the state of the case." Should Douglass today "chime in" with the "tumultuous joy" surrounding the celebration of the Fourth of July, it "would be treason most scandalous and shocking, and would make a reproach before God and the world." (368) Douglass, the speaker, cannot appropriately speak.

To those who say that abolitionists should "argue more, and denounce less," Douglass replies that "where all is plain there is nothing to be argued" (369). He says he has "better employments for my time and strength" than to make such arguments (370); "at a time like this," he declares, defining the moment, "scorching irony, not convincing argument, is needed" (371). In his argument for the impossibility of argument, he repeatedly suggests propositions and then strikes himself dumb at their utter self-evidence. Using the masculine pronouns of his time, Douglass declares that he need not argue that blacks are men, because the Southern states' own black laws confirm it; he need not argue for equal manhood, because already blacks across the nation are engaged in all imaginable human pursuits; he need not argue that men are entitled to liberty, because "you have already declared it" (370); he cannot bring himself to argue that it is wrong to make men brutes. The audience thus is invited to experience the description of degeneration that follows as an unmediated prophetic revelation.

Douglass closes his encomium on the Founding Fathers by noting that "their solid manhood stands out the more as we contrast it with these degenerate times" (365). As Douglass views them, these times are degenerate indeed. He declares that "the character and conduct of this nation never looked blacker to me than on this 4th of July" (368) and that "for revolting barbarity and shameless hypocrisy, America reigns without a rival" (371). This is prefatory to the centerpiece of the speech, the cinematic tour of what Douglass refers to as the "Internal Slave Trade." This is not argument; its persuasive potential stems not from its logic but from its appeal as a presentation of fact. Douglas does not argue explicitly that these scenes must be understood in a particular way but relies upon the paratactic strategy of irony: he presents American ideals and American practice in close proximity and then relies upon his audience to decry the disparity.[24]

Leroux notes that this "display tour of the American slave market is a sensory experience of observation for Douglass's audience" and has summarized the many references to the senses:

> Behold . . . you will see . . . I will show you . . . Mark the sad procession . . . Hear his savage yells . . . There, see the old man . . . Cast one glance . . . See, too . . . Suddenly! you hear . . . your ears are saluted . . . The crack you heard . . . Fellow this drove . . . Attend the auction . . . Tell me, citizens, where, under the sun, you can witness a spectacle more fiendish and shocking. Yet this is but a glance at the American slave-trade, as it exists, at this moment, in the ruling part of the United States.[25]

"Americans!," Douglass sums up, "your republican politics, not less than your republican religion, are flagrantly inconsistent" (382).

Douglass declares that "hope is much needed, under the dark clouds which lower above the horizon" (360). "The eye of the reformer is met with angry flashes, portending disastrous times," he continues, "but his heart may well beat lighter at the thought that America is young" and "that high lessons of wisdom . . . will yet give direction to her destiny" (360–61). This wisdom and direction are to be found in the Constitution— specifically, in a radical recovery of the Constitution. He differs, he says, "from those who charge this baseness [slavery] on the framers of the Constitution of the United States. *It is a slander upon their memory,* at least, so I believe." When interpreted "as it ought to be interpreted," Douglass assures his listeners, "the Constitution is a GLORIOUS LIBERTY DOCUMENT" (385). The jeremiad, like many rhetorical forms, has a cyclical structure—the final promise that will resolve the current chaos depends upon a revivification of the foundational ideals and attitudes with which the speech begins. Douglass declares that he is ending "where I began, with hope."[26]

Prophetic Interpretation

But there is an apparent slippage in the location of this hope. In the beginning of the speech, Douglass hoped his white audiences would emulate the revolutionary attitudes of the Founding Fathers; here, at the end, the hope seems to reside in the founding document itself. But this is not a slippage so much as a reframing and perhaps a redoubling—Douglass is instructing his audience to read the Constitution in a revolutionary way, to bring the indecorous attitudes of the Founding Fathers to bear upon a reinterpretation of the founding document. His audience is to pay no heed to the pervasive norms of interpretation used by both proslavery and antislavery factions to understand the Constitution as sanctioning slavery. Such norms label the Founding Fathers "the veriest impostors that ever practised [*sic*] on mankind" (384) and thus reject the source of the very attitudes required to give the Constitution a proper reading. Douglass reminds his audience that "there are certain rules of interpretation, for the proper understanding of all legal instruments. These rules are well established." The rules that Douglass is referring to are radically democratic: "They are plain, common-sense rules, such as you and I, and all of us, can understand and apply, without having passed years in the study of law. I scout the idea that the question of the constitutionality or unconstitutionality of slavery is not a question for the people." "Read its preamble," Douglass says of the Constitution, "consider its purposes. Is slavery among them? Is it at the gateway? or is it in the temple? It is neither" (385). With the proper interpretive attitude, the antislavery bias of the Constitution is self-evident.

This right and obligation to read the Constitution for oneself imply a right and obligation to encourage others to share in this same reading. "I hold that every American citizen," Douglass declares, "has a right to form an opinion of the constitution, and to propagate that opinion, and to use all honorable means to make his opinion the prevailing one" (385). But Douglass the speaker, ironically, cannot speak in this way. He and the blacks whom he represents cannot recover the ideals of the Founding Fathers, because those are ideals from which African Americans have been divided. The declension from those ideals is vividly present in the existence of the internal slave trade and in the relative silence of the American church. Redemption is available through an interpretive recovery of the Constitution by whites, and this recovery entails a revivification of the revolutionary attitudes of the Founding Fathers. Like the American jeremiad, Douglass's Fifth of July oration urges its audience toward the revitalization of dormant principles. But these principles are not, as they are for most American Jeremiahs, the property of the prophet. Douglass can help to teach his white audience how to read the Constitution, but they must do the reading.

Douglass does not present these interpretive strategies as his own; he demurs that he does not have "time now to argue the constitutional question at length" but refers his audience to others—Lysander Spooner, William Goodell, Samuel E. Sewall, "and last, though not least, by Gerritt Smith, Esq."—by whom the "subject has been handled with masterly power" and who have "fully and clearly vindicated the Constitution from any design to support slavery for an hour" (384). Douglass thus invites his audience to perform critical tasks based upon external models. In other words, the pattern of judgment being modeled for the audience belongs to Douglass only to the extent that he has chosen to agree with conclusions previously reached by others. In the Fifth of July oration, the interpretive and inventional processes of judgment that he is urging his audience to adopt occur offstage, in the writings of Spooner, Smith, and the others. Douglass's text, then, models for his audience a form of judgment that consists in casting off one set of interpretive methods and becoming aligned with another, much as Malcolm X's rhetoric while a Nation of Islam minister schooled his black audiences in modes of interpretation that consisted in becoming aligned with the teachings of Elijah Muhammad.

W. E. B. Du Bois: Nationalist Prophet

Frederick Douglass offers an example of the sort of jeremiad that an African American rhetor might address to a white audience, one that signals a "virtually complete acceptance of and incorporation into the national cultural norm of millennial faith in America's promise."[27] White Americans are a chosen people, and in order to fulfill their destiny they must reenact the nation's founding ideals. Other variations of the African American jeremiad, however, were addressed to black audiences. Some of these comprise what Howard-Pitney refers to as "the dominant black American jeremiad tradition," which "conceives of blacks as a chosen people *within* a chosen people."[28] Still other variations "embraced exclusive black nationalist myths . . . which posit a messianic destiny for blacks apart from, or even in opposition to, the national mission imagined by Anglo-Americans."[29] In these black nationalist jeremiads, African Americans have fallen short of their promise, and African American values must be revivified in order to realize their particular destiny. These nationalist jeremiads are not necessarily implicated in the larger narrative of American exceptionalism, because the future they prophesy concerns the exceptional fortunes of the black race. And because racial oppression has rendered their own history and culture unavailable to African Americans, these oppositional jeremiads cannot merely recall a covenant that is common social knowledge. They must shoulder the additional burden of reacquainting their audiences with values and practices that have been forgotten, displaced, and maligned. Only then can they call their people home.

There were significant differences between the nationalism delivered to lower-class black audiences and that delivered to middle-class black audiences. Most commonly, especially in the late nineteenth and early twentieth centuries, black nationalist ideas addressed to the lower classes were associated with emigrationist schemes. Always the number of African Americans interested in relocating to Africa was quite small, but the end of Reconstruction and a rising tide of racial violence reawakened interest in hearing emigrationist rhetoric. In the 1890s, "Bishop Henry McNeal Turner was, without doubt, the most prominent and outspoken American advocate of black emigration. By constant agitation he kept Afro-Americans aware of their African heritage and their disabilities in the United States."[30]

Inspired by early black nationalist Alexander Crummell, Turner was a tire-less proselytizer and organizer, speaking throughout the nation but prima-rily among the southern rural poor. "I would make Africa the place of refuge," Turner declared in 1883, "because I see no other shelter from the stormy blast, from the red tide of persecution, from the horrors of Ameri-can prejudice."[31] The white press dubbed Turner a "Black Moses," an ap-pellation later given to Marcus Garvey.[32]

But Turner, like other emigrationist rhetors, found much less enthusias-tic audiences among African Americans who were more educated and fi-nancially secure. "Like other black nationalists," Edwin Redkey writes, Turner "called for a virtual separation of the races, a segregation approved by many whites, although most articulate Afro-Americans—the black middle-class—would rather have integration into American society."[33] This created a dilemma typical of all such emigrationist ideas. The ideal Liberia that Turner hoped for required that only the most ambitious and successful people emigrate. "Unfortunately for the bishop's plans," Redkey points out, "those who came closest to meeting his specifications were the ones least likely to forsake the gains they had made in the United States."[34]

Nationalist rhetoric addressed to middle-class blacks tended instead to urge the preservation of African American art and culture without suggest-ing that moving to Africa was a prerequisite for doing so. This discourse in-vited middle-class blacks to think of themselves as a people worthy of preservation and empowerment; it also addressed individuals who often actually were in a position to locate cultural resources and render them salient through the publication of newspapers, magazines, and academic essays. Such rhetoric emphasized the preservation and deployment of cul-tural resources toward the founding of, as W. E. B. Du Bois would put it in 1934, "a Negro nation within the nation."[35]

In 1897, Du Bois delivered a prototypical example of the sort of nation-alist discourse that would be addressed to middle-class blacks throughout the early twentieth century. In "The Conservation of Races," he argues that people of African descent cannot fulfill their exceptional destiny unless they preserve and celebrate a distinction between white culture and their own.[36] Du Bois delivered this speech to seventeen African American intel-lectuals who comprised the American Negro Academy; at this meeting the academy had just elected as its president Alexander Crummell, who had so inspired Bishop Turner, after a laudatory nomination speech from Du Bois.[37] "The Conservation of Races" calls upon its audience to assume leadership roles in the "conservation" of a racial identity defined not by biological or physical characteristics but by a shared culture. Du Bois assumes that his audience has access to the appropriate resources and assumes cultural ties binding African American elites with those less fortunate. And this address recalls its audience back toward cultural conceptions of race that have been rendered unavailable in the current milieu but which are necessary in order to continue the expected progress of African Americans.

Du Bois was speaking in response to three central exigencies. The first of these is the rising tide of nineteenth-century racial science, which attempted to classify human beings based upon cranial measurements, skin color, facial features, and other empirically verifiable physical traits. Kirt Wilson points out two effects of this line of research: to render lines of racial difference "certain, stable, and unavoidable" and to inscribe "the binary of white superiority and black inferiority into the very bones of humanity."[38] A third effect was to undermine any notions that African Americans possessed a "culture" that was worthy of recognition or preservation; biology was both definition and destiny. Du Bois, as a Harvard-trained sociologist, was well aware of this academic and popular discourse, and "The Conservation of Races" was an effort, in part, to counter its logic. The innovation of Du Bois's argument is perhaps best testified to by the continuing debate over the degree to which he was successful.[39]

The 1890s also saw an increase in emigration agitation. In 1889, the American Colonization Society (ACS) invited Edward Wilmot Blyden to travel from his home in Liberia to lecture in the United States about the glories of that country. His reception was mixed; predictably, lower-class blacks showed the most interest, but only a small minority even of these audiences were interested in moving to Africa. Nonetheless, Blyden's lectures in the North and South, as well as his book, *Christianity, Islam and the Negro Race,* were used during Senate debates as evidence of African American desire for emigration. A bill was introduced, the Butler Bill, that would have provided federal aid to African Americans who wanted to leave the country, but it was never brought to a vote. The heated debate that it sparked in the Senate, however, together with Blyden's agitation, focused widespread public attention on the prospect of African American emigration. Du Bois, like most middle-class blacks, rejected emigration; "The Conservation of Races" is a plea to develop and maintain a praiseworthy African American culture within the United States.

This address also, and particularly after its publication as a pamphlet, represented one of Du Bois's first statements as a public intellectual in counterpoint to the ubiquitous voice of the "Wizard of Tuskegee," Booker

T. Washington. Washington's famous and epoch-marking address at the Atlanta Exposition of 1895 might itself be seen as a response to the emigrationist ideas then stirring among both blacks and whites. "To those of my race who depend on bettering their condition in a foreign land or who underestimate the importance of cultivating friendly relations with the Southern white man, who is their next-door neighbour," Washington told his audience, "I would say: 'Cast down your bucket where you are'—cast it down in making friends in every manly way of the people of all races by whom we are surrounded."[40] Du Bois initially joined many leading African Americans in praising Washington's speech but then parted ways with him, particularly with regards to the inherent assimilationism of the Tuskegee program. "The Conservation of Races" and an essay published in the August 1897 issue of the *Atlantic Monthly* entitled "Strivings of the Negro People" (later revised to serve as the first chapter of Du Bois's monumental *The Souls of Black Folk*) do not attack Washington directly, but they do provide an alternative nonemigrationist rationale for constituting a viable African American identity within the United States.

The Conservation of Races

Du Bois notes, in his opening remarks, that the "American Negro" has "been led to deprecate and minimize race distinctions, to believe intensely that out of one blood God created all nations, and to speak of human brotherhood as though it were the possibility of an already dawning tomorrow." This is perhaps Booker T. Washington's color-blind assimilationism, and Du Bois's speech is an attempt to counter this vision. The awareness of race, for Du Bois, is not to be transcended or minimized, for doing so would negate the opportunity to address what he would later call "the problem of the Twentieth Century."[41] Du Bois argues that "we must acknowledge that human beings are divided into races; that in this country the two most extreme types of the world's races have met, and the resulting problem as to the future relations of these types is not only of intense and living interest to us, but forms an epoch in the history of mankind" (73). Du Bois will not offer a programmatic resolution to specific social problems but instead will attempt to orient the values and beliefs of his listeners so that they are in accord with appropriate racial conceptions.

Central to this reorientation is Du Bois's conception of "race." He reviews the various "criteria of race differences" (74) that have been proposed by modern science and finds them wanting. The conception of race that Du Bois would "conserve" is not exhausted by "the grosser physical differences of color, hair and bone," for such classifications "go but a short way toward explaining the different roles which groups of men have played in human progress" (75). "What, then, is a race?" he asks: "It is a vast family of human beings, generally of common blood and language, always of common history, traditions and impulses, who are voluntarily and involuntarily striving together for the accomplishment of certain more or less vividly conceived ideals of life" (75–76). This is a remarkable notion of "race" for 1897. Blood and language may play a role, but the "common history, traditions and impulses" and the striving toward "more or less vividly conceived ideals" are primarily responsible for constituting the African American people. While "race differences have followed mainly physical race lines . . . no mere physical distinctions would really define or explain the deeper differences," the "spiritual, psychical, differences" that are "undoubtedly based on the physical, but infinitely transcending them" (77).

Du Bois provides as an example the "forces that bind together the Teuton nations," which are "first, their race identity and common blood; secondly, and more important, a common history, common laws and religion, similar habits of thought and a conscious striving together for certain ideals of life" (77). These are precisely the forces that are being ignored within the African American "nation," and Du Bois would have his audience turn their attention to their conservation. These forces have allowed other races to contribute to the world community: the English have contributed "liberty and commercial freedom," the Germans "science and philosophy," and the Romance nations "literature and art." But "some of the great races of today—particularly the Negro race—have not as yet given to civilization the full spiritual message which they are capable of giving." And, Du Bois asks, "how shall this message be delivered; how shall these various ideals be realized? The answer is plain: by the development of these race groups, not as individuals, but as races" (78). "For the development of Negro genius," Du Bois argues, "of Negro literature and art, of Negro spirit, only Negroes bound and welded together, Negroes inspired by one vast ideal, can work out in its fullness the great message we have for humanity" (79).

African Americans, like all races, are "chosen." Anthony Appiah, whose analysis in some ways parallels mine, points out that in Du Bois's system, each race possesses a "'message' for humanity—a message which derives, in some way, from God's purpose in creating races." But Appiah thinks that "we do not need the theological underpinnings of this argument," because the "essential" point is "the thought that through common action Negroes can achieve, by virtue of their sociohistorical community, worthwhile ends which will not otherwise be achieved."[42] To ignore Du Bois's conviction that African Americans are a chosen people, however, would be to ignore his appropriation and manipulation of the myth of American exceptionalism that undergirds his entire argument. It is important to conserve a race, culturally defined, only insofar as it helps that race to achieve some preordained plan. This plan, in turn, relies upon some degree of racial separation—a direct attack on Washington's stance as well as on emigrationist nationalism. The "advance guard of the Negro people," the most educated and financially stable Talented Tenth that Du Bois would spend the next several decades cultivating, "must soon come to realize that if they are to take their just place in the van of Pan-Negroism, then their destiny is *not* absorption by the white Americans" (79).

For Du Bois, assimilation is the single greatest obstacle that stands between African Americans and their destiny, and its ascension as the predominant theory of race relations has precipitated the declension from a productive, cultural conception of race. It fosters two distinct threats: inaction and vice. The first clearly is the result of the color-blind ideal, for this ideal places African Americans in a dilemma: "Am I an American or am I a Negro? Can I be both? Or is it my duty to cease to be a Negro as soon as possible and be an American?" (79–80). "It is such incessant self-questioning and the hesitation that arises from it," Du Bois declares, "that is making the present period a time of vacillation and contradiction for the American Negro; combined race action is stifled, race responsibility is shirked, race enterprises languish, and the best blood, the best talent, the best energy of the Negro people cannot be marshaled to do the bidding of the race." Thus, paradoxically, this lack of race pride renders the race susceptible to the wiles of "every rascal and demagogue who chooses to cloak his selfish deviltry under the veil of race pride" (80). Du Bois's response to this first threat is to demarcate rather firm lines of separation between white and black Americans: African Americans should identify themselves as Americans "by birth . . . citizenship . . . political ideals . . . language . . . [and] religion," he argues, but "farther than that, our Americanism does not go. At that point, we are Negroes, members of a vast historical race . . . which is yet destined to soften the whiteness of the Teutonic today" (80–81). African Americans must "conserve our physical powers, our intellectual endowments, our spiritual ideals" within the confines of their own racial borders and apply them only toward "the realization of that broader

humanity which freely recognizes differences in men, but sternly depre-
cates inequality in their opportunities of development" (81).

The second threat to African American advancement concerns the cultural impurities of the race itself. Darsey argues that prophetic rhetoric is
characterized by a "desire to bring the practice of the people into accord
with a sacred principle, and an uncompromising, often excoriating stance
toward a reluctant audience."[43] "There is no power under God's high
heaven," Du Bois declares, "that can stop the advance of eight thousand
thousand honest, earnest, inspired and united people. But—and here is the
rub—they *must* be honest, fearlessly criticizing their own faults, zealously
correcting them" (81). In a remarkable passage, Du Bois warns that if the
black race is to realize its potential, "it *must* be inspired with the Divine
faith of our black mothers, that out of the blood and dust of battle will
march a victorious host, a mighty nation, a peculiar people, to speak to the
nations of earth a Divine truth that shall make them free" (81–82). As
Douglass asked his white audience to act in accordance with the principles
of their Founding Fathers, so Du Bois asks his black audience to act in accordance with the ideals represented by their black mothers.

Du Bois continues to paint a vivid picture of the current declension from
the African American potential and ideal. His people should be united, but
"not merely united for the organized theft of political spoils, not united to
disgrace religion with whore-mongers and ward-heelers; . . . but united to
stop the ravages of consumption among the Negro people, united to keep
black boys from loafing, gambling, and crime; united to guard the purity of
black women and to reduce that vast army of black prostitutes that is today
marching to hell" (82). The members of the American Negro Academy
must not only "unflinchingly and bravely face the truth," but they must
also "sound a note of warning that would echo in every black cabin in the
land: *unless we conquer our present vices they will conquer us;* we are diseased,
we are developing criminal tendencies, and an alarming large percentage
of our men and women are sexually impure." In an almost apocalyptic vision, Du Bois argues that the academy must "fight an army of devils that
disgraces our manhood and our womanhood" (83). Yet despite the current
depravity, there is much reason to hope that African Americans can realize
the potential inherent in their uniqueness, for "there does not stand today
upon God's earth a race more capable in muscle, in intellect, in morals,
than the American Negro," but African Americans must "bend [their] energies in the right direction" (84). Du Bois's peroration consists of a proposed "Academy Creed," seven points to which he would ask the members

of the academy to pledge themselves, designed to bring to realization the dormant African American potential.

Cultural Conservation

The interpretive models that Du Bois provides can be usefully compared with other protonationalist discourse. When the emigrationist Edward Wilmot Blyden delivered his black nationalist ideas to African American audiences, his message was one brand of "Ethiopianism," which Wilson Moses describes as "a prophecy of African glory" that framed Africans as a chosen people and that "involved not only Christianizing the continent, but liberating it from foreign domination."[44] Blyden outlined three stages in the modern providential history of the black race. The first was slavery, which brought blacks out of Africa so that they could be of service to the rest of the world; the second phase was education and refinement, which commenced with emancipation; and the third phase would involve emigration and repatriation, which would eventuate in the fulfillment of Africa's manifest destiny.[45] Ethiopianist discourse shares with the jeremiad an assumption that the audience is a chosen people and that the present is a time of declension from the promised ideal, which compromises this people's ability to fulfill its destiny. The key difference, of course, is that for Ethiopianists like Blyden, the ideals that would enable Africa to achieve its promised glory are imported from white culture rather than revivified through a refreshed exploration of the chosen people's own past. Du Bois's address—like speeches later delivered by Marcus Garvey and Malcolm X—requires instead that his American audience look to their black culture itself as a source of strength and innovation within the United States.

Frederick Douglass, in his Fifth of July speech, calls upon his white audience to perform a textual interpretation. He presents his audience with a method—one borrowed from Spooner, Goodell, Sewall, Smith, and perhaps the Founding Fathers themselves—and with a text in need of rereading, the Constitution. It is through this act of rereading that the American promise might be achieved.

Du Bois, however, schools his audience in an art of cultural interpretation. There is not a fundamental text that needs to be reinterpreted but rather cultural practices that need to be reviewed and preserved. Du Bois is urging his black audiences to turn their attention back upon their own history, to recover it and think about it and use it in a potentially empowering way.

In its effort to urge its audience to appreciate their own past as worthy of study and preservation and in its constitutive nature as discourse that addresses a group that had not, until that moment, existed as a collective identity, Du Bois's rhetoric resembles Malcolm's. Both rhetors were dissatisfied with the assimilationist status quo, both thought that the loss of African American culture was too high a price to pay for admission to the white middle class, and both believed that the eventual rise of a strong African American "nation" required a reinterpretation of the black past. And, like Malcolm's Nation of Islam rhetoric, "The Conservation of Races" is a discourse of prophecy. Du Bois's audience is schooled in interpretive strategies designed to hasten the fulfillment of a preordained destiny—African Americans exist because they have a message to deliver to the world, and the conservation of race is the best way to see to it that this message is delivered.

David Walker: Apocalyptic Appeal

Peter Hinks notes that "the years 1800–1831 comprised the period of the most active and carefully planned slave conspiring and rebelling in American history."[46] One factor contributing to this increase in slave resistance was that, like the 1840s and 1850s, the period surrounding the Missouri Compromise of 1820 was characterized by an inflammation of sectional conflict over slavery. The compromise offered ostensible resolution to what had been an unusually rancorous two-year debate by establishing the southernmost border of Missouri as the northernmost extent of slavery. But the instability of the compromise, along with the continued incendiary potential of the slavery question, was evident only a year later, when tensions flared again over Missouri's proposed state constitution that would have excluded free blacks and mulattos.[47] The slave cabins were no better insulated against white political wrangling than they were from the weather, and rumors, both promising and catastrophic, circulated swiftly. Herbert Aptheker reports, for example, that some slaves believed that the Missouri Compromise debates included an emancipation proclamation.[48]

Another factor contributing to slave unrest was the 1804 revolution in Haiti, which created the world's first independent black nation. This news undoubtedly increased anxiety among Southern American whites just as it surely was of particular interest among the slaves. Partially in response, laws were passed that strictly constrained the "freedom" of free blacks, and the ACS was formed in 1817 to attempt to remove free blacks from the

United States. Add to this volatile mixture the fact that the 1820s also were a time of severe economic distress, especially in the agrarian South, because the market prices of goods such as cotton had dropped precipitously, and it is perhaps not surprising that the cataclysmic images of apocalyptic rhetoric seemed appropriate rhetorical resources for rhetors seeking a fitting response.

In the same way that Douglass and Du Bois echoed the forms of the jeremiad in their effort to give shape to a rhetoric that encouraged a rearticulation of the past as a means to ameliorate the present declension from a promised goal, these slave revolt discourses call upon apocalyptic forms to shape their visions of divine intervention and eventual jubilee. These are revolutionary texts, calling for cataclysmic change to the social order, a violent and sudden transformation that would irrevocably disrupt the dominant culture. Apocalyptic discourse predicts "the catastrophic destruction of world or current society," and these texts sanction actions that would, if successfully completed, precipitate the end of the social world as it then existed.[49] The effects of a full-scale slave revolt on the antebellum Southern culture of the United States could only be described through a discourse of complete and merciless upheaval.

David Walker's most significant rhetorical work, published in 1829—its full title was *Appeal, in Four Articles; Together with a Preamble, to the Coloured Citizens of the World, but in Particular, and Very Expressly, to Those of the United States of America*—provides a valuable bridge between discourses that share an essential optimism concerning America's potential redemption, such as Douglass's and Du Bois's, and discourses that are more richly informed by an apocalyptic pessimism.[50] The *Appeal* offers some promise that white America may be redeemed if it revivifies its egalitarian potential, but it also casts American wretchedness as so thorough that only direct divine intervention can resolve it. These mixed motives are among its qualities that make it a valuable comparison to Malcolm X's oratory.

Historical evidence concerning Walker's early years is somewhat scanty, but it seems that Walker was born in Wilmington, South Carolina, about 1796. He was the son of a slave father and a free black mother, and according to the legal tangle of the slave codes of the day, this made Walker free. There is some speculation that he may have taken part in Denmark Vesey's foiled slave uprising in Charleston, South Carolina, in 1821.[51] Sometime before 1825, Walker moved to Boston and opened a used-clothing store, probably catering to the needs of sailors in search of relatively cheap and durable goods. Walker became one of the founding

members of the Massachusetts General Colored Association (MGCA) and
was a frequent contributor to *Freedom's Journal*, the first black newspaper
in America. Along with black churches, the MGCA fostered connections
among the black educated elite in cities throughout the North, and the
nearly universal opposition among this social class to the ACS provided another goad toward unity. As Hinks puts it, in 1829 "Walker's *Appeal* issued
naturally out of this matrix of solidifying black communities, interconnected leaders, and high hopes for black improvement and freedom."[52]
The pamphlet was distributed throughout the eastern states and into the
Deep South, aided by the easy access to the highly mobile and multicul-
tural maritime class afforded by Walker's used-clothing trade. The *Appeal*
went through three editions in the face of increasing agitation among
whites; in the summer of 1830 Walker died suddenly at his home.[53]

To the Coloured Citizens of the World

Though, as Peter Hinks notes, "Most of the principal themes Walker under-
took in his work did not originate with him and had been mined by previous authors, . . . they were rarely expressed with the high-pitched intensity
so common in his rhetoric."[54] Sean Wilentz suggests some of the density of
the *Appeal*, noting that in "a concise pamphlet—concise enough to be
smuggled in batches inside a sailor's coat—Walker combined political argument, racial theorizing, historical reflection, and pre-millennial black
Christianity in a stunning rebuke of the United States as he knew it."[55] The
Appeal is, for the most part, a litany of the horrors entailed by being black
in America at the beginning of the nineteenth century, interspersed with
promises of divine intervention. Its dramatic locutions and liberal use of
exclamation marks lend it an urgent tone, while it also includes footnotes
to some of the scholarly work of the day. Its four articles predict themes
that also are developed by Douglass and Du Bois; they are titled "Our
Wretchedness in Consequence of Slavery," "Our Wretchedness in Consequence of Ignorance," "Our Wretchedness in Consequence of the Preachers of the Religion of Jesus Christ," and "Our Wretchedness in
Consequence of the Colonizing Plan." Each of these four articles follows a
similar loose structure, opening with a few pages of descriptions of the
present state of African American degradation and gradually shading into
warnings of retribution against whites if they do not repent. The argument
proceeds not linearly but cyclically, repeating themes and images and
sometimes even whole passages.

The brief notes that form a sort of preface to the third and final edition of the *Appeal* are typical of the work as a whole; indeed, much of this preface is repeated, in close paraphrase, at the beginning of the preamble and in each of the four articles. Walker juxtaposes the emerging American civil religion against the reality of its present practice, but while the motive is similar to Douglass's two decades later, the tone is much more harsh and confrontational. Walker begins by assuming an audience familiar with previous editions of the *Appeal:*

> It will be recollected, that I, in the first edition of my "Appeal," promised to demonstrate in the course of which, viz. In the course of my Appeal, to the satisfaction of the most incredulous mind, that we Coloured People of these United States, are, the most wretched, degraded and abject set of beings that ever lived since the world began, down to the present day, and, that, the white Christians of America, who hold us in slavery (or, more properly speaking, pretenders to Christianity,) treat us more cruel and barbarous than any Heathen nation did any people whom it had subjected, or reduced to the same condition, that the Americans (who are, notwithstanding, looking for the Millennial day) have us.

Walker provides a generous role for divine providence, promising that "though our cruel oppressors and murderers, may (if possible) treat us more cruel, as Pharaoh did the children of Israel, yet the God of the Ethiopeans [*sic*], has been pleased to hear our moans in consequence of oppression; and the day of our redemption from abject wretchedness draweth near." But at the same time, he warns his readers that "there must be a willingness on our part, for God to do these things for us, for we may be assured that he will not take us by the hairs of our head against our will and desire, and drag us from our very, mean, low and abject condition."[56] God and humans shall work together, it seems, to cleanse the world of slavery.

The main body of the *Appeal* develops these themes through repetition and accretion; as with Douglass, a cool, logical argument seems inappropriate to the crisis of the situation. The effect of reading the text is difficult to describe, with the rapid and unexpected shifts among a jumble of horrific description and cataclysmic retribution suggesting a textual approximation of Picasso's *Guernica*. A summary of the first article may suggest the experience of reading the whole. It begins by repeating the description from the preface and the preamble that African Americans are *"the most wretched, degraded* and *abject* set of beings that *ever lived* since the world began" (7), and then Walker details the cruelties inflicted on the people of Israel in Egypt as illustration that "the condition of the Israelites was better under the Egyptians than ours is under the whites" (10). Next comes an assertion of race pride, that blacks are "as thankful to our God, for having made us as it pleased himself, as they, (the whites,) are for having made them white." God is "on our side," and blacks should not, therefore, be afraid to fight (12). There follows a review of the degradation of the Helots at the hands of Sparta, which also is found not to be as severe as American slavery (13). The willingness to fight is reasserted, for Walker himself "would rather die, or be put to death, than to be a slave to any tyrant" (14). Walker then provides a biting critique of Thomas Jefferson's thoughts on the inferiority of African Americans, complete with a footnote to *Notes on the State of Virginia;* he pauses to promise divine intervention, because "God will not suffer us, always to be oppressed"; and then he offers a provocative call to action by arguing "that unless we try to refute Mr. Jefferson's arguments respecting us, we will only establish them" (15). Drawing the article to its conclusion, Walker rebukes his black audience for being submissive to mere (white) men instead of to the laws of God and wonders if white Christians can be, given the great disparity between their ideals and their actions, "*as good by nature* as we are or not" (17).

Wilson Moses argues that "Walker's jeremiadic prophecy was a conscious and deliberate response" to Jefferson's "racial theories and apocalyptic prophesies," and David Howard-Pitney suggests that Walker's "skillful use of jeremiadic rhetoric reflected his active participation in the highest ideals of American society."[57] But because Walker's discourse is so thoroughly saturated with apocalyptic visions, its relationship to the jeremiad is complex. It may be useful to differentiate between two broad genres of apocalyptic discourse—*premillennial* and *postmillennial*—each with a different view of human agency. Premillennialism, as its name implies, assumes that the apocalypse must occur *before* the millennial Golden Age can arrive. As Daniel Wojcik explains, premillennialism "has been identified as involving an interpretation of humanity and the world as unrecuperably evil," so that it might be redeemed "only through catastrophe and supernatural intervention."[58] Humans cannot affect the preordained end of the present chaos but can prepare for the arrival of the Golden Age. Postmillennialism, on the other hand, promises that the apocalypse will come *after* the Golden Age. This discourse "is characterized by an expectation of the gradual transformation of society brought about by Christian ideals, the belief in the idea of human progress and perfection, and a relatively liberal perspective."[59] It calls upon its audience to engage in works that gradually will hasten the arrival of the millennium. Evil, in this view, is not something impervious to all but divine power but instead is something that might be overcome through "recognition, reform, and education."[60] Postmillennial prophecy, then, bears some resemblance to the jeremiad—except that the jeremiad asks its hearers to repent and change so that the world will change, and "postmillennialists argue that one needs to change oneself so as to join with history's inevitable progress that will eventually transform the world."[61]

In Walker's *Appeal*, the mixture of premillennial and postmillennial prophecy makes it seem at times that the end is inevitable and that the only human action required or possible is preparation, and at other times that both whites and blacks can avert disaster if they bring themselves into alignment with the proper doctrines. For example, speaking of Spain in his preamble, Walker warns that whites "forget that God rules in the armies of heaven and among the inhabitants of the earth . . . and a just and holy Being will at one day appear fully in behalf of the oppressed, and arrest the progress of the avaricious oppressors" (3). Whites "have always been an unjust, jealous, unmerciful, avaricious and blood-thirsty set of beings" (16), irredeemable "*devils*" (25) who are "our *natural enemies ! ! ! ! !*" (23). The frequent suggestions that America does not compare favorably with Sodom and Gomorrah further reinforce the impression that hope for white redemption is slim (53, 59, 73). It is not surprising, then, that the *Appeal* calls repeatedly for separation from this doomed white race; Walker declares that he "would not give a *pinch of snuff* to be married to any white person I ever saw in all the days of my life" and further declares that any "black man, or man of colour, who will leave his own colour . . . and marry a white woman, to be a double slave to her, just because she is *white*, ought to be treated by her as he surely will be, viz: as a NIGGER! ! ! !" (9). His black readers otherwise are urged only to allow the "person whom God shall give you" to "go his length," for "God will indeed, deliver you through him from your deplorable and wretched condition under the Christians of America" (20). "I assure you," Walker promises, God "will hurl tyrants and devils into *atoms* and make way for his people. But O my brethren! I say unto you again, you must go to work and prepare the way of the Lord" (30). Near the end of the pamphlet, Walker notes that some whites "represent us to be the greatest set of cut-throats in the world, as though God wants us to take his work out of hand before he is ready." But such is not the case, for: "Does not vengeance belong to the Lord?" (69).[62]

But at the same time that the apocalypse seems both inescapable and destined to be wholly the work of a divine hand, Walker also repeatedly suggests that it might be staved off if whites and blacks work to recover forgotten or dormant ideals. Walker quotes from the Declaration of Independence, for example, and asks his white readers, "Do you understand your own language?" (75). White Americans are warned that "unless you speedily alter your course" to bring your actions in line with your doctrine, then "*you* and your *Country are gone! ! ! ! ! !*" (38–39). Walker's black readers are reminded that "a groveling servile and abject submission to the lash of tyrants" is not "natural" for blacks but that "God has suffered our fathers to be enveloped" in these "misfortunes" in "consequence of their disobedience to their Maker" (21). People "my colour," Walker says, "all over the world, have a mean, servile spirit." Why is it, he asks, "that those few weak, good-for-nothing whites, are able to keep so many able men . . . in wretchedness and misery? It shows at once, what the blacks are, we are ignorant, abject, servile and mean" (62). Black pride has been beaten out of them by the whites, and they will only be able to achieve their promised glory if they can recapture their "natural" strength of character (61). Blacks are urged to fight, not merely to wait for the Lord to appear, for the "man who would not fight under the Lord and Master Jesus Christ, in the glorious and heavenly cause of freedom and of God . . . ought to be kept with all of his children or family, in slavery, or in chains, to be butchered by his *cruel enemies*" (12).[63] Blacks sufficiently reacquainted with their natural prowess are nearly invincible: "[I]f you can only get courage into the blacks, I do declare it, that one good black man can put to death six white men." "The reason is," he goes on, "the blacks, once you get them started, they glory in death. . . . Get the blacks started, and if you do not have a gang of tigers and lions to deal with, I am a deceiver of the blacks and of the whites" (25). Walker himself would "meet death with avidity far! far!! in preference to such *servile submission* to the murderous hands of tyrants" (14) and announces that he is ready to die "at any moment" for the cause, for "what is the use of living, when in fact I am dead" (72).

Walker's black audience, then, is told on the one hand that nothing is to be done except to prepare themselves for Armageddon and on the other that the end might be postponed or even averted if they, or the whites, begin to act in accordance with moral codes—and yet they are told that they should be willing to fight, if necessary, to obtain their freedom. This simultaneous presentation of multiple options, with no sense of contradiction, resembles the well-known doctrine of "by any means necessary" that emerged in Malcolm's post-Nation of Islam rhetoric. But as with Douglass and Du Bois, Walker's discourse functions within a predetermined mythic narrative. The universe is governed by predictable trajectories, and the Last Days will arrive as scheduled—the only question is whether humans can affect or even know when this event will occur. There may be multiple appropriate responses to the world, and among those responses may be an impulse to alter the world so that it is realigned with natural and authentic laws, but the foundational laws and narratives themselves remain unchallenged. This is a prophetic discourse, and Walker frames himself as merely the messenger. He appeals "to Heaven for my motive in writing" (2), for example, and acknowledges that "the final result of all future events are [*sic*] known but to God Almighty alone" (38). As such, this prophetic discourse bears much in common with Malcolm's rhetoric before he left the Nation of Islam.

Among the similarities between Walker's discourse and Malcolm's Nation of Islam discourse is the emphasis on the potentially emancipatory effects of education. Education makes a person unenslaveable: "[F]or coloured people to acquire learning in this country," Walker declares, "makes tyrants quake and tremble on their sandy foundation" (31). "Do you suppose," he asks, "one man of good sense and learning would submit himself, his father, mother, wife and children, to be slaves to a wretched man like himself, who, instead of compensating him for his labours, chains, hand-cuffs and beats him and family almost to death, leaving life enough in them however, to work for, and call him master? No!" Such education also would enable the oppressed to make the whites' "infernal deeds of cruelty . . . known to the world" (32). The sort of education that Walker envisions would also increase race awareness, so that blacks will act in their collective self-interest. Blacks who say that they are happy while still serving whites, for example, are "ignorant and wretched"; it is an "unshaken and for ever immovable *fact*, that your full glory and happiness . . . shall never be fully consummated, but with the *entire emancipation of your enslaved brethren all over the world*" (29). He excoriates blacks who aid whites, such as those who seek out runaway slaves and return them to bondage, attributing such behavior to "servile deceit, combined with the most gross ignorance: for we must remember that *humanity, kindness* and *the fear of the Lord*, does not consist in protecting *devils*" (24–25). "Ignorance and treachery," Moses points out, "were almost synonymous in Walker's vocabulary."[64]

Revolutionary Reading

Walker violates the general class divisions associated with black nationalist discourse, for though he was addressing slaves, his message was not emigrationist. He was, however, addressing literate slaves—and literate free blacks and literate whites. At one point, he advises his readers to "get Sheridan's Dictionary" to look up the meaning of "apathy" (52). Walker's literate audience also is evident in his critique of the ACS, which consists of an extended and careful rhetorical critique of speeches by Henry Clay, Elias B. Caldwell, and John Randolph at an 1816 ACS meeting.[65] He quotes Clay at great length, showing Clay declaring that it is not the object of the ACS to agitate for "emancipation" or "the abolition of slavery" (47). Walker then translates this for his readers: "That is to say" that colonization is "a plan to get those of the coloured people, who are said to be free, away from among those of our brethren whom they unjustly hold in bondage." Clay says this because he knows that "if the free are allowed to stay among the slaves, they will have intercourse together, and, of course, the free will learn the slaves *bad habits,* by teaching them that they are MEN, as well as other people, and certainly *ought* and *must* be FREE" (47). In this passage, consistent with the tone throughout the *Appeal,* Walker through his qualified terms ("who are *said* to be free"; "they *unjustly* hold") invites his audience to share an attitude suspicious of the dominant white culture. Walker is positioning his audience so that they can read the absurdity in the discourse of white domination. Caldwell's speech, Walker writes, "will be taken for the speech of a friend, without close examination and deep penetration, as I shall now present." He quotes Caldwell saying that "Americans ought to be the last people on earth, to advocate such slavish doctrines, to cry peace and contentment to those who are deprived of the privileges of civil liberty." "The real sense and meaning" of Caldwell's speech, Walker argues, is that the free blacks should be taken away to Africa so that "those who we hold in slavery, will be contented to rest in ignorance and wretchedness" (52). Randolph's speech is given similar treatment: it is excerpted at length and then translated as "demonstrative proof" that the ACS was created by "a gang of slave-holders to select the free people of colour from among the slaves" (55).

Walker's literate black audience is advised to stay in the United States; of those "who are ignorant enough to go to Africa, the coloured people ought to be glad to have them go" (64). Like Du Bois, he urges the members of his literate black audience to turn a critical and recuperative eye upon their own culture. But Walker also encourages his black audience to critique the discourse of white domination, which is a far more revolutionary act, an act of empowerment that relies neither upon white redemption, divine intervention, nor physical force. Such critique requires a systemic shift in attitude and consciousness and an appreciation of the discursive nature of political power.

Walker's *Appeal* displays perhaps the most pointed and eloquent antebellum attempt to craft this critical attitude, and its mixed jeremiadic and apocalyptic impulses are central to the effort. If a recovery of an authentic black identity alone could bring about the end of slavery, then such an attitude would be unnecessary. But close attention to the *Appeal* reveals that Walker understood these attitudes as insufficient; blacks had to be willing to fight, if need be, to secure their freedom, and blacks also had to learn to interpret the discourses through which they were oppressed. Of these options—perhaps because, as Hinks suggests, Walker understood well the power of the white Southern adversary—the latter is privileged. And it is this interpretive attitude, grounded in the mixed motives of Walker's discourse, that is his most salient contribution to the African American rhetorical landscape within which Malcolm X worked and against which he innovated.

Nat Turner: Black Messiah

It is possible that the slave called Nat Turner knew of Walker's *Appeal*. If so, then this would complete a genealogy of radical prophecy from Denmark Vesey through Walker and to Turner. *The Confessions of Nat Turner* does not mention either Vesey or Walker, however, and historical data concerning the circulation of particular pieces of literature among slaves is difficult to obtain. At any rate, as Vincent Harding puts it, "contact was not necessary, for Nat Turner had long been convinced that the God of Walker's *Appeal* had always been in Southampton."[66] Nat Turner's rebellion is the most notorious of the slave uprisings. Unlike Walker, Turner, as a slave, was a member of the same class he was addressing, and perhaps as a result there is little ambiguity in his prophetic vision—he and his recruits were to take actions that would initiate a racial Armageddon and thus hasten the end of the white-dominated world.

Details of Turner's life can be only roughly outlined. He was born October 2, 1800, in Southampton County, Virginia, where he would spend his entire life; he passed between owners until eventually his master was Joseph Travis, a carriage-maker;[67] his bloody rebellion began on Monday morning, August 22, 1831. The plan was for his small band of men to move from farm to farm, killing all the whites they encountered and enlisting recruits from among the slaves until eventually their forces would be sufficient to take control of the small town of Jerusalem, just across the Nottoway River. Turner's band eventually would grow to over forty members, and they would kill nearly sixty whites—men, women, and children.[68] Turner's account of the uprising is contained in *The Confessions of Nat Turner.* This remarkable text, produced by local lawyer Thomas R. Gray from interviews with Turner over a period of three days soon after his capture, marks the most apocalyptic point along the continuum of African American prophetic protest that I have been tracing. As Stephen H. Browne points out, some elements of this narrative may owe as much to the melodramatic expectations of the day as to Turner's actual words.[69] Nonetheless, *Confessions* provides the best record available of a slave uprising based upon a premillennialist apocalyptic vision. The text begins with the story of Turner's life, a biography in the first person in which considerable rhetorical effort is expended to establish a prophetic persona. The middle section is a detailed account of the uprising, the scattering of Turner's recruits, and Turner's efforts to avoid capture. The final section primarily is in Gray's voice, describing Turner's demeanor while in jail and corroborating his story.

Nat Turner's Confession

To explain the events, Turner tells Gray and, through Gray, his readers, "I must go back to the days of my infancy, and even before I was born."[70] "In my childhood," he continues, "a circumstance occurred which made an indelible impression on my mind, and laid the ground work of that enthusiasm, which has terminated so fatally to many, both white and black, and for which I am about to atone at the gallows." At about three or four years old, Turner described to his young playmates "something" that had happened before he was born. Turner does not say what this thing was but does tell us that he "related somethings [sic] which went," in his mother's opinion, "to confirm it." Others were called in to witness the miracle and "were greatly astonished." They told Turner that he "surely would be a prophet, as the Lord had shewn me things that had happened before my birth." This childhood event, Turner declares, is "the commencement of that belief which has grown with time, and even now, sir, in this dungeon, helpless and forsaken as I am, I cannot divest myself of." Nat's mother and father supplemented this revelation by sharing with young Nat their conviction that he "was intended for some great purpose, which they had always thought from certain marks on my head and breast" (44). Gray parenthetically dismisses these marks as merely "a parcel of excrescences . . . not at all uncommon, particularly among negroes."[71] But in its first few pages, *Confessions* already has offered a preponderance of evidence that Nat Turner is the chosen one.

Turner's purity is emphasized throughout. As a youth, he did not partake in the illicit activities of the other boys; but they recognized his "superior judgment" and "would often carry me with them when they were going on any roguery, to plan for them." He was a sort of participant observer of his own culture, not entirely integrated with it and yet at the same time not alienated from it. He describes himself as "[g]rowing up among" the slaves, rather than *as* a slave. "Having soon discovered to be great," he continues, "I must appear so, and therefore studiously avoided mixing in society, and wrapped myself in mystery, devoting time to fasting and prayer" (45). Even during the uprising itself, Turner portrays himself as unable to "give a death blow" to his own master (49) and as having "never got to the houses . . . until the murders were committed, except in one case" (51). He kills only one white person, and while his recruits visit several stills during the insurrection, Turner remains sober.

Apocalyptic discourse largely is an interpretive genre, characterized by a rhetor's attempts to invite an audience to share her or his understanding of some foundational text.[72] An apocalyptic vision entails extracting a meaning from some text or set of signs that others have observed but not understood. Apocalyptic rhetors must "demonstrate the rationality of their interpretation" and therefore "must depict himself or herself as learned, scholarly, or expert enough to interpret the grounding text and lay claim to its credibility."[73] The apocalyptic prophet is the medium through which the audience reads the underlying text; she or he provides a model reading of that text and encourages the audience to generate similar readings on their own. As such, an apocalyptic rhetor may emerge "as a leader, often a charismatic one, for followers of his or her discourse."[74]

Turner models multiple interpretive acts for audiences of the *Confessions*. He seems hyperaware, gifted with preternatural faculties of observation, so that signs and omens appear to him at every turn. Turner describes his own mind as "restless, inquisitive and observant of every thing that was passing," and though religion principally occupied his thoughts, "there was nothing that I saw or heard of to which my attention was not directed." He learned to read suddenly and without any apparent instruction, which "was a source of wonder to all in the neighborhood, particularly the blacks." But reading books, for Turner, was supplementary to his own powers of observation and invention: "many things . . . would present themselves" to his imagination while he was working, "and whenever an opportunity occurred of looking at a book . . . I would find many things that the fertility of my own imagination had depicted to me before" (45).

Attending a religious meeting, he says, he was "struck with that particular passage which says: 'Seek ye the kingdom of Heaven and all things shall be added unto you'" (45). Turner "reflected much on this passage [Luke 12:31] and prayed daily for light on this subject," until eventually he heard "the spirit that spoke to the prophets in the former days" repeat back to him the same passage, "which fully confirmed me in the impression that I was ordained for some great purpose in the hands of the Almighty" (45–46). Naming this biblical passage, which asks its readers to remain fixated upon ultimate salvation and to be willing to sacrifice earthly comforts, as central to his spiritual development contributes to Turner's prophetic persona. It also rounds out his interpretive strategy; Turner is not attempting to understand the meaning of the text, but rather he is attempting to understand what action the text is asking him to take. This is not an exercise in exegesis but the sighting of an omen. As Barry Brummett puts it, the apocalyptic prophet "claims attention as the one who can tell what the Revelation or Daniel has to do with us, *not* as one to whom God has directly revealed history's plan. The rhetor knows that plan as an interpreter of the grounding text."[75]

As he reached adulthood, Turner determined to "direct my attention to this great object, to fulfill the purpose for which, by this time, I felt assured I was intended." He began to share his revelations with other slaves, who "believed and said my wisdom came from God," and he "began to prepare them for my purpose, by telling them something was about to happen that would terminate in fulfilling the great promise that had been made to me." Turner's preparation was guided by apocalyptic visions, such as seeing "white spirits and black spirits engaged in battle, and the sun was darkened—the thunder rolled in the Heavens, and blood flowed in streams—and I heard a voice saying, 'Such is your luck, such you are called to see, and let it come rough or smooth, you must surely bare it'" (46). Turner responds by withdrawing "as much as my situation would permit" from his fellow slaves, so as to "obtain true holiness before the great day of judgment should appear." He tells us that he "began to receive the true knowledge of faith" and eventually was "made perfect; and the Holy Ghost was with me" (47).

Other omens appeared with increasing frequency. Turner saw lights in the sky "to which the children of darkness gave other names" but which he knew actually were "the Savior's hands, stretched forth from east to west, even as they were extended on the cross on Calvary for the redemption of sinners." While working in a field, he "discovered drops of blood on the corn as though it were dew from heaven" and "found on the leaves in the woods hieroglyphic characters, and numbers, with the forms of men in different attitudes, portrayed in blood." These he interpreted as signs showing "that the Savior was about to lay down the yoke he had borne for the sins of men, and the great day of judgment was at hand." Over the next several years, Turner's power grew. He told a white man, Etheldred T. Brantley, about his visions, and Brantley immediately "ceased from his wickedness" and blood began to ooze "form the pores of his skin" (47). On May 12, 1828, Turner heard "a loud noise in the heavens," and the spirit appeared and informed him that "Christ had laid down the yoke he had borne for the sins of men" and that Turner himself should take it up "and fight against the Serpent." Signs in the heavens "would make it known to me when I should commence the great work." Gray interjects himself into the text at this point, to ask Turner if he does not "find yourself mistaken now," jailed and facing execution. Turner answers: "Was not Christ crucified?" (47–48).

Confessions then segues into a narrative of the uprising itself. A solar eclipse in February signaled the beginning of the Last Days, and "the seal was removed" from Turner's lips so that he could begin to spread the word among his compatriots. They were "instructed" to begin the work on the Fourth of July, but planning difficulties and a sudden illness forced Turner to postpone until "the sign appeared again, which determined me not to wait longer" (48). On Saturday, August 13, he and other residents of Southampton County witnessed a strange atmospheric phenomenon that caused the sun to seem to change colors in the sky. In addition, August was the time of "jubilee," a relatively quiet period between the planting and the harvest when slaves might be afforded more free time. Far from representing *the* Jubilee, long a slave marker for a millennium purged of slavery (probably a reference to the Mosaic prophecies in Leviticus, especially chapter 25), the association still may have been strong. Oates notes that, for whatever reason, "Negroes both in Southampton and in adjoining counties in Virginia and North Carolina received word that something apocalyptic was in the wind, but did not know when or how Nat intended to move."[76]

The following Sunday, August 21, six slaves met in the woods for a feast of roast pig and apple brandy. Nat arrived late, for "the same reason that had caused me not to mix with them for years before" (48). They put their plans into action beginning at about 2:00 Monday morning, beginning by killing the entire household of Joseph Travis, Turner's owner. As the day wore on and they lost the advantage of surprise, Turner's insurrection became increasingly difficult to sustain. Vincent Harding describes "a growing sense of confusion, disarray, and sometimes drunkenness among some of Nat's men."[77] With his recruits scattered and the bridges blocked, Turner's plan to attack Jerusalem was thwarted, and he was forced into hiding. During the time before his capture, "the outraged, terrified white forces struck back in overwhelming fury. Estimates range from scores to hundreds of black people slaughtered, most of whom evidently had no intimate connection with the uprising."[78] Turner, discovered and apprehended without resistance after some six weeks in hiding, was accorded a speedy trial and was hanged on Friday, November 11. His body was given to surgeons for dissection.[79]

Apocalyptic Observation

The Confessions of Nat Turner offers important additions to our understanding of African American prophetic protest. For example, Turner is systematically relieved of direct responsibility. His messianic role is thrust upon him; he cannot even choose when the rebellion is to begin but must wait until propitious signs appear on the cornstalks and in the sky. Gray comments on the "calm, deliberate composure with which he [Turner] spoke of his late deeds and intentions" (54), and indeed throughout, with few exceptions, the horrors are related in a relatively detached tone in marked contrast to the often melodramatic style of Walker's *Appeal*. Stephen H. Browne reads within the *Confessions* two Turners: Gray's Turner is "unique, alien, mad, local, and containable"; Turner's Turner, to the extent that Turner's voice breaches the constraints of Gray's authorial voice, is "a tropological figure of universal significance, generated from within the community but ultimately destructive of it, justified if not by man then by God."[80] Browne thinks that these two figures stand in "sharp contradistinction" to one another, and so they do in many aspects—but they both cue us to understand Turner as irrational and thus not entirely responsible for his actions. He was acting under the influence of madness or a divine hand, either of which dramatically circumvents Turner's agency. Turner's actions actually were merely *reactions* to the visions and omens that appeared around him, not inventions in the sense of reasoned or reasonable corollaries to critical observation and study. Turner assures Gray that the omens are primarily responsible for the mayhem and that the "strange appearances about this time in the heaven's [*sic*] might prompt others, as well as myself, to this undertaking" (54).

This mode of agent-less interpretation is one aspect of the "universalism" that Browne ascribes to Turner; anyone in a similar position, Turner seems to suggest, would respond to these hieroglyphs, lights, and eclipses in exactly the same way. The signs commanded, and Turner responded in the only way allowed. These signs are concrete markers, and their meaning is self-evident to those who know how to read them. They carry none of the ambiguity of metaphor or allusion. For Turner, the biblical passage from Luke 12:31, "Seek ye the kingdom of Heaven and all things shall be added unto you," does not model a possible response to generic situations of woe. It refers to Turner's concrete situation specifically; he must seek the kingdom of heaven, he must take concrete steps to do so, and he must take these as soon as possible. The other passage from Luke that Turner discusses—"For he who knoweth his Master's will, and doeth it not, shall be beaten with many stripes, and thus have I chastened you"—is taken to refer specifically and concretely to Turner himself, as though Luke was written with Turner in mind.[81]

Turner is not encouraging an emancipatory rereading of a foundational text, or an empowering conservation of a culture, or the critical appraisal of oppressive discourses; his audiences are schooled in a style of reading that literalizes symbols into omens. This mode of interpretation differs from that modeled and advocated by Douglass, Du Bois, or even Walker. Each of those prophets believed that African Americans were a chosen people with a fixed and attainable destiny that might be realized at some point in the future; for Turner, the time was at hand, and he was the chosen one.

Conclusion

My purpose in this chapter has been to use examples of African American prophetic protest to set out a backdrop against which other discourses might bet set for the purposes of interpretation and assessment. Frederick Douglass's "What to the Slave Is the Fourth of July?" calls upon some forms similar to characteristics of the American jeremiad to urge his white audience to bring their actions in line with a revivified version of their heritage and by doing so to redress the dangers and moral chaos of the present day. Douglass relies upon the rich ironic potential of the situation—an ex-slave addressing a crowd of whites in celebration of their independence—to place the onus squarely on the shoulders of that white audience; if the situation is to be repaired, it is the whites who must repair it. W. E. B. Du Bois's "The Conservation of Races," addressed to an African American audience, also presents jeremiadic echoes. He is urging his audience to avoid the dangers of the present through a revivification of their past, and he operates from an established faith in the exceptional destiny of those he addresses. But he is addressing a black audience, and so the past he calls them toward is not shared with the dominant white culture. This is a nationalist discourse, constituting a people defined by a viable and worthy African American culture.

David Walker's *Appeal* is a hybrid discourse, incorporating many of the forms and themes associated with the jeremiad within an apocalyptic rhetorical vision. The *Appeal* addresses multiple audiences and, as a result, exhibits mixed motives and an ambiguous role for human agency. It can perhaps best be described as a rhetoric of preparation: the end of slavery is inevitable, and it will be brought about through divine intervention. While it is unclear what role the *Appeal*'s audience is to play in the apocalypse itself, this text does consistently urge its audience toward race pride and solidarity through education.

The Confessions of Nat Turner charts the most purely premillennial apocalyptic rhetoric among the discourses reviewed in this chapter and as such presents a role for its audience that, however radical, also is remarkably narrow. Turner does not conceive of the present situation as amenable to education or to gradual change; only a catastrophic and violent confrontation can bring about the end of slavery. Human beings may act only in accordance to the directions provided by signs and omens, and the only interpretive skills required are those that allow these signs and omens to be recognized. The actions of Turner and his followers are reactions, scripted responses to stimuli intended to further human history along a predetermined course.

In each of these four nodal points along the continuum of African American prophetic protest, an act of interpretation is central to the emancipatory project. Each of these discourses schools its audience in a mode of reading—either explicitly, as an object of advocacy for the rhetor, or implicitly, through the rhetor's modeled interpretive practices. Douglass explicitly urges his white audience to recapture the attitudes of the Founding Fathers and provides a brief sample of the sort of "plain reading" of the Constitution that would recover it as an antislavery document. Du Bois urges his black listeners to attend to their own cultural history, to become aligned with its attitudes just as Douglass's white audience is to become aligned with the attitudes of the Founding Fathers; the interpretive act, for Du Bois, is one of cultural "conservation" rather than textual exegesis. Walker, like Douglass, points out to his white audience their ironic declension from their own ideals and warns them that they need to reinterpret their founding documents. Like Du Bois, Walker urges his black audience to recover a nationalist pride through an appraisal of their own history. But Walker also demonstrates a critical engagement with oppressive discourses that is absent from Douglass and Du Bois, because their faith in America's ability to effect a progressive resolution to racial tensions is foreign to Walker. For Walker, white discourses are fundamentally corrupt, and emancipation means being able to discern their corruption. For Nat Turner, interpretation entails understanding texts and signs as concrete and literal references to specific actions; what is needed is not critical thinking or cultural recuperation but a steely resolve to carry out divine edicts.

Each of these interpretive strategies appears in Malcolm's Nation of Islam rhetoric. Like Douglass, when Malcolm X addressed white audiences he played the ironist, asking them to view their current practices in light of their fundamental promises. Like Du Bois, Malcolm urged his black audiences to reinterpret their own cultural heritage and warned them against the dangers of assimilation. Like Walker, Malcolm modeled thoughtful critique of the discourses of white power. And like Turner, Malcolm taught his audiences to read the world for signs and omens that heralded the apocalypse.

All of these various strategies of prophetic interpretation mark out for their audiences confining patterns of judgment. These audiences are trained to read or to reread texts according to specific and articulated teleological commitments. For these prophetic rhetors, history shall—or should—follow a predetermined arc, and the appropriate strategy is to bring the interpretation of texts, cultures, and signs into alignment with that arc. These rhetors deliver addresses that are disciplined within that arc, and in turn these discourses discipline their audiences. The pattern of judgment being modeled is a matter of decorous alignment, because the most appropriate action always is the thing that will further human progress along its inevitable journey—whether that be toward redemption through the revivification of cultural ideals or toward destruction through the cataclysm of divine intervention. Once the *telos* of human advancement is known, rhetorical invention is limited merely to discovering the best way to pursue it. For these rhetors and audiences, the available means of engaging, resisting, and interrogating the dominant culture occupy a fairly narrow range. In the next chapter, I examine these restraints as they were manifest for Malcolm X while he was a minister for the Nation of Islam.

3

Limits of Prophecy

◇ ◇ ◇ ◇ ◇

In the first decades of the twentieth century, black separatist and nation-alist discourse found its most ready audience in northern urban centers.[1] The promise of increased respect, freedom, and opportunity had spurred the so-called Great Migration of African Americans out of the South. The resurgence of racial violence and hate organizations such as the Ku Klux Klan (KKK) further fueled the flow, as did, eventually, the promise of good jobs in northern factories during World War I. Advertisements in such black newspapers as the *Chicago Defender,* distributed hand-to-hand throughout the South, touted life in the North. But these northern ghettos proved not to resemble Canaan, and when whites reclaimed the factory jobs after the war, racial tensions began to mount. As E. David Cronon puts it, African Americans' "initial feeling of delight at the comparative equality of treatment in the North rapidly gave way to a wave of discouragement as it became apparent that even in the fabled North Negroes were still only second-class citizens, herded into black ghettos, the last to be hired and the first to be fired."[2] Escalating incidents of racial violence culminated in the "Red Summer" of 1919 and helped to create a poor, displaced, and frus-trated black audience unusually receptive to radical rhetoric of social uplift.

Cronon continues: "[B]y 1919 American Negroes were ready for any program that would tend to restore even a measure of their lost dignity and
self-respect."[3]

The Nation of Islam finds its roots in these fertile conditions, specifically
among the disappointed and displaced African Americans in "Paradise Val-
ley" in 1930s Detroit. In 1938, Erdmann Beynon interviewed two hundred
Nation of Islam members and found that "with less than half-a-dozen exceptions all were recent migrants from the rural South."[4] The story of the
founding of the Nation of Islam is an oft-told tale, of how the mysterious
W. D. Fard appeared in black Detroit as a traveling salesman, how he began
to gain a reputation for preaching an "Islamic" doctrine that he said was
the true and rightful religion of black people, and how he vanished one
day in 1934, leaving his fledgling Nation in the initially unsteady hands of
Elijah Muhammad. There is little need for me to recount this story in detail.[5] Instead, I describe the impact of the two organizations that seem most
directly to have influenced the early doctrine of the Nation of Islam. Then
I focus on representative speeches by Malcolm X that illustrate vividly both
the possibilities and the limitations of Nation of Islam rhetoric.

I make two central arguments in this chapter. First, the specific historical
antecedents of the Nation of Islam—Marcus Garvey's Universal Negro Improvement Association (UNIA) and Noble Drew Ali's Moorish Science
Temple of America (MSTA)—present the conduits through which characteristic elements of African American prophetic discourse find their way
into the Nation of Islam. The previous chapter developed a continuum of
African American prophetic discourse against which other discourses
might be understood; collectively, Douglass, Du Bois, Walker, and Turner
provide a textual landscape within which to situate and evaluate Malcolm's
discourse while he was a Nation of Islam minister and against which to
gauge the remarkable rhetorical innovations of his last year. In this chapter, I begin by situating Garvey's UNIA and Ali's MSTA within that landscape, suggesting some of their points of direct and indirect influence upon
the Nation of Islam as well as their particular contributions to its prophetic
rhetoric. Specifically, the UNIA emphasizes themes characteristic of what I
have described as a secular nationalist jeremiad, while MSTA discourse is
more typically apocalyptic. Thus is the prophetic stance of the Nation of
Islam informed by two potentially contradictory types of rhetoric, and it is
the tension between them that is partially responsible for the Nation of
Islam's unusual longevity.

My second argument is that as Malcolm's fame grew and he addressed increasingly diverse audiences, he produced increasingly secular discourse, eventually abandoning a discourse of prophecy altogether. In this chapter, I do not mean to present a linear trajectory that takes Malcolm from addressing audiences primarily inside the Nation of Islam's mosques to addressing audiences primarily outside, but I intend to illustrate an incremental incompatibility that was a consequence of Malcolm's continuing efforts to address these two audiences. Malcolm's well-known chafing against the limitations of Elijah Muhammad's Nation of Islam can only partly and inadequately be accounted for by understanding the eventual split as a tale of youthful rebellion against senior authority (as it is depicted in the *Autobiography*) or as a case of bureaucratic inertia shucked off by a revolutionary thinker (as George Breitman would have it). Rather, it is essential to understand the split as being driven by shifts in Malcolm's discourse and specifically by the incompatibility of a rhetoric of prophecy with the emancipatory strategies of interpretation that eventually would become central to his rhetoric. To illustrate a growing incompatibility, I attend carefully to representative speeches by Malcolm X delivered during his last year as a Black Muslim, exploring within these texts the various and often conflicting prophetic visions that constitute the core of the Nation of Islam's rhetorical power.

Marcus Garvey

Marcus Moziah Garvey read Booker T. Washington's *Up From Slavery* in 1912; at that moment, he declared years later, "my doom—if I may so call it—of being a race leader dawned upon me."[6] Garvey was born in Jamaica, where he honed his oratorical skills by attending the churches of successful preachers and listening carefully to the open-air speakers common in Kingston. Garvey arrived in Harlem in 1916, a year after Washington's death, to find a power vacuum in African American leadership, especially among the lower classes who were not attracted by Du Bois's polished prose. Garvey was determined to "see how American Negroes would receive his program of race improvement," and after a false start, the response was overwhelming.[7] As Manning Marable describes it:

> Within several brief years, the UNIA initiated the Black Star steamship line, the Universal African Legion, and the *Negro World* newspaper. The popularity of "Garveyism" spread at a phenomenal rate. At its peak, the UNIA had fifty two branches in Cuba, over thirty in Trinidad and Tobago, eleven in

Jamaica, six in the Dominican Republic, six in Panama, and four in British Honduras. . . . Garvey's greatest successes occurred in North America, which had more than seven hundred official UNIA branches by the early 1920s. The organization claimed thirty-five thousand dues-paying members in New York City alone.[8]

In 1922, after rousing successes and high-profile failures, Garvey was arrested for mail fraud. A "Garvey Must Go!" movement was begun, led by A. Philip Randolph and Chandler Owen and supported by W. E. B. Du Bois, and Garvey eventually was convicted, imprisoned in Atlanta's Tombs prison, and deported back to Jamaica.

Most historians of the Nation of Islam note the importance of Garvey's influence. C. Eric Lincoln, for example, writes that in the Nation of Islam's "commitment to racial uplift and to the unification of black peoples . . . the echo of Garveyism is loud and distinct."[9] Many of the Nation of Islam's early converts were former Garveyites casting about for leadership after Garvey's deportation in 1927. Karl Evanzz makes a well-documented argument that Elijah Muhammad—then Elijah Pool, a recent arrival from Sandersville, Georgia—was a member of the UNIA. And Malcolm X tells of his Garveyite parents in his autobiography and theorizes that his father's black nationalist sermons contributed to his murder.[10] Some also have argued that Garvey may have helped to open the door to Islam among African Americans. Louis A. DeCaro Jr., for example, suggests that Garvey was "influenced by Edward Wilmot Blyden's earlier, positive assessment of Islam" and that "Garvey provided Muslim missionaries in the United States with a friendly platform. Indeed, some members of the UNIA were themselves converts to Islam."[11]

Harold Cruse draws a direct line of descent from Booker T. Washington through Marcus Garvey and then to Malcolm X, and Manning Marable suggests that "the Garvey movement transformed the Tuskegee philosophy by discarding accommodationist rhetoric and expanding into the urban working class for both support and leadership."[12] Garvey himself claimed that his "new ideal includes the program of Booker T. Washington and has gone much further."[13] But as Garvey's program developed in the United States, especially after he witnessed violent race riots such as those in East St. Louis and Chicago during the summer of 1919, he seems to have lost much of Washington's optimism about the prospects for African Americans in America. Garvey's program might be most profitably understood as a revision of Washington's, one that combined the "self-help, community development, industrial education aspects of Washington's philosophy" with an "internationalist pan-Africanism" that was more similar to Du Bois's.[14]

In situating Garvey against the continuum of black prophetic protest outlined in the previous chapter, it is evident that his rhetoric shares little in common with that exemplified by Douglass's Fifth of July oration— Garvey was not motivated by a faith in America's ultimate promise and never imagined that the destiny of African Americans was to remain in this country. He also rarely addressed white audiences.[15] When Garvey does ask if "the soul of liberal, philanthropic, liberty-loving, white America is not dead," it is to suggest that white Americans should support the efforts of African Americans to "have a country and a nation of [their] own."[16]

Garvey's discourse does share some of the mixed motives of Walker's prophecy. At times, Garvey seems to offer nearly a pre-millennial vision of inevitable divine retribution, inviting his black audience to "work and pray, for surely our day of triumph and authority to mete out justice will come and Africa may yet teach the higher principles of justice, love and mercy, yea, true brotherhood." He promises that "with the Almighty Power of God and with the guidance and mercy of our Blessed Lord we feel that one day Ethiopia shall stretch forth her hand, and whether it be at the second coming or before, we shall all sing our Hosannas, shout our praises to God for freedom, for liberty, for life." "Our consolation should be," he says, "that each and every race will have its day; and there is no doubt that the Negro's day is drawing near."[17] But Garvey also makes it clear that he is not offering a strategy of reading signs and omens. Real leadership, Garvey explains, comes from African Americans "who will not blame Nature, who will not blame Fate for his condition; but the man who will go out and make conditions to suit himself." "Oh, how disgusting life becomes," he continues, "when on every hand you hear people . . . telling you that they cannot make it, that Fate is against them, that they cannot get a chance."[18] Generally, the historical trajectories that Garvey describes are guided by science rather than religion and display a more active role for human agency. Garvey argues, for example, that "evolution and human progress bring changes," but when he tells his audience to "prepare yourselves for the higher life, the life of liberty," he does not mean that they should prepare themselves for some divine cataclysm but rather that they should work "industrially, educationally, socially and politically" to bring about the proper elevation of the black race. "Man is the individual," Garvey writes, "who is able to shape his own character, master his own will, direct his own life and shape his own ends."[19]

But it is to Du Bois's discourse that Garvey's bears most similarity, and thus it is Du Bois who is most useful in locating Garvey along the continuum of prophetic black protest that I have outlined. That Garvey's position is substantially similar to Du Bois's as exemplified in "The Conservation of Races" is deeply ironic, given that Du Bois and Garvey were bitter enemies, trading public jabs at each other in one of the most spectacular rhetorical duels in the history of African American public address. Though in many ways a continuation and escalation of the conflict between Du Bois and Washington, it also was a peculiar reversal: Du Bois thought Garvey was a dangerous nationalist radical, while Garvey thought Du Bois was an accommodationist sellout.[20]

Nonetheless, a good part of the conflict seems to have stemmed from some fundamental points of similarity.[21] Wilson Moses, for example, places them under the same heading, suggesting that "black nationalists like Garvey and Du Bois hoped for a dramatic shift in the balance of world power, a rise in the status of the colored peoples that would correspond to the decline of the West."[22] Both men espoused a national homeland in the form of an "Africa for the Africans," and both men frequently argued for the importance to African Americans of an independent African homeland.[23] Arnold Rampersad summarizes other similarities: "Both men saw the world as comprising separate cultures, each reflecting a distinct heritage and demanding freedom of expression. By the early twenties both believed that there are not superior and inferior races in the twentieth century, only temporarily backward peoples. Both saw the speciousness of the Anglo-Saxon claim to superiority based on technological progress usually of a destructive sort."[24] This is not to say, of course, that Garvey and Du Bois were identical. The fact that Garvey, and not Du Bois, was the most direct historical influence on the early Nation of Islam is significant. Garvey's similarities to Du Bois help to place him within a landscape of black prophecy, but his differences with Du Bois provide an insight into the shaping of the Nation of Islam's particular brand of black nationalism.

There are three particularly salient points of comparison and contrast between Garvey and Du Bois. As Pan-Africanists, first, both men advocated that African Americans form a relationship with Africans. Du Bois states in "The Conservation of Races" that African Americans represent "the advance guard of the Negro people," so that a revivification of the cultural definition of "race" that he advocates in that speech would enable the uplift not only of African Americans but also of blacks worldwide. In Garvey's vision, African Americans should ideally have a complementary two-way relationship with Africa. On the one hand, Garvey supported a free and independent Africa because such a state could prove politically useful for African Americans. "Do they lynch Englishman, Frenchmen, Germans or Japanese?" Garvey asks. "No. And why? Because these peoples are represented by great governments, mighty nations and empires, strongly organized." On the other hand, for Garvey, "Back to Africa" meant that African Americans had an obligation to their home continent; that is, he was in essential agreement with Du Bois's sense of the special burden to be shouldered by enlightened African Americans. As Garvey put it: "We, the Negroes in this Western Hemisphere are descendents of those Africans who were enslaved and transported to these shores. . . . Should we not, therefore, turn our eyes toward Africa, our ancestral home and free it from the thralldom of alien oppression and exploitation?"[25] For Garvey, then, Africans and African Americans needed to develop a mutually dependent relationship for the good of both. "The Negroes of Africa and America are one in blood," Garvey declared. "They have sprung from the same common stock. They can work and live together and thus make their own racial contribution to the world."[26]

The rhetoric of the Nation of Islam exhibits many of these Pan-Africanist notions and particularly shows the influence of Garvey's vision of a two-way relationship between African Americans and Africans. But again, part of the peculiar rhetorical genius of the Nation of Islam was its ability to constrain severely the perspective and scope of its audience, and it did so by cloaking its Pan-Africanism in a mystic narrative of racial origins. An effort to broaden this scope—and to cast off the confining mysticism—becomes a hallmark of Malcolm's post-Nation of Islam rhetoric.

A second key point of convergence and variation between the rhetoric of Garvey and Du Bois has to do with audience. While Du Bois primarily published in magazines and periodicals directed to the rising black middle class, Garvey, like the early Nation of Islam, explicitly directed his rhetoric to the urban poor. Indeed, Garvey critiqued Du Bois on this issue, accusing him of wanting to build up a "'blue vein' aristocracy and to foster same as the social and moral standard of the race." Late in his career, Garvey compared his accusers, including Du Bois, to "Good Old Darkies" doing the bidding of whites, foreshadowing Malcolm X's famous distinction between "House Negroes" and "Field Negroes."[27] This tendency to paint the world in violently contrasting colors was a rhetoric of division in which one was either black or white and either with black people or against them. Such a rhetoric was troubling to Du Bois, of course, because it seemed to cut across the cultural definition of race he had begun to outline in "The Conservation of Races"; while Du Bois became increasingly nationalist and separatist throughout his long activist life, in the 1920s he played the moderate to Garvey's radical.

But a neatly bifurcated worldview likely would have been highly attractive to urban audiences with very limited resources who were weary of negotiating the continuous and seemingly capricious demands of being black in America. Elwood Watson suggests that "Garveyism made such a grand impact on working class African Americans in the 1920s because it elevated all things African and diminished all things Eurocentric. . . . For every white organization, Garveyism offered an African American counterpart—from the black shipping fleet to a black Christ. Everything of virtue was linked to blackness."[28] Of course, much of the pomp and circumstance of the UNIA—the lofty titles bestowed upon its officers, the extravagant uniforms, the elaborate parades through Harlem—was designed to appeal to people for whom the more sedate and white-normed demeanor of the National Association for the Advancement of Colored People (NAACP) held little attraction.[29] And as Edwin S. Redkey suggests, "Garvey's followers . . . were the same Southern black marginal farmers who had responded to the emigration appeals of [early black nationalist] Bishop Turner and his followers a generation earlier."[30] This, again, is the same displaced audience who eventually would respond most enthusiastically to the rhetoric of the Nation of Islam, so it is perhaps not surprising that the Nation of Islam also provided a discourse that relied upon a racially bifurcated worldview and an essentialized theory of race.

Finally, a third key difference between Garvey and Du Bois was that Garvey crafted a messianic role for himself. Recall that, for Du Bois, the African American intelligentsia were to be primarily responsible for the "conservation of races" that would allow blacks to contribute meaningfully to world progress. Like David Walker, Du Bois positioned himself more as cultural critic and man of letters than as a political leader; like Walker, Du Bois intended for the most well educated African Americans to lead the rest of the race. Garvey, on the other hand, imagined himself—and made himself—a leader, if not a savior. Like Bishop Turner, Garvey was called a "Black Moses," and much of his rhetorical success stemmed from his ability to personify messianic leadership.[31] As Elijah Muhammad would do within the Nation of Islam, Garvey imbued his movement with religious overtones that emphasized the authority of his leadership. Garvey did not reject Christianity outright, as did the Nation of Islam, but instead worked toward a black recovery of what he viewed as a dysfunctional white Christianity.[32] He boldly asserted the right to worship a black god, noting that "it is human to see everything through one's own spectacles" and that "we Negroes believe in the God of Ethiopia, the everlasting God," and so "shall worship Him through the spectacles of Ethiopia."[33] "Unwittingly," Cronon points out, "Garvey demonstrated a keen awareness of social psychology when he used a black God or Israel to stimulate racial nationalism among the Negro masses."[34] Whether unwitting or cunning it is perhaps impossible to know, but clearly Garvey—like Elijah Muhammad—was positioning himself as a prophet of Mosaic proportions, not merely declaiming a righteous vision but leading his followers in an effort to render that vision manifest.

Noble Drew Ali

There is some disagreement regarding the details of Noble Drew Ali's life and his Moorish Science movement, and a definitive history is yet to be written. However, it seems well established that he was born Timothy Drew in North Carolina in 1886.[35] Evanzz suggests that Ali may have become a devoted follower of Mufti Muhammad Sadiq, who himself was a missionary of Hazrat Mirza Ghulam Ahmed, who in turn had proclaimed himself the Mahdi, or Islamic messiah, in India in 1889. In this account, Ali grew dissatisfied after about a year of studying with Sadiq and then produced his own tract, the *Holy Koran of the Moorish Holy Temple of Science*, which I discuss in detail below. It is certain, at any rate, that Ali founded his first Moorish Science temple in 1913 in Newark, New Jersey—two years before the death of Booker T. Washington and three years before Garvey arrived in Harlem. By 1928, Ali had moved his headquarters to Chicago and had established temples in fifteen states. Ali's followers were drawn from the same recently transplanted, poor, urban African Americans who constituted the primary audience for Garvey's UNIA and, later, Elijah Muhammad's Nation of Islam. All members paid initiation fees and yearly dues, and numerous products were specially produced for their consumption.[36] Eventually, this potential income became an irresistible prize, and in a struggle for leadership, one of Ali's rivals was murdered. Ali was arrested, charged, and later died while out on bail—perhaps as a result of a police beating, perhaps killed in retribution for the murder, perhaps of natural causes.[37]

The MSTA disintegrated after the death of its leader, though several of the splinter groups believed they were being led by a reincarnation of Ali.[38] It is possible that the leader of one of these splinter groups was W. D. Fard, the door-to-door silk peddler who founded the Nation of Islam.[39] Evanzz argues that W. D. Fard also was David Ford, who joined Ali's movement shortly before Ali's death and rapidly rose through the ranks to become head of the Chicago Temple. In any case, and whoever Fard was, a careful reading of Ali's *Holy Koran* suggests a number of similarities to the rhetoric of the early Nation of Islam.

This *Holy Koran* is a curious document. Its sixty-four pages are divided into fifty-eight short chapters, and each chapter consists entirely of a numbered list of short statements. Most of the first half of Ali's *Holy Koran* is plagiarized from Levi H. Dowling's *Aquarian Gospel of Jesus the Christ*, a mystical emendation to the New Testament that follows Jesus of Nazareth on journeys to India, Persia, Egypt, Rome, and Greece. Along the way, Jesus learns from Moslems, teaches Hindus, meets with Apollo, and in Heliopolis joins a "Secret Brotherhood" that bears a striking resemblance to the Masons.[40] Ali retained Dowling's elaborate, simulated King James diction but discarded many of Dowling's chapters. He also has changed "God" to "Allah" in most places, resulting in some awkward moments, such as when Pontius Pilate, while washing his hands, proclaims Jesus "Son of the Most High Allah."[41] Most of the remainder of Ali's *Holy Koran* consists of brief instructions for maintaining relationships based on rigid hierarchies, such as between men and women (XXI and XXII) and masters and servants (XXVIII), or meditations on virtues such as "Justice" (XXXI) and "Gratitude" (XXXIII). The last few chapters describe a Pan-Africanist apocalypse.

Because of the eclectic nature of Ali's *Holy Koran*, it defies easy categorization. Its prophetic form, however, is clearly established in the frontispiece, which proclaims the text to be "Divinely prepared by the Noble Prophet Drew Ali, by the guiding of his father God, Allah; the great God of the universe. To redeem man from his sinful and fallen stage of humanity back to the highest plane of life with his father God, Allah." And the revelatory tone is continued in the prologue: "The reason these lessons have not been known is because the Moslems of India, Egypt and Palestine had these secrets and kept them back from the outside world, and when the time appointed by Allah they loosened the keys and freed the secrets, and for the first time in ages have these secrets been delivered in the hands of the Moslems of America." A messianic impulse also is explicit, as Ali draws a parallel between his relationship to Marcus Garvey and Jesus' relationship to John. "In these modern days," he explains, "there came a forerunner of Jesus, who was divinely prepared by the great God-Allah and his name is Marcus Garvey." Garvey "did teach and warn the nations of the earth to prepare to meet the coming Prophet; who was to bring the true and divine Creed of Islam, and his name is Noble Drew Ali who was prepared and sent to this earth by Allah, to teach the old time religion and the everlasting gospel to the sons of men" (XLVIII).

Ali's *Holy Koran* echoes several themes presented in the texts of Douglass and Du Bois, but generally it is an apocalyptic discourse more similar to Nat Turner's *Confessions*. Like Frederick Douglass, for example, Ali seems to teach that the current state of sin was a result of a declension from historical models. "Through sin and disobedience," he says, "every nation has suffered slavery, due to the fact that they honored not the creed and principles of their forefathers" (XLVII). Unlike Douglass, however, Ali does not call upon his followers to revivify a radical attitude toward cultural change but to accept the status quo as the will of Allah. Wives should obey their husbands, and children should honor their parents, just as the poor and the rich, and the master and the servant, should glory in their fulfillment of their divinely appointed roles. The "state of servitude," Ali declares, "is the appointment of Allah" (XXVIII).

Like Du Bois, Ali emphasizes the necessary moral purity of the black race. Du Bois argued that African Americans "*must* be inspired with the Divine faith of our black mothers" and "*must* be honest, fearlessly criticizing their own faults, zealously correcting them."[42] For Ali, moral purity involves strict adherence to an ascetic code of personal behavior. Young men must "beware of all the allurements of wantonness" and should guard against the "madness of desire" for from its "blindness . . . thou shalt rush upon destruction" (XX). Young women are warned to "[g]ive ear . . . to the instructions of prudence and let the precepts of truth sink deep in thy heart; so shall the charms of thy mind add luster to the elegance of thy form; and thy beauty, like the rose it resembleth, shall retain its sweetness when its bloom is withered" (XXI). But while Du Bois perceives the moral impurity of the race to stand in the way of political advancement, Ali sees a need to bring African American behavior into line with celestial precepts. Ali's goal is otherworldly, and he urges his followers to focus their attention inward. After some Moors in Chicago precipitated racial confrontations by displaying their Moorish Science identity cards to whites—they apparently "believed that the mere sight of the card would be sufficient to restrain a white man who was bent on disturbing or harming its

holder"[43]—Ali issued edicts requiring the Moors to "cease all radical or ag-
itating speeches" and to "stop flashing your cards before the Europeans as
this only causes confusion."[44] And like the Black Muslims, the Moors were
encouraged to concentrate their energies in collective self-improvement
rather than individual advancement.

Ali's *Holy Koran* resembles Turner's *Confessions* in three significant ways:
its repeated subordination of human agency to divine will, its Manichaean
division of the world into black and white halves, and its explicit description of an interpretive mode limited to the reading of signs. Human agency
is subordinated to divine will because Ali's universe, like Turner's, is governed by an explicitly divine plan, and it is the duty of all humans, and
particularly of African Americans, to align themselves with this plan. "Pay
therefore to His wisdom, all honor and veneration; and bow down thyself
in humble and submissive obedience to His supreme discretion" (XXXV).
People should not be tempted to take full credit for their actions, because
in all things the individual is merely making Allah's will manifest: "Let him
who doeth well," warns Ali, "beware how he boasteth of it, for rarely is it
of his own will" (XLI).

Both Ali and Nat Turner divide the world between those with dark skins
and those without, and they both rely upon biblical imagery to describe an
inevitable clash between the races. But for Ali, this division is aligned with
a sometimes vague differentiation between Christianity and Islam. Though
he does argue that "Jesus himself was of the true blood of the ancient
Canaanites and Moabites and the inhabitants of Africa" (XLVI), the central
thrust of the second half of his *Holy Koran* is that all of the people of the
world, except white Europeans, are properly Islamic. For the Moors, not
only the "fallen sons and daughters of the Asiatic Nation of North America" belong properly to the black race but also the ancient Moabites, the
Egyptians, and the Arabians; the Japanese, the Chinese, and the "Hindoos
of India"; "the Moorish Americans and Mexicans of North America";
"Brazilians, Argentinians [*sic*], and Chilians [*sic*] in South America";
"Colombians, Nicaraguans, and the natives of San Salvador in Central
America"—"All of these are Moslems" (XLV).

Like Turner, Ali models an interpretive practice that attends to signs and
omens to predict events and mark propitious moments for action. Ali's
Moors know themselves to be in the End Days, for example, because "a
sign, a star within a crescent moon, had been seen in the heavens, and . . .
this betokened the arrival of the day of the Asiatics, and the destruction of
the Europeans (whites)."[45] "The last Prophet in these days is Noble Drew

Ali," states the *Holy Koran,* "who was prepared divinely in due time by Allah to redeem men from their sinful ways; and to warn them of the great wrath which is sure to come upon the earth" (XLVIII). But unlike Turner, Ali does not ask his followers to do anything other than to continue to observe the signs and to strive toward fulfilling the laws and virtues contained within the *Holy Koran.* It seems that Allah has implanted in each individual a knowledge of divine will, and the directive to "know thyself" (XXXVI) is translated as a directive to know this divine internal presence. "He who made virtues what they are," explains Ali, "planted in thee a knowledge of their pre-eminence. Act as thy soul dictates to thee, and the end shall be always right" (XLII). This inward-directedness is one of the features that distinguishes Ali's prophecy from those reviewed in the previous chapter and presents one of his most enduring legacies to the Nation of Islam.

Elijah Muhammad's Nation of Islam would adopt many characteristics of Noble Drew Ali's Moorish Science temples. Like the Moors, members of the early Nation of Islam referred to themselves as "Asiatics," were encouraged to imagine themselves as a part of a brotherhood of dark-skinned people, were required to follow strict behavioral and dress codes, and were required to change their names (Moors by adding an "el" or a "bey" to their names, members of the Nation of Islam by replacing their last names with an "X"). Both the Moors and the members of the Nation of Islam were told that Christianity is the proper religion of white people, while Islam is the rightful religion of people of color. And, most important, the doctrines of both the Moors and the Nation of Islam were based on prophetic calls to recapture a mystical and esoteric black past.

The Nation of Islam

The Nation of Islam grew out of and appealed to the same audiences as both Marcus Garvey's UNIA and Nobel Drew Ali's MSTA. The Black Muslim doctrine apparently developed by W. D. Fard and eventually entrusted to Elijah Muhammad bears significant resemblances to both. Claude Andrew Clegg III suggests that whatever Fard's direct relationship to these previous organizations, "the ideological landscape of Detroit, shaped by Garvey, Noble Drew Ali, the black church, and other forces, made the messianism, nationalism, and millenarianism of the Nation of Islam acceptable to a certain segment of the African American community."[46] And C. Eric Lincoln reports that many of the early converts to the Nation of Islam "consider Muhammad a natural successor to both Garvey and Noble Drew Ali, and they have had little difficulty in making the transition" from membership in those organizations to membership in the Nation of Islam.[47]

Through Garvey, the Nation of Islam received a politically charged and messianic black nationalism based in a Pan-Africanist vision of mutual support and communication between Africans and African Americans and presented with bravado and pomp. Through Ali, the Nation of Islam received an inward-looking apocalyptic vision based in an esoteric gospel of quasi-Islamic influences and vestigial Christianity and presented along with severely restrictive moral and behavioral codes.

Garvey's rhetoric, through its similarities to Du Bois's, found its roots near the jeremiadic end of the continuum I described in the previous chapter; Ali's eclectic vision references more comfortably the apocalyptic end. These two influences do not smoothly mesh. The jeremiad assumes that authentic cultural norms and mores lie dormant in the audience and need to be "conserved," in Du Bois's terms, or "awoken" in Garvey's; apocalyptic rhetoric, on the other hand, assumes a world in which old paradigms and attitudes no longer hold and are slated to be replaced. The first fosters political action intended to revivify the past and to bend the present into alignment with dormant ideals, while the latter encourages a violent overthrow of the oppressors, as in the case of Nat Turner—or, as in the case of the Moors, an apolitical withdrawal from the doomed dominant culture. Through its ability to position itself precisely at the juncture of these two rhetorical responses to racism and to maintain a static tension between them, the Nation of Islam has experienced unprecedented success and longevity.

The peculiarly generative potential of this static tension is best illustrated in the Nation of Islam's foundational mythic narrative. Lincoln notes that "Muslim philosophy is limited, and the temple lectures are, without exception, rephrasings of statements already made in printed materials, interviews or public lectures"; some Federal Bureau of Investigation (FBI) agents complained that they had trouble keeping informants interested in attending Nation of Islam meetings "because the speeches were repetitive and dull."[48] What was being repeated, for the most part, was "Yacub's History." This was "the central myth of the Black Muslim Movement," and versions of it were repeated regularly in each Nation of Islam temple in order to attract new followers and to reinforce the faith of the converted.[49] Its core content was expected to be memorized by the members of the Nation of Islam, who periodically were quizzed on it. "Yacub's History," in its fully realized form, begins as a genesis myth, describing the origins of the white race in an evil scientist's plot to rule the world; it finishes as an eschatology, predicting a cataclysmic race war eventuating in the end of white domination. Broadly, the narrative begins with a call for its audience to recover a black past as a resource through which to engage contemporary American racial tensions and then shades into a series of apocalyptic warnings that promise the inevitable destruction of the white race.

"Yacub's History" summarizes the rambling revelations of Elijah Muhammad. Within the cosmology of the early Nation of Islam, W. D. Fard was Allah in the flesh. Though often instructing his ministers to downplay his divine status, possibly for fear of alienating potential converts, Fard's most able and enthusiastic student and "Supreme Minister," Elijah Muhammad, had no doubts.[50] When Fard disappeared mysteriously in 1934, "challenges to the leadership of Elijah Muhammad bubbled to the surface quickly," and the Nation of Islam was on the verge of disintegration. But Fard bestowed the title of "Messenger of Allah" upon Elijah Muhammad, significantly bolstering his credibility and helping to ensure that the Nation of Islam splinter group led by Elijah Muhammad would become the most powerful.[51] "You don't need me anymore," Fard is reported to have told his followers, "hear Elijah."[52] Thus was Elijah Muhammad christened a prophet.

It was the job of all Nation of Islam ministers, including Malcolm X, to translate Elijah Muhammad's teachings into effective rhetorical prose. This was a challenge. As Barbara Ann Norman puts it, "Malcolm . . . extracted, from Muhammad's diffuse and often confusing rhetoric, themes he deemed salient to contemporary urban Blacks."[53] Malcolm described his relationship to the words of Elijah Muhammad this way: "When you hear Charlie McCarthy speak, you listen and marvel at what he says. What you forget is that Charlie is nothing but a dummy—he is a hunk of wood sitting on Edgar Bergen's lap. . . . This is the way it is with the Messenger [Elijah Muhammad] and me. It is my mouth working, but the voice is his."[54] Hakim Jamal remembers Malcolm saying that he had "often heard brothers and sisters say to me, they like the way I speak, but somehow they can't get the same feeling by listening to the Messenger." "This is normal," Malcolm explains, "but also it is training by the devil." Whites have told them to pay attention only to "eloquent" people, and this is "the biggest trick yet." His relationship to Elijah Muhammad is like the relationship between Aaron and Moses, he explains. As Jamal puts it: "Malcolm was cleaning up for Elijah."[55] In fact, Malcolm's discourse while a minister of the Nation of Islam, like that of all Nation of Islam ministers, was doubly removed from its source. Malcolm spoke for Elijah Muhammad, and Elijah Muhammad spoke for W. D. Fard. The range of Malcolm's inventional activities was limited to a repackaging of previously developed truths, and the strategies of interpretation that he could model for his audiences were limited to reiteration and paraphrase.

The Nation of Islam's foundational mythic narrative, like most mythic narratives, was intended to explain the world rather than critically engage it. It did not invite its audience to perceive a complex world characterized by multiple motives in need of evaluation and critique, but instead it attempted to subsume and simplify African American experience within its bifurcated worldview. In other words, as long as Malcolm X spoke inside the Nation of Islam, he could encourage his audiences to engage in judgment and critique only to the extent that he encouraged them to reject their previous knowledge and to accept "Yacub's History."

Black Man's History

On December 1, 1955, Rosa Parks was arrested in Montgomery, Alabama, for refusing to give up her bus seat to a white rider. The ensuing bus boycott, in which African Americans organized and refused to ride the city buses until they were desegregated, catapulted a young preacher named Martin Luther King Jr. to national attention and, of course, set in motion what would become recognized as the civil rights movement of the 1960s. But those events may have seemed strangely disconnected from the daily experience of the residents of northern black ghettos, many of whom were long accustomed to riding integrated buses to and from subsistence-level jobs servicing relatively affluent whites. One of the key events of the middle 1950s in the lives of many of these people took place much closer to home and reflected much more strongly the realities under which they were forced to live. It also significantly raised the profile of the Nation of Islam within the black community.

On a Sunday evening in April 1957, a young member of the Nation of Islam's Harlem Mosque named Hinton Johnson happened upon two New York City policemen beating an African American man. Johnson protested and, as a result, was beaten and then arrested. In a show of Nation of Islam force, dramatically re-created in Spike Lee's film, Malcolm led a large and orderly group of the Nation of Islam's paramilitary guard, the Fruit of Islam, down to the Twenty-eighth Precinct station.[56] These men stood at attention along the street and attracted a sizeable crowd of the curious and the enraged—estimated by some to have been in the thousands, many of whom had never heard of Malcolm X or the Nation of Islam—while Malcolm requested to see Johnson to find out if he needed hospitalization. Malcolm did see him, and Johnson was sent to the hospital. A metal plate had to be placed in his skull, and he eventually won $70,000 in a police brutality lawsuit against the city.[57] This dramatic incident established the Black Muslim's uncompromising stance and refusal to flinch in the face of white power and led to unprecedented growth of Mosque #7 as well as to Malcolm X's notoriety. With this incident, the Nation of Islam began its transformation from merely a quiet and insular religious cult into an insular religious cult with a stern nationalist public demeanor. As what Peter Goldman calls the "Parable of Hinton Johnson" elevated the profile of the Nation of Islam within the black ghettos of Chicago and Detroit, the group eventually attracted the attention of white America. A series of studies and documentaries followed, all focused primarily on Malcolm X and the Harlem Mosque: the Mike Wallace television documentary, *The Hate That Hate Produced*, was broadcast in 1959; C. Eric Lincoln's *The Black Muslims in America* was published in 1960; E. U. Essien-Udom's *Black Nationalism* was published in 1962; and Louis Lomax's *When the Word Is Given* was published in 1963. As Malcolm's audiences expanded, they became more diverse, until he was speaking to white audiences at least as often as he was speaking to black audiences. The resulting incompatibility between the Nation of Islam's narrow rhetoric of prophecy and the expectations of Malcolm's wider audiences eventually would contribute to his split with Elijah Muhammad and the Nation of Islam. In this speech, however, Malcolm X is safely within the mosque.

Malcolm delivered "Black Man's History" in December 1962 at the Nation of Islam's Mosque #7 in Harlem. This was the Nation of Islam's flagship mosque, and Malcolm X, ten years after his release from prison, was the Nation of Islam's most eloquent and influential speaker. He had been given command of the Harlem post as a reward for his hard work and leadership in helping the Nation of Islam grow from about four hundred members in 1952 to over forty thousand in the early 1960s.[58] "Black Man's History" primarily is a retelling of the first part of the story of Yacub, focusing on the origin of the black race. Even breaking off the narrative at this midpoint makes this a very long speech. At some fourteen thousand words and taking into account Malcolm's typically deliberate rate of delivery, the speech would have been a lengthy one; it is reasonable to assume that

"Yacub's History" often was presented in segments, as it is here. I rely upon several other speeches and statements, primarily from Malcolm but also from other sources, to round out the apocalyptic end of the narrative.

"Narrative," in fact, should not be too strictly applied. Themes and examples circulate within Malcolm's text in ways that echo strongly the disjointed and cyclical discourse of Elijah Muhammad. As the topics shift and shade into one another in nearly a stream of consciousness, the effect also is reminiscent of David Walker's *Appeal* and presents similar connotations of urgency and pending chaos. This was a standard recruiting speech, and Malcolm X must have delivered many versions of it. Goldman quotes "a former Muslim" who says that "the first lesson I ever heard him [Malcolm X] teach . . . was The History of the End of the World." "We called it history," he goes on, "but it was more like prehistory—something that's written before the thing takes place."[59] Benjamin Karim recalls, also, that the first time he saw Malcolm preach he was delivering a version of this same speech."[60]

This is a narrative intended to provide for its audience an explanatory template through which to make sense of a seemingly arbitrary world, and as Malcolm delivers it in "Black Man's History," he offers many asides that urge upon the audience the usefulness and application of this interpretive resource. He invites his audience to perceive a bifurcated universe that is progressing toward a predetermined end so that adequate preparation requires only patience, introspection, and withdrawal. Like Du Bois, Malcolm in this speech calls upon his black audiences to recover a lost racial identity—but this racial identity is rooted in part in a biological definition of race like those that Du Bois was laboring to reject. As in Walker's *Appeal,* this speech argues for the importance of education as a means toward emancipation—but it equates education with the recitation of Elijah Muhammad's esoteric catechism. Like Turner's *Confessions,* this speech demonstrates a mode of interpretation that culminates in discerning signs and omens—but unlike Turner, neither Malcolm X nor any Nation of Islam minister ever urged his congregation to take immediate violent action. This a discourse, then, that most closely resembles Noble Drew Ali's *Holy Koran.* It is a peculiarly hermetic brand of prophecy, severely limiting the role for human agency. It is designed to spur its audience not toward political action but instead toward self-improvement and collective self-control.

In addition, it was delivered to audiences that were stringently homogenous. The early Nation of Islam was evangelical but also selective. White people, of course, were not permitted to attend services.[61] The Nation of

Islam did, however, send its male members on compulsory "fishing" expeditions looking for converts among the poor and dispossessed throughout the black ghettos that surrounded each mosque.[62] A great many converts also were made in prison, where Malcolm X was first introduced to the faith, and Lomax speculates on the possible common attraction of Elijah Muhammad's teachings to those in prison and to the people on the streets who were "in something of a prison, too; they see themselves as failures and need some accounting for why they are what they are, why they are not what they are not."[63]

Once enticed to attend a meeting, the prospective member would find that entrance into the mosques was strictly monitored by the Fruit of Islam. Those wishing to go inside were thoroughly questioned and searched, and if the individual did not pass muster or if the guards suspected that she or he was there to cause trouble, that person would be turned away.[64] All objectionable personal belongings, such as liquor, cigarettes, or anything that potentially could be used as a weapon, were placed into a paper sack and returned at the end of the service. The entire process seemed designed to increase the sense that the mosques were sacred places and to optimize the probability that the message would reach those most inclined to accept it.

Entering the mosque, the faithful and the curious were visually prepared for the strictly bifurcated worldview to which Nation of Islam rhetoric shortly would introduce them. Men were dressed in black suits, women in white robes. Men sat on one side of a broad center aisle, women on the other. On a stage at the front of the room there generally was a chalkboard, divided into halves—on one side, recalls Benjamin Karim, "was an American flag with each of four words in capital letters—CHRISTIANITY, SLAVERY, SUFFERING, DEATH—at each of its four corners. Opposite it, at each corner of a red flag emblazoned with a crescent moon and a star, had been printed ISLAM, FREEDOM, JUSTICE, EQUALITY." "Between the two flags," Karim continues, "had been written the question 'Who will survive the War of Armageddon?'"[65] In stark and self-conscious contrast to the participatory Christian churches with which most of the audience would have been familiar, the proceedings were subdued and formal. The audience was expected to sit quietly and attentively, and the Fruit of Islam circulated among the rows of folding chairs ensuring that a properly solemn mood prevailed.[66]

Generally, an assistant minister would open the proceedings with a welcome in Arabic and an overview of Elijah Muhammad's teachings and then would yield the floor to the main speaker. Benjamin Karim "opened up" on the day Malcolm delivered "Black Man's History" and remembers that Malcolm "was wearing his blue suit and red tie. This was his 'burning suit,' which he wore when he was fully prepared and intended to give a very deep lecture."[67] Malcolm typically would approach the lectern with a handful of three-by-five-inch cards, some newspaper clippings, the Bible, and perhaps two or three other books; he would repeat the Arabic welcome—*As-Salaam-Alaikum,* Peace be unto you—and begin.[68]

History

Malcolm prepares his audience for Yacub's genesis myth by reminding them of the need to understand their own history and supplying some rather startling biblical exegeses designed to legitimate Nation of Islam doctrine and to elevate Elijah Muhammad to near-divine status. He begins by establishing the bifurcated, racialized worldview common to Nation of Islam discourse. "Today dark mankind is waking up and is undertaking a new type of thinking," and "by black man we mean, as we are taught by The Honorable Elijah Muhammad, we include all those who are non-white."[69] "If you're here at the Mosque you're black," Malcolm continues, "because the only ticket you need to get into Muhammad's Mosque is to be black. So if you got in you know you're black" (24).

Our contemporary ears may miss the significance of Malcolm referring to his audience as "black." Hakim Jamal recalls that when he heard Malcolm X for the first time at the Nation of Islam mosque in Boston, "Many of us recoiled at being called black. I know that I did. . . . Sure, it was easy for Malcolm to call us black, most of us looked black, but his skin was light. Light skinned people in Boston or in the United States always called people darker than themselves black, but not as a compliment."[70] One of Marcus Garvey's missteps may have been his exploitation of a skin-color hierarchy among African Americans; he distrusted those with light skin and once characterized Du Bois as a tragic mulatto "who bewails every day the drop of Negro blood in his veins, being sorry that he is not Dutch or French."[71] The Nation of Islam would make no such mistake—its vision of blackness owes more to Noble Drew Ali's extreme inclusiveness, so that virtually everyone not of European descent is "black." The Nation of Islam also retained Ali's insistence that Islam is the true religion for all "black" people. "We don't separate our color from our religion," Malcolm tells his audience. "So the religion that we have, the religion of Islam, the religion that makes us Muslims, the religion that The Honorable Elijah Muhammad is teaching us here in America today, is designed to undo in our minds what the white man has done to us" (25). But the Nation of Islam has amended Ali's global black vision, as we shall see, with a quasi-scientific genetic mythology that has significant implications for the role for human agency it provides.

"The thing that has made the so-called Negro in America fail," Malcolm continues, "more than any other thing, is your, my, lack of knowledge concerning history" (26). The argument for the need to attain this proper understanding of black history consists, for the most part, of a cautionary list of individuals whose lack of such knowledge accounts for the relative lack of respect they are accorded by whites. "What made Dr. George Washington Carver a *Negro* scientist instead of a scientist?" Malcolm asks. "What made Paul Robeson a *Negro* actor instead of an actor? What made, or makes, Ralph Bunche a *Negro* statesman instead of a statesman?" The answer is that "they don't know the history of the black man" (27). The emphasis on the need to know one's history echoes David Walker's emphasis in the *Appeal* on education as a means through which to attain emancipation: "But when you and I wake up," Malcolm says, "as we're taught by The Honorable Elijah Muhammad, and learn our history . . . then the white man will be at a disadvantage and we'll be at an advantage" (28). This is why this knowledge has been kept from African Americans and why Elijah Muhammad has come to share it.[72] The call for a chosen people to revivify their useable past suggests a parallel to Du Bois's "Conservation of Races," but the history that Malcolm presents to his audience is unlike anything that Du Bois might have imagined. Religion and history are not only interrelated but are synonymous, and the repository for this history is the Bible.

Black Muslim theology explicitly is a program of biblical interpretation. "The Honorable Elijah Muhammad's mission," Malcolm tells his audience, "is to teach the so-called Negroes a knowledge of history, the history of ourselves, our own kind, showing us how we fit into prophecy, Biblical prophecy" (33). DeCaro notes that "if anyone ever honed Black Muslim biblical application into a fine art, it was Malcolm X" and that in the early days "neither Malcolm nor the rest of the Nation had paid much attention to the Qur'an's text and message."[73] W. D. Fard "apparently recognized that no successful liberation movement among African Americans could afford to divorce itself from the Bible as an authoritative canon." But the Bible presented something of a dilemma, for at the same time that it was presented as a foundational and authoritative text, it also was "constantly maligned [by the Nation of Islam] as a book poisoned, skewed, and perverted by white people."[74] This dilemma is resolved through peculiarly literal and concrete reading strategies similar to, but more exaggerated than, those that characterize Nat Turner's *Confessions*. The Bible is not understood as a compendium of metaphors or parables but instead as a predictive history referring distinctly and directly to the Nation of Islam. The job of Nation of Islam ministers, then, was to unmask the Bible so that it was no longer understood as a mystical or religious tract but instead as a reference book of future and past African American history.

Like all prophets, Malcolm is interpreting texts that already have been written—but his interpretations are Elijah Muhammad's, not his own. Malcolm's reading of the Exodus story, for example, is illustrative. Michael Walzer points out that "wherever people know the Bible, and experience oppression, the Exodus has sustained their spirits and (sometimes) inspired their resistance," and David Howard-Pitney notes that the "biblical motif of the Exodus of the chosen people from Egyptian slavery to a Promised Land of freedom was central to the black socio-religious imagination."[75] But for Elijah Muhammad's Nation of Islam, the Exodus story presents not an opportunity to draw instructive parallels between black and Jewish history but instead is a direct reference to a key moment in black history. "Not *these* things that you *call* Jews," teaches Malcolm X. "They weren't in Egypt, *they* weren't the people that Moses led out of Egypt, and the Jews know this. But the Bible is written in such a tricky way, when you read it you think that Moses led the Jews out of bondage" (36). Moses is not merely an exemplar for future black leaders; he *was* a black leader, leading out of bondage in Egypt the actual tribe that later would become the black race. Whites do not want African Americans to know this, of course, but "thanks to Almighty God, The Honorable Elijah Muhammad knows their secret, and he told it to us and we're going to tell it to you" (36).

The book of Genesis is given similar treatment. Malcolm quotes, for example, Genesis 15:13–14: "And he said unto Abram, Know of a surety that thy seed shall be a stranger in a land that is not theirs, and shall serve them; and they shall afflict them four hundred years; and also that nation, whom they shall serve, will I judge: and afterward shall they come out with great substance" (34).[76]

"Now The Honorable Elijah Muhammad," Malcolm continues, "teaches that the so-called Negro is the one that the Bible is talking about" (34). As in Noble Drew Ali's *Holy Koran*, Masonic ritual also plays a role in Nation of Islam doctrine and is given a similarly literal interpretation. These rituals are "a sign of what happened to the white man six thousand years ago" (60). They illustrate a historical event; specifically, they refer to the moment when Adam was cast out of the Garden, which itself actually is a reference to the time "the white man was run out of the East by the Muslims six thousand years ago into the caves of Europe." "The white man," Malcolm explains, "they tell the white man what it means: a white Shriner, a white Mason, what it means. A Negro never learns what it means" (61). But they do now, because Malcolm X is transmitting to them the interpretive conclusions reached by Elijah Muhammad.[77]

Perhaps the boldest appropriation is the direct insertion of Elijah Muhammad into biblical narrative. Noble Drew Ali may have figured himself as Christ to Marcus Garvey's John, but Ali regarded the New Testament relationship only as an instructive metaphor. The Nation of Islam establishes a more directly messianic role for its leader, similar to that occupied by Nat Turner—the Bible refers directly and immediately to current world events and specifically predicts the rise of Elijah Muhammad out of the cotton fields of Georgia. Elijah Muhammad is the one who has been promised, and his presence in North America is itself a fulfillment of prophecy. The "Bible is a book of history," Malcolm assures his listeners, and then quotes from Deuteronomy 18, in which "God told Moses: 'I will raise them up a Prophet'" (37). This Bible story, like the others, is "talking about you and me" and promising "a prophet like Moses whose mission it would be to do for you and me the same thing that Moses did back then." Malachi, further, prophesied that the name of this prophet would be called Elijah and that this prophet would "turn the hearts of the children to the fathers and the hearts of the fathers to the children" (37). And this, Malcolm continues, "is something that The Honorable Elijah Muhammad is doing here in America today" (38).

In other speeches that Malcolm delivered during this time, the connection is even more explicit. At Harvard University in 1960, Malcolm declared that Black Muslims "believe that the presence today in America of the Honorable Elijah Muhammad, his teachings among the 20 million so-called Negroes, and his naked warning to America concerning her treatment of these 20 million ex-slaves is all the fulfillment of divine prophecy."[78] In June 1963, Malcolm reminded an audience at Adam Clayton Powell's Abyssinian Baptist Church that "Jesus did prophesy" that "Elijah would guide you with truth and Elijah would protect you with truth and make you free indeed. And brothers and sisters, that Elijah, the one whom Jesus has said was to come, has come and is in America today in the person of The Honorable Elijah Muhammad."[79] And in a speech that Elijah Muhammad himself delivered in 1961 in Atlanta, he explicitly shoulders the mantle of prophecy: "I stand before you as a man who has been chosen for you by God Himself. I did not choose myself. This must be made clear! . . . I did not see Him in a vision and receive my mission in a vision as others before me received theirs. I was in the Presence of God [W. D. Fard] for over three years, and I received what I am teaching you directly from His Mouth." He warns his listeners that they should not be "too proud, as others were in former times; they were too proud to follow the words of the prophets. I don't want you to be like that. . . . Accept Allah and His religion and follow me and I will lead you to Him and to a heaven right here on this earth."[80]

Yacub's History

The path toward that earthly heaven lies through "Yacub's History," which all Nation of Islam ministers, including Malcolm X, revealed faithfully to their flocks. Malcolm's retelling of this history follows closely, and sometimes is indistinguishable from, Elijah Muhammad's own rendition.[81] The tale begins sixty-six trillion years ago, before the white race existed, when the world was populated exclusively by black scientists. One of these scientists had a disagreement with the other black scientists about what language the people of Earth should speak, and he determined to destroy civilization when the others rebuffed him. "So this scientist drove a shaft into the center of the Earth and filled it with high explosives and set it off." The explosion did not destroy civilization—"the black man can't destroy himself" (45)—but instead only created the moon.[82] "All of this," says Malcolm, meaning the orbit of the moon and the fluctuation of the tides, "was done by man himself, not some Mystery God. A black man set this up. And you and I have been running around in the trap that the white man put us in, thinking that the only one who can do anything is a Mystery God and what the Mystery God doesn't do the white man does" (47). The potential value in the Nation of Islam's literalization of metaphor is apparent: it allows Malcolm's audience some sense of agency. *They* (or their ancestors) were the gods who created the universe, so they do not need to wait for whites or for anyone else to set things right. Despite this elevation to nearly divine status, however, the role for human agency within "Yacub's History" also is severely limited. As we shall see, the myth unfolds so that the members of the Nation of Islam actually cannot influence the arc of history—the End Times are coming with or without their help, and the most they can do is prepare for them.

Returning to Malcolm's retelling of the story, we find that it is time to introduce the devil. Just as the black race is naturally intelligent—"black men have always been the wisest things in the universe" (44)—and divinely empowered, so are whites naturally backward and irredeemably evil. Whites are this way as a result of a mixture of divine providence and genetic engineering. The explosion that created the moon also destroyed one of the original thirteen tribes of black scientists. Whites, then, were created six thousand years ago by Yacub, an evil black scientist—who Malcolm reveals actually to be John, the author of the Book of Revelation (53)—as a replacement for this missing tribe. This new tribe was "a weak tribe, a wicked tribe, a devilish tribe, a diabolical tribe, a tribe that is devilish by nature" (47). Through a process of "grafting the brown one from the black one so that it became lighter and lighter," Yacub found he could eventually create a white race out of a black one (51). As the blackness was gradually diluted, generation by generation the emerging white race became weaker, "and then Yacub could take that weak man that he made and teach him how to lie and rob and cheat and thereby become the ruler of all of the rest of the world" (52).

Yacub/John set up "a birth control law" that involved a combination of selective breeding and infanticide and which over the course of six hundred years created a white race that was inherently wicked: "at the outset the nurses had to kill the little black babies, but after a while it got so that the mother, having been brainwashed, hated that black one so much she killed it herself. . . . So that at the end of the six hundred years . . . by the time they got the white man, they had someone who by nature hated everything that was darker than he was" (56–57). White people are so far removed from the black humanity out of which they were rendered that "you're not using the right language when you say the white man," Malcolm urges.

> You call it the devil. When you call him devil you're calling him by his name, and he's got another name—Satan; another name—serpent; another name—snake; another name—beast. All these names are in the Bible for the white man. Another name—Pharaoh; another name—Caesar; another name—France; French; Frenchman; Englishman; American; all those are just names for the devil. (57).

A narrative more starkly divided between dark good and white evil would be difficult to imagine. The audience has been called upon to recall their past and to use that past as a resource through which to rectify the short-comings of the present day; but that past consists of a racially bifurcated and overdetermined narrative, and the only solution is separation from the corrupt white culture.

As the narrative unfolds, the newly created white race eventually emerged from the island of Patmos with instructions from Yacub in the science of "tricknology," which whites then used to "divide and conquer" the rest of the world. "You see," explains Malcolm, "the white man" is "an underdog. He's a minority, and the only way a minority can rule a majority is to *divide* the majority. This is the trick that the white man was born to execute among the dark mankind here on this Earth" (58). He created divisions among the Native Americans, "South Korea–North Korea, South Vietnam–North Vietnam," and elsewhere. "He always dis-courages unity among others but he encourages unity among his own kind" (59). This characterization of the white race as a great disrupter is consonant with its nature, within Nation of Islam theology, as funda-mentally evil—the white race is the snake in the Garden. Themes of whites as an obstacle to black unity recur throughout Malcolm's dis-course, even after he left the Nation of Islam and stopped relying upon Elijah Muhammad's mythology.

The first target of white disruption is Arabia, which was a peaceful and Edenic place until "they started telling lies, started confusion, and in six months' time they had turned heaven into hell" (59). Whites were soon banished to Europe, where they lived in caves for two thousand years. While there, whites reverted to walking on all fours and even grew tails and excessive hair, and eventually they "amalgamated" with the dogs that lived with them. Moses, at last, was dispatched from Mecca to "put the white man back on the road to civilization" (64). It had been proph-esied that whites should rule for six thousand years, but they were late in getting started and thus in danger of not fulfilling their destiny. With Moses's help, though, they finally were able to assume their rightful po-sition of world domination. Their reign expired in 1914, and they origi-nally were slated for destruction at that time, but "you and I were here in their clutches and God gave them an extension . . . to give the wise men of the East the opportunity to get into this House of Bondage and 'awaken' the Lost Sheep" (65). This is the work that Elijah Muhammad is doing today.

End of History

This is where "Black Man's History" ends, with a prayer acknowledging
that Elijah Muhammad is the "True Servant and Last Apostle" of Allah. But
this is not the end of "Yacub's History." Elijah Muhammad supplies the full
story in his book *Message to the Blackman in America,* published in 1965 after
Malcolm's split from the Nation of Islam and at the height of the feud between Malcolm and Elijah. Though this book was, in part, Muhammad's
preemptive response to the release of Malcolm's *Autobiography,* it is an anthology of speeches and writings from throughout Muhammad's career. In
it, Muhammad describes the book of Revelation as a direct and concrete
reference to the imminent "downfall" of America. In a halting prose style
that accurately transcribes his oral delivery, Elijah Muhammad's text reveals that "Allah (God) has found His people (the so-called Negroes), and is
angry with the slave-masters for the evil done by them to His people (the
so-called Negroes). Allah (God) is going to repay them according to their
doings." This period of repayment is already under way: "Texas and Kansas
were once two of the nation's proudest states," for example, but "are today
in the grip of a drought, continuous raging dust storms; their river beds lie
bare, their fish stinking on the banks in dry parched mud."[83] Rain "does
more damage than good"; snow brings only "death and destruction"; and
"hail stones the size of small blocks of ice" will soon start to fall, "breaking
down crops, trees, the roofs of homes, killing cattle and fowl." This will be
followed by earthquakes, sickness, and death. "Now she (America) puts on
a show of temptation with their women (white women) in newspapers,
magazines, in the streets half nude, and posing in the so-called Negroes
faces in the most indecent manner that is known to mankind," but "the so-
called Negroes" will not be tricked "to death and hell along with them." Indeed, the destruction will be selective: "Only that on the earth (the devils)
which has sinned against Allah and His laws will be destroyed."[84]

"When God appeared to me," Elijah Muhammad says, "in the person of
Master Fard Muhammad, to whom all praises are due forever, in 1931 in
Detroit. He said that America was His number one enemy on his list for destruction."[85] The hailstorms and earthquakes, however, are only prelimi-
nary to the actual apocalypse, which will occur soon according to signs in
the sun and the moon. This version of the end takes as its central motif a
typically concretized vision from the prophet Ezekiel: "Ezekiel's vision has
become a reality," proclaims Muhammad, in the form of a "wheel-shaped
plane known as the Mother of Planes, [that] is one-half mile by a half mile
and is the largest mechanical man-made object in the sky." It carries fifteen

hundred small round planes, each equipped with bombs that will drill into the earth to a depth of one mile before detonating with enough force to produce "a mountain one mile high." "The final war between Allah (God) and the devils is dangerously close," Muhammad warns. Like dry tinder, the "very least amount of friction can bring it into action within minutes. There is no such thing as getting ready for this most terrible and dreadful war; they are ready." "The small circular-made planes called flying saucers, which are so much talked of being seen, could be from this Mother Plane. . . . Believe it or believe it not!" After this racial apocalypse will dawn the millennium, "the righteous will make unlimited progress; peace, joy and happiness will have no end. War will be forgotten; disagreement will have no place in the hereafter. . . . The earth, the general atmosphere will produce such a change that the people will think it a new earth. It will be the heaven of the righteous forever!"[86]

This history sometimes seems inevitable and at other times seems avoidable. "This is all known to the world, but why are they trying to build up a defense against God. It is useless. America has it coming."[87] But at the same time, the whites who may be overhearing this message to the Blackman seem to be offered—like the whites that David Walker was addressing indirectly in his *Appeal*—a last chance at redemption. "What America needs to win," Muhammad explains, "is to give freedom and equal justice to her slaves (the so-called Negroes)."[88] Malcolm sounds a similar bivalent theme in some of his speeches, even when addressing whites. At Harvard in 1960, for example—in a speech in which Archie Epps notes that "the prophetic style was very pronounced"—Malcolm declares that "now today, God has sent Mr. Elijah Muhammad among the downtrodden and oppressed so-called American Negroes to warn us that God is again about to bring about another great change . . . only this time, it will be a FINAL CHANGE! This is the day and the time for a COMPLETE CHANGE."[89] "God has come to close out the entire Old World . . . the Old World in which for the past 6,000 years practically the entire earth has been deceived, conquered, colonized, ruled, enslaved, oppressed and exploited by the CAUCASIAN RACE." At the same time, though, "God is giving America every opportunity to repent and atone for the crime she committed when she enslaved our people, just as God gave Pharaoh a chance to repent before He finally destroyed him because he was too proud to free his slaves and give them complete justice."[90] White repentance would involve provisioning a new nation for African Americans. "Just give us a portion of this country that we can call our own," Malcolm warns. "Otherwise America will reap the full fury of God's wrath, for her crimes against our people here are many." "Do justice by your faithful ex-slaves. Otherwise: all of you who are sitting here, your government, and your entire race will be destroyed and removed from this earth by Almighty God, ALLAH."[91]

Celeste Condit and John Lucaites note that "Elijah Muhammad's myth . . . constructed great limitations for itself. Its authenticity came at the price of disengagement from this-worldly ways of thinking. It required a mythic consciousness that placed evidence and causality outside human time. It thereby removed the possibility for collective human action in the world."[92] This is true if what is meant by "collective human action" is the sort of political action that defined movements such as the Southern Christian Leadership Conference (SCLC) or legal action such as that sponsored by the NAACP. In 1962, the year in which Malcolm delivered "Black Man's History" and the year that Taylor Branch has called the "last year of postwar innocence," Martin Luther King Jr. led a difficult and costly fight for desegregation in Albany, Georgia, considered by many at the time to be the SCLC's first major failure. This was the year of the Cuban Missile Crisis, of continued bombings of black churches in Birmingham and throughout the South, of James Meredith's first classes at the University of Mississippi, and of "the last militant race rally among respectable whites for at least a generation" at an Ole Miss football game.[93] In November, John F. Kennedy finally signed an executive order ending racial discrimination in federal housing; in December, King and other African American leaders met with Kennedy to request a "Marshall Plan" of economic aid for newly independent nations. From within the confines of "Yacub's History," Malcolm could not respond to, or encourage his audience to respond to, any of these things.

Yet the Nation of Islam faithful were, certainly, called through this discourse to engage in a great deal of collective action of other types. I already have noted that a common criticism of the Nation of Islam, as voiced by Charles Kenyatta, a close associate of Malcolm X's, was that "they clean people up, don't drink, don't smoke, but they don't *do* anything. Don't even vote."[94] Malcolm himself noted in his autobiography that "it could be heard increasingly in the Negro communities: 'Those Muslims *talk* tough, but they never *do* anything, unless somebody bothers Muslims.'"[95] And Louis Lomax, writing in 1963, notes that "the Negro masses are beginning to indict the Black Muslims for impotence."[96] But these assessments deflect our attention from the fact that Black Muslims were required to alter their personal lives significantly: diet, friendship, dress, reading habits, spending patterns, courtship and marriage, and leisure activities were all dictated by the rules of the Nation. Indeed, Nation of Islam membership required almost constant motion.[97] As Peter Goldman puts it: "Islam, if it is narrowing, still fills the days."[98] Building Muslim-owned businesses, attending meetings and lectures almost every night of the week, praying five times a day, and selling a prescribed number of copies of the weekly Nation of Islam newspaper, *Muhammad Speaks,* made many members more visible in their communities than they were before joining.[99] But this is the sort of activity inspired by a rhetoric of preparation; the goal is purification of the self and the group rather than intervention into political culture.

Ronald Stokes

Malcolm's increasing dissatisfaction with Elijah Muhammad's leadership is universally recognized among historians of the Nation of Islam, and one incident, not mentioned in the *Autobiography,* often is cited as a representative anecdote for this dissatisfaction.[100] It parallels, in some ways, the "Parable of Hinton Johnson" described earlier. But I wish to emphasize the way that this incident illustrates the extremely narrow range of rhetorical invention allowed to Black Muslim ministers and members that was at the root of this dissatisfaction and frustration.

The central and brutal fact of this incident is that in April 1962, a member of the Los Angeles Mosque, Ronald X Stokes, was shot to death by the Los Angeles police. It seems that a pair of officers had driven past some Muslims unloading dry cleaning and apparently suspected foul play; they confronted the Muslims, a crowd gathered, and shots were fired. All but one of the wounded were Nation of Islam members. Stokes was killed, and another Muslim was paralyzed for life. Malcolm X had helped to found the Los Angeles Mosque, knew many of the members personally, and helped to raise money to pay for a motorized wheelchair for the paralyzed man.

But Stokes's death particularly enraged Malcolm—his first response, like many of the Muslims, was to seek revenge. He flew to Los Angeles to preach at Stokes's funeral and to plan the counteroffensive, but Elijah Muhammad reigned him in. Hakim Jamal remembers hundreds of Black Muslims and their supporters gathering at the Los Angeles Mosque, awaiting the word from Elijah Muhammad to begin "Armageddon" but instead hearing a Nation of Islam official read out Elijah's disappointing message that they were to "[h]old fast to Islam" and that "we are not going out into the street now to begin war with the devil . . . no, we are going to let the world know he is the devil: we are going to sell newspapers."[101] Jamal and some of the other men formed small vigilante groups and roughed up white drunks, and Malcolm told them to stop. Jamal feels that "if he [Malcolm] had been free to act as he felt instead of having to speak for Elijah Muhammad he would probably have gone with us."[102] Karim argues, perhaps more persuasively, that Malcolm "would have liked to have been able to retaliate against the police violence in a politically consequential way."[103] But there would be no revenge and indeed no public and official Nation of Islam response of any kind save for a few relatively insignificant protest rallies.

Years later, Malcolm would cite this incident as one of the reasons he split with the Nation of Islam. In a speech delivered on January 1, 1965, Malcolm told an audience: "That's what caused the Black Muslim movement to be split. Some of our brothers got hurt and nothing was done about it. Those of us who wanted to do something about it were kept from doing something about it. So we split."[104] Jamal admits that he and a number of other Muslims left the Nation for the same reason: "I kept my belief in Islam, but I could no longer function in that way, the way of turning the other cheek or waiting for Allah to kill the devil. The group of black men I left the mosque with wanted vengeance."[105] But Malcolm did wreak vengeance, of a rhetorical sort, later that year. On June 4, a plane carrying many members of the white cultural elite of Atlanta crashed on its way to Paris, and at a press conference Malcolm proclaimed that "a very beautiful thing . . . has happened." "I got a wire from God today," he continues, " . . . somebody came and told me that He really had answered our prayers in France. He dropped an airplane out of the sky with over 120 white people on it because the Muslims believe in an eye for an eye and a tooth for a tooth. We call on our God, and He gets rid of 120 of them at one whop."[106]

In part, of course, Malcolm's chafing reflects the bureaucratic entrapment that many inventive rhetors would feel within a rigid hierarchical organization like Elijah Muhammad's Nation of Islam. But both Elijah Muhammad's pacifist decree and Malcolm's heartless response indicate that these limitations are rooted in the Nation of Islam's founding apocalyptic mythology. When Malcolm frames that French plane crash as an answer to Black Muslim prayers, he is appealing to one of the very few forms of action available to him and to his audiences—a reformulation of their identities as Allah's most favored and chosen people.

Rhetorical invention, in these circumstances, becomes merely an exercise in crafting more engaging and efficient ways of restating the formula: according to Elijah Muhammad, Allah will provide. The interpretive dimension of rhetorical invention is, for Malcolm X as for other Nation of Islam ministers, limited to the artful paraphrasing of Elijah Muhammad's doctrine. It is true that the doctrine itself features interpretation, since the Bible is understood as brimming with direct historical references to past and future events in African American history. But like the prophetic interpretation modeled by Nat Turner, Nation of Islam doctrine transforms these biblical passages into the same sort of data as the drought in Texas—omens to which the collectivity must react, not opportunities for judgment or critique. These are the only interpretive strategies that can be modeled for the audience and in which the audience themselves might be encouraged to engage. The only judgment to be made is whether the end is inevitable, since this seems to be only the point upon which there seems to be some degree of uncertainty—all else was delivered from Allah to Fard to Muhammad to Malcolm and is not open to interpretation. But when Malcolm X spoke outside the mosques, as he did with increasing frequency in the early 1960s, he was not so severely constrained, and his rhetoric often reflected a tendency toward a broader and more flexible perspective.

Michigan State University

Malcolm addressed the predominantly white student body of Michigan State University on January 23, 1963.[107] This was the beginning of what would effectively be Malcolm's last year in the Nation of Islam, for Elijah Muhammad would "silence" him in December following Malcolm's remarks that the assassination of President Kennedy was a case of the "chickens coming home to roost."[108] This speech is typical of those that Malcolm X delivered on college campuses during the early 1960s, before his break with the Nation of Islam. Separated from "Black Man's History" by only about a month, the marked differences between the speeches should not be ascribed merely to a trajectory of Malcolm's thought but to Malcolm's efforts to adjust simultaneously to the expectations of two very different audiences. Karim remembers that "Malcolm didn't preach Nation of Islam doctrine in his college lectures," and in no surviving transcripts of his speeches to whites does Malcolm X review "Yacub's History" in detail.[109] This is hardly surprising, since a sharply bifurcated worldview, in which blacks are angels incarnate and whites are irredeemably evil, would play poorly before a white audience. Malcolm also was not addressing these white college students indirectly, as David Walker's *Appeal* or Du Bois's "Conservation of Races" indirectly addressed whites. And Malcolm's audience was largely sympathetic—or at least not necessarily already convinced of his wickedness, like those addressed by Nat Turner. When Malcolm X stepped outside the mosque, then, he was breaking largely new ground both for the Nation of Islam and for prophetic black nationalism more generally.

In the first moments of this speech at Michigan State, Malcolm X reinforces his prophetic role: "It should be pointed out at the outset that I represent the Honorable Elijah Muhammad." Malcolm frames his speech as an attempt "to try and spell out what the philosophy and aims and motivations of the Honorable Elijah Muhammad happen to be and his solution to this very serious problem that America finds herself confronted with." As in the mosque, Malcolm will be speaking for another. But these opening moments also subtly distinguish this speech from those delivered inside the mosque. In this speech, Malcolm is not delivering the message of Allah but of Elijah Muhammad; the final solution will not be Allah's decision to rain destruction upon white America but Elijah Muhammad's program of self-help and black pride. In a word, this speech is more *secular* than "Black Man's History"—Malcolm even enlists the earthbound authority of Robert F. Kennedy to help him establish the importance of race issues: "In almost every speech he's been involved in, especially during the past few months and even today, he [Kennedy] has pointed out that the race problem is America's most serious domestic problem" (25). As such, this speech draws more strongly on the secular, nationalist, Garveyite jeremiad in the Nation of Islam's ideological DNA than on the more apocalyptic Islamic elements drawn into the Nation by way of Noble Drew Ali.

Comparing this speech at Michigan State briefly to earlier speeches that Malcolm delivered to college students illustrates the changes in his approach to addressing these audiences. At a Harvard Law School Forum in 1960, for example, Malcolm related much of the Black Muslim doctrine contained in "Black Man's History." He does not deliver "Yacub's History" in full, but he does declare that "God is giving to America every opportunity to repent and atone . . . even as God gave Pharaoh a chance to repent before He finally destroyed that king."[110] And at Yale in 1962, he told his audience that "it takes God Himself to solve this grave racial dilemma" and that when we "face these facts, we see the necessity for DIVINE intervention . . . we see the necessity for a DIVINE SOLUTION." "The handwriting is on the wall for America," he continues, and the question is: "will America blindly reject God's Messenger [Elijah Muhammad], and in so doing bring on her own Divine Destruction?"[111] At Michigan State, however, the apocalyptic tone is attenuated, and the solutions explored are more political and less rigidly divisive.

At first blush, it may seem unremarkable that Malcolm should deliver a somewhat more flexible and secular discourse at a public university than he does inside a Nation of Islam mosque. But the distinction is significant. As we have seen in "Black Man's History" and in some of Elijah Muhammad's and Malcolm's other discourse, the doctrine and rhetoric of the Nation of Islam are thoroughly permeated with religious and mystical qualities; it is a carefully balanced and hermetically sealed system in which history, religion, and rhetoric are one integrated whole. The Bible is a book of black history and prediction, and proper discourse is that which conveys these truths most efficiently. Malcolm's efforts to address more diverse audiences force him to privilege some aspects of Nation of Islam doctrine over others, so that the unity of the doctrine is imperiled. And with that unity, so is the doctrine's coherence: a discourse that allows the dissociation of history and religion can no longer be recognized as Elijah Muhammad's. Malcolm declares, for example, that he is "professing to speak for Black people by representing the Honorable Elijah Muhammad" (27), but he does not make the argument found in Ali's *Holy Koran* and in "Black Man's History" that all black people are naturally Muslims and that those who are interested in locating their true history/religion should turn to Islam. Inside the mosque, Malcolm tells his audience that if you know history then you "know the right religion."[112] But outside the mosque, the essential unity of Nation of Islam doctrine fails, and history and religion become two separate entities.

Most of this speech centers on an extended differentiation between the "Old Negro" and the "New Negro." Malcolm describes the "Old Negro" as the "bourgeois type" who is blind to the conditions of most African American people and is satisfied with "token solutions"; the "New Negroes," on the other hand, are "the masses . . . who really suffer the brunt of brutality" and who "are represented by the leadership of the Honorable Elijah Muhammad" (27). Malcolm, of course, is speaking for the "New Negroes." "Some Negroes don't want a Black man to speak for them," he argues. "Now that type we don't pretend to speak for. You can speak for him. In fact," he tells his white audience, provoking laughter, "you can have him" (28). Further, this speech makes this division based upon political inclinations rather than a religious and scientific determinism—it may be possible, at least in theory, for "Old Negroes" to become "New Negroes," but whites never can become blacks. This differentiation among African Americans is presented just as vigorously as the differentiation between blacks and whites in "Black Man's History." Just as vehemently as that speech identifies all nonwhite peoples together, this speech sunders some blacks from others.

This political distinction among African Americans was a common theme for Malcolm when speaking outside the mosque during 1963. Later in the year, for example, Malcolm appeared on a radio program in Philadelphia to respond to a recent article in the *Saturday Evening Post* called "Merchants of Hate," and he used much of his time to summarize a speech he delivered to more than three thousand people at the University of Pennsylvania earlier that day; that speech, apparently, also primarily was concerned with contrasting the "New Negro" and the "Old Negro."[113] At the University of California at Berkeley on October 11, 1963, Malcolm again differentiated for his predominantly white audience the "old Uncle Tom–type Negro" and the "New Negro" who "won't hesitate to pay the price" for freedom.[114] Outside the mosque, it seems, Malcolm understands his task as educating white Americans about political gradations within the African American community, thus complicating the leadership of Martin Luther King Jr. and other integrationist African Americans that might have seemed, to many whites, to present the complete gamut of African American leadership. This multiperspectival motive, which encourages an audience to perceive a more complex world rather than a simpler one, will become a central and defining component of Malcolm's discourse in his last year, after he split with the Nation of Islam.

Malcolm's most vivid depiction of the differences between the "Old Negro" and the "New Negro" is one of his stock formulations, or set pieces, aligning the elites and the masses with the social ranks of plantation slaves. The "House Negro," according to Malcolm X, "lived close to his master . . . dressed like his master . . . ate food that his master left on the table," and finds a counterpart in the "twentieth-century Uncle Tom" (29). The only difference is "that [earlier] Uncle Tom wore a handkerchief around his head. This Uncle Tom wears a top hat" (30). These "Old Negroes" present several dangers, most of which stem from their lack of knowledge concerning their own history. Like George Washington Carver, Ralph Bunche, and Paul Robeson in "Black Man's History," the "Old Negro" that Malcolm is describing to his audience at Michigan State "believes in exactly what he was taught in school. That when he was kidnapped by the white man, he was a savage in the jungle someplace eating people and throwing spears and with a bone in his nose." But here, outside the mosque, the history with which Malcolm would replace that "jungle" history is not the story of how Yacub created the white race on the island of Patmos. Instead, these "Old Negroes" are disempowered because they don't know anything about "the ancient Egyptian civilization on the African continent. Or the ancient Carthaginian civilization on the African continent. Or the ancient civilizations of Mali on the African continent." These were, Malcolm points out, "[c]ivilizations that were highly developed and produced scientists," but these were not the same scientists who created the moon and the white race (37). "Old Negroes" are dangerous to their own race, as a result, because they fawn over a white culture that they believe is superior to their own. Like a dog on a white person's porch, this "Old Negro" has been "been trained by his master to think in terms of what's good for his master." "He hasn't been educated," Malcolm repeats, "he's been trained" (36).

The "New Negroes" for whom Malcolm speaks lack such "training." They historically are aligned with the "Field Negroes": "If someone came to the house Negro and said, 'Let's go, let's separate,' naturally that Uncle Tom would say, 'Go where? What could I do without boss?' . . . But if you went to the field Negro and said, 'Let's go, let's separate,' he wouldn't even ask you where or how. He'd say, 'Yes, let's go'" (29). "This new type Black man," ideologically descended from these slave laborers, "he doesn't want integration; he wants separation. Not segregation, separation" (38).

Malcolm rehearses almost verbatim this same distinction in his well-known address "Message to the Grass Roots," delivered in November 1963 to a predominantly black and non-Muslim audience. But he includes in that later address a particularly telling analogy to illustrate the dangers of the "Old Negro" to African Americans. "It's like when you go to the dentist," Malcolm explains,

> and the man's going to take your tooth. You're going to fight him when he starts pulling. So he squirts some stuff in your jaw called novocaine, to make you think they're not doing anything to you. So you sit there and because you've got all of that novocaine in your jaw, you suffer—peacefully. Blood running all down your jaw, and you don't know what's happening. Because someone has taught you to suffer—peacefully.

"The white man does the same thing to you in the street," Malcolm continues. "To keep you from fighting back, he gets these old religious Uncle

Toms to teach you and me, just like novocaine, to suffer peacefully. Don't stop suffering—just suffer peacefully."[115] The "Old Negro" is, quite literally, bad medicine. At Michigan State, Malcolm tells his white audience that the "Old Negro" is "sick," "intoxicated by the white man" (35). The "New Negro" is not blinded by "the white man's Christian religion" and therefore "recognizes the real enemy" and rejects the notion of "turning his other cheek to his enemy." This "New Negro" "doesn't believe in any kind of peaceful suffering" (39).

For his white audience at Michigan State, Malcolm points out that this miseducated "Old Negro" also presents a danger to them. This is because he wants "to eat with you . . . to sleep with you . . . to marry your woman" (31). Malcolm repeats this threat of race mixing several times throughout the speech, bolstering his claim by naming various African American celebrities who have white spouses, including "Lena Horne, Eartha Kitt, Sammy Davis, and you could name 'em all night long" (34). This echoes David Walker's assertion that the properly politicized black man "would not give a *pinch of snuff*" to marry a white woman, as well as Garvey's fear that "an unrestricted intercourse of miscegenation" eventually would destroy the black race.[116] Directed toward a white audience, however, these echoes acquire a different meaning, neatly inverting the threat that always is implied in black nationalist discourse. Malcolm and the Black Muslims, because they desire to avoid race mixing, are presented as a safer alternative to the more dangerous integrationists. Further, "if white people get the impression that Negroes all endorse this old turn-the-other-cheek cowardly philosophy of Dr. Martin Luther King, then whites are going to make the mistake of putting their hands on some Black man, thinking that he's going to turn the other cheek, and he'll end up losing his hand and losing his life in the try" (40).

At the beginning of his address at Michigan State, Malcolm told his audience that he was going to argue that the "unity of Africans abroad and the unity of Africans here in this country can bring about practically any kind of achievement or accomplishment that Black people want today" (25). This argument was laid aside while he differentiated between the "Old Negro" and the "New Negro" but reemerges in his peroration. In this way, the arrangement of this speech enacts a part of its argument—possibilities for international identification and Pan-African unity occupy space on all sides of the domestic disagreements between "Old Negroes" and "New Negroes," but only the "New Negroes" are able to take advantage of these possibilities. Like the education that David Walker advocates in his *Appeal,* which would raise race awareness and so render an individual unenslaveable, Malcolm argues that the "New Negro," because of a more sophisticated and authentic understanding of race history, cannot be contained within domestic borders. The "Old Negro" thinks only "locally" and thus thinks of himself or herself as the "underdog" or "minority": "by his thinking and desires being confined to America, he's limited." But "the masses of Black people who have been exposed to the teachings of the Honorable Elijah Muhammad, their thinking is more international." This "New Negro" "speaks as one who outnumbers you. He sees that the dark world outnumbers the white world. That the odds have turned today and are in his favor, are on his side" (45). In his later discourse, after he left the Nation of Islam, Malcolm further develops his effort to reverse the arithmetic of oppression through an internationalist perspective; eventually, both themes would form the basis of organizations that Malcolm founded on his own.

Of particular interest to understanding the development of Malcolm's later rhetoric is a curious instability of agency within the speech at Michigan State concerning the responsibility for resolving America's racial tension. When speaking to African Americans inside the mosque, as in "Black Man's History," Allah is described as holding the ultimate power to resolve the crisis by destroying the white race; the white race, at best, might be able to avert this disaster by giving African Americans some land of their own. When speaking to white audiences, such as the students of Michigan State University, Allah assumes none of this burden. Indeed, the responsibility for solving the problem seems to shift by the end of the speech even from the shoulders of Elijah Muhammad to those of the white students. Though Malcolm says at the outset that his purpose is to describe Elijah Muhammad's "solution to this very serious problem that America finds herself confronted with" (25), it becomes clear that it is the white audience who actually is being called upon to act. One reason it is important for whites to comprehend the diversity of opinions within the African American movement is that "once you know there's more than one type, then you won't come up with just one type solution" (26). Malcolm also tells the white students that "the reason the problem can't be solved today is you try and dress it up and doctor it up and make it look like a favor was done to the Black man by having brought the Black man here. But when you realize that it was a crime that was committed, then you approach the solution to that problem in a different light and then you can probably solve it." Malcolm elaborates, making it clear that he is engaging in a direct address to his white audience: "If you stick a knife in my back, if you put it in nine inches and pull it out six inches, you haven't done me any favor. If you pull it all the way out, you haven't done me any favor" (41).

As was the case for Frederick Douglass when he was addressing a white audience on the fifth of July in 1852, Malcolm insists that his white audience must take responsibility for repairing their own culture's shortcomings. He tells them, for example, that "you don't realize what a crime your forefathers have committed" (41). The present-perfect verb tense—"a crime your forefathers *have committed*"—indicates an action initiated in the past and continuing into the present. These crimes happened in the past and continue to happen in the present, and Malcolm's white audience must accept responsibility. "So you have to take the blame," he tells them, and "once you take the blame, then its [*sic*] more easy. Its [*sic*] easier for you to approach the problem more sensibly and try and get a solution" (42). Like Douglass, Malcolm assigns to his white audience the work of transforming their own culture; he and those for whom he speaks have not committed these crimes and thus cannot atone for them. While Douglass urges his white audience to atone for their present crimes by revivifying the activist attitudes of their own revolutionary forebears, Malcolm X urges his white audience to take responsibility for the crimes that their forebears committed.

Limits of Prophecy

The doctrine of the Nation of Islam was directly influenced by two precursor organizations—Marcus Garvey's UNIA and Noble Drew Ali's MSTA. Garvey's rhetoric sometimes presented a nearly premillennial vision of an inevitable Golden Age and divine retribution but for the most part urged a secular program of self-help and economic independence together with a need to refurbish African American identity through establishing ties to its own past and to the black Diaspora. Ali's organization presented an eclectic Islam and an apocalyptic vision in which Allah would effect divine retribution for sins against African Americans. Through Garvey, the Nation of Islam felt the influence of both the incipient nationalism of Booker T. Washington and explicit nationalism of Du Bois and the emphasis on education present in both. Through Ali, the Nation of Islam inherited a worldview in which cultural trajectories are predetermined, and, as a result, the faithful should turn their attention resolutely inward in an effort to purify their collective selves in preparation for the coming millennium. Garvey's

worldly political perspective and Ali's esoteric asceticism make for peculiarly contradictory bedfellows; early Nation of Islam doctrine requires its
followers to engage in frenetic identity-shaping activity, but only within
rather severely limited boundaries. They must renounce their "slave
names" and alter their diet, but they are not allowed to vote.

These tensions are managed within the Nation of Islam through a discourse that collapses history and religion. Inside the mosques, the political
world *is* the religious world, so that becoming aligned with one entails becoming aligned with the other. The reason to learn history is to make evident the proper religion for African Americans; the reason to read the Bible
is to learn the history—and predicted future—of the black race. The ability
to manage these tensions is one reason for the Nation of Islam's resound-
ing success as a black nationalist organization. Where previous black nationalist efforts from Bishop Henry McNeal Turner to Marcus Garvey had
foundered in part because the audiences most attracted by such rhetoric
were precisely those without access to the tremendous financial resources
required to build a nation (either at home or abroad), the early Nation of
Islam succeeded because it required no such resources. To be sure, the
faithful were required to finance a relatively lavish lifestyle for Elijah
Muhammad and a few of the most senior Nation of Islam officials. But
they were not asked to fund emigrationist projects or international shipping lines. As it was for Ali's Moors, the focus was inward, on purifying the
collective self. Within the carefully segregated world that was the Nation of
Islam, Allah would provide.

But Malcolm's fame and oratorical skills increasingly presented opportunities for him to speak outside the mosque, and these situations disrupted
the careful balance that allowed Nation of Islam doctrine to cohere. In
front of these audiences, most often the predominantly white student bodies of public universities, the eschatological mythology of "Yacub's History"
was a wildly inappropriate rhetorical choice. It is true that this narrative
may provide a sort of symbolic liberation, in that it is a history unfettered
by what the dominant culture deems acceptable. It is also true that such a
narrative may create "a state of mind or a perceived condition [of freedom]
. . . through a complex manipulation of symbolic images."[117] E. U. Essien-
Udom notes that "the need for 'roots,' which seriously concerns the Negro
masses, especially those in the northern cities, is a problem that respectable
Negro circles have shunned and long ignored," and "Yacub's History" provides roots in the form of a compelling mythic tale that elevates the black
race above the white.[118] Lincoln, further, suggests that the attraction of the

Black Muslims is related to "the lure of personal rebirth. The true believers who become Muslims cast off at last their old selves and take on a new identity."[119]

But the demonstrated potential for this narrative to refurbish egos damaged by generations of racial oppression did not translate well to the relatively privileged audiences that Malcolm increasingly encountered. A more secular rhetoric was called for, one that opened a space for multiple voices by resisting the picture of a single-minded black integrationist coalition headed by Martin Luther King Jr. The more Malcolm spoke outside the mosque, the more he emphasized the secular elements of Black Muslim doctrine. In such speeches, like the one he delivered at Michigan State University, Malcolm still assured his audience that he was speaking on behalf of Elijah Muhammad, though relatively little of what he said resembled Muhammad's rambling apocalyptic visions. In these speeches, rather, the influence of Garvey's nationalist rhetoric is predominant.

Both "Black Man's History," which is typical of the speeches that Malcolm delivered to the Nation of Islam faithful, and the speech at Michigan State, which is typical of the speeches Malcolm delivered on college campuses, call upon their audiences to recover a more authentic history as the basis for constructing their identities. Though in neither case does the specific history being recovered very closely resemble the racial identity that Du Bois was seeking to "conserve" or the radical actions that Douglass was urging his white audiences to emulate, they do exhibit a consonant *attitude* regarding the necessity of revivifying the past in order to better address the vicissitudes of the present. Within the mosque, the Black Muslim audiences are provided a quasi-scientific definition of race that seems an inversion of the racist biological determinism that Du Bois is critiquing in his "Conservation of Races," but still these audiences receive a rather Du Boisian warning regarding their inability to realize their destiny if they continue to neglect this history. At Michigan State University, authentic membership in the black "race" seems predicated upon a particular set of political convictions that perhaps bear some resemblance to those of the Du Bois of 1897 (they more closely resemble the convictions of the later and more radically nationalist Du Bois of the 1950s), but again the governing attitude is that proper preparation for the present and future requires an appropriate recovery of African American history. Certainly, the nationalist political convictions that Malcolm ascribes to the "New Negro" could be understood as an example of one of the "more or less vividly conceived ideals of life" that are central to Du Bois's cultural definition of "race."[120]

The reading strategies through which this past is to be recovered are those generally associated with a rhetoric of prophecy. This is true of the interpretive practices presented both to the black audience and to the white one. I have already mentioned the peculiarly concrete and literalized reading style presented in "Black Man's History" and other Black Muslim discourse, in which biblical references are not symbolic illustrations but direct references to specific historical moments—and predictions of specific future moments—in black history. Supporting this reading style are insistent references to *sight*. In "Black Man's History," for example, Malcolm commands his audience within the mosque to "look at it" when he offers a reading of John 8:32–33 to support Elijah Muhammad's claim that Islam was the religion of Abraham (36). Elijah Muhammad, Malcolm promises, "will open the people's eyes up so wide that from then on a preacher won't be able to talk to them—and this is really true" (39). "It's all right," Malcolm goes on, "to believe when you were a little baby that God made a little doll out of the sand and mud and breathed on it and that was the first man. But here it is 1962 with all this information floating around in everybody's ears—you can get it free. . . . Today it's time to listen to nothing but naked, undiluted truth" (40).

In the *Autobiography*, Malcolm recalls Elijah Muhammad explaining to him how best to preach the Black Muslim message: "One day . . . a dirty glass of water was on a counter and Mr. Muhammad put a clean glass of water beside it. . . . 'Don't condemn if you see a person has a dirty glass of water,' he said, 'just show them the clean glass of water that you have. When they inspect it, you won't have to say that yours is better.'"[121] James Darsey argues that this is a characteristic rhetorical strategy of prophecy and refers to it as a "rhetoric of self-evidence" that "has no power of invention; it can only reveal that which was already there, the sempiternal; it is always the rhetoric of the messenger."[122] It may be more useful to say that such rhetoric can model for its audience only a very narrowly limited sort of invention. Malcolm can invent new ways of showing people that glass of water, but he need not produce arguments about it or interpretations of it; he cannot illustrate for people how to interpret that glass of water. Malcolm, like Nat Turner, can show his audience the signs and omens in the Bible and in the skies, but he cannot show them how to make *judgments* concerning this evidence. This meaning already is fixed, encoded into Nation of Islam doctrine, and Malcolm can at best help his audience merely to apply the proper decoding filter.

The interpretive practices that Malcolm models for his white audiences *outside* the mosque, where the confines of Nation of Islam eschatology were temporarily and incompletely relaxed, are more complex. Like Frederick Douglass in his Fifth of July oration, Malcolm X at Michigan State is schooling his white audience in particular patterns of interpretation. He is urging them toward a more careful and nuanced understanding of African American political thought, and he is asking them to engage in a critical evaluation of their own cultural history. The students are to discern a diversity in African American voices that they may not have seen before and thus challenge the seemingly monolithic leadership of Martin Luther King Jr.[123] The students are also to discern their complicity in their own history, taking responsibility for what their ancestors have done. Neither of these interpretive motivations would have been possible before a black audience inside the mosque, of course, and both also strain against the limitations of Elijah Muhammad's teachings; the doctrine of the Nation of Islam is not designed to help whites understand blacks but to help blacks to appreciate themselves. As such, both of these interpretive motivations forecast characteristics that will inform much of Malcolm's rhetoric after he left the Nation of Islam.

For our purposes, however, the most significant feature of the interpretive strategies modeled by Malcolm X at Michigan State and elsewhere during his last year with the Nation is their narrow range. That is, the interpretive strategies he demonstrates for his white audiences retain the prophetic limitations of those he presents to his black audiences. The members of Malcolm's audience at Michigan State are not being invited to reach their own conclusions, and they are not invited to critique or interpret any specific political action. They certainly are not being invited to think of the facts that Malcolm is revealing to them about black discourse or their own culpability as provisional or contingent. Malcolm is not telling his audience *how* to make judgments but instead is telling them *what* conclusions to reach: the Nation of Islam is a better alternative to King's leadership; they, as whites, are as guilty as their forebears. These are stable and revealed truths, hidden, perhaps, under generations of misinformation but ultimately self-evident through plain-thinking reading strategies able to brush away the accumulated grime. Malcolm's discourse at Michigan State—as in "Black Man's History"—contains few of the startling reversals and outrageous metaphors that mark his later oratory. Malcolm's address at Michigan State, every bit as much as "Black Man's History," is a discourse of prophetic revelation.

Such discourse can offer its audiences radical visions of utopian—or dystopian—futures; it can provide potentially empowering vocabularies through which an audience might redefine themselves; it can offer useful analysis of social structures; and it can urge its audience to reexamine fundamental and problematic truths about itself and its past. These all are valuable motives of protest discourse, and the rhetoric of Malcolm X often has been understood as providing these resources to his audiences. But this form of rigid prophecy cannot model for its audiences any form of radical judgment or critique. Its hearers can be encouraged only to act in accordance with values and standards that previously were obscured.

This sort of discourse enacts what Darsey describes as a central characteristic of prophetic rhetoric, the division between "invention" and "action": "Contrary to the assumptions of traditional Graeco-Roman rhetorical theory, prophecy shatters the unity of rhetoric. *Inventio* and *actio* are not products of the same agent. Prophecy is in a significant respect a performance from script."[124] In other words, a rhetoric of prophecy displays only a relatively narrow sense of invention as a process of adapting revealed truths for effective delivery to a particular audience.[125] For the prophet—and for the audience of prophecy—"judgment" refers to conclusions either already reached in the past or predicted for the future; "invention" is limited to the exegeses that will reveal these judgments. There is no need to engage particularities or contingencies present in specific circumstances. There need be no particular connection between invention and action, because the audience of prophecy is barred from inventional activities. In prophetic discourse in general, and perhaps especially in the severely constrained form of prophecy that Malcolm was required to deliver while a Nation of Islam minister, the goal is not an audience that is prudent because it can discern but rather an audience that is righteous because it knows.

4

Radical Judgment

◇ ◇ ◇ ◇ ◇

Malcolm X's prophetic Black Muslim rhetoric was characterized by a rigid adherence to a predetermined narrative and a persistent call to recover an authentic historical black identity. It presented interpretive strategies intended to foster allegiance to this stable and codified identity as a way to prepare for inevitable future events, and it intended to equip the audience to be able to discern the omens that portended these events. Rhetorical invention was confined to a narrow range, because these identities and omens are self-evident, and thus one's attention need only be directed toward them. And once they are observed, there is little to be done except to come into collective alignment with them; their meanings and their proper applications already were firmly established. Malcolm's rhetoric after he left the Nation of Islam, in contrast, is characterized by a radical flexibility, a suspicion of constraint and of commitment, and a rejection of formulaic programs. History becomes an open-ended product of human construction rather than the predetermined creation of a divine hand. Identity construction depends on recovering the power to manage its continual remaking to one's own advantage rather than on assimilating a revealed sense of self that is stable and unchanging.

I have two central arguments in this chapter. First, Malcolm's rhetoric during the last year of his life should not be understood exclusively, or even primarily, as a developmental trajectory. As I suggested in the first chapter, that is the predominant model for making sense of Malcolm, and it positions his speeches as points along a path toward an end that was never reached. Reading his texts as *merely* pointing us toward some hypothesized final position deflects our attention from those texts themselves, and the focus is shifted from what Malcolm said to what he *might* have said had he lived. In contrast, I argue that key texts from Malcolm's last year should be understood as complementary elements in a coherent rhetorical practice. My second argument, a corollary of the first, is that Malcolm's discourse in this last year worked to break his audiences free from the confines of the dominant white culture while at the same time helping them to avoid becoming trapped within another set of restrictions. He modeled and advocated patterns of thought that suspended himself and his audiences among positions of confining stability, in a conceptual space within which they might begin to nurture the faculties of judgment which for so long had been suppressed. In particular, Malcolm's listeners are urged to discern the available possibilities that are inherent in any given situation, including those possibilities that are far beyond what the dominant white culture deems acceptable.

I develop these arguments primarily through close attention to key texts from near the end of Malcolm's life. The first is Malcolm's last speech as a Nation of Islam minister, which displays persistent themes of entrapment, echoed both in image and arrangement, thus eloquently marking the tension between the narrow prophecy of the Nation of Islam and the expansive critical rhetoric that Malcolm was developing. The next text I discuss is perhaps Malcolm's best-known oration, "The Ballot or the Bullet," which was his most important speech between his break with the Nation and his journey to Mecca. In it, Malcolm articulates for the first time a critical rhetorical vision unencumbered by prophecy, and he demonstrates some of the outrageous figures and disruptive definitions that characterize his most radical discourse. Malcolm's famous "Letter from Mecca" generally is given a place of great significance in his biography but scant attention as a rhetorical document. I understand this text as a masterful effort to lead his audience through his experiences in Mecca in a way that prepares them not for Islamic conversion but instead for political engagement. The final text discussed in detail in this book also is one of the last speeches that Malcolm delivered. A version of a set speech that he developed after his return from his second African trip, this text, addressed to a racially mixed crowd in Rochester, New York, just days before he was assassinated, demonstrates in rich detail the emancipatory strategies of interpretation in which Malcolm would have his audiences engage.

My textual analyses in this chapter are set against two historical narratives—the increasing tensions between Malcolm X and the Nation of Islam and the harbingers of fragmentation within the mainstream civil rights movement. There are some striking parallels in these two stories, and both are driven in different ways by the emerging frustration of more radical voices. But to say that my analyses are set *against* these narratives is quite accurate. Malcolm spent most of the last year of his life out of the country, and he was almost completely independent from the civil rights movement. There is some evidence that his conflict with the Nation of Islam became a source of almost paranoiac personal anxiety—and, of course, there is irrefutable evidence that this was a well-justified paranoia—but Malcolm's public speeches and statements mostly avoided the topic. Malcolm seems intent on developing a rhetoric that would emancipate his audiences from cultural and political limitations, and he rarely dwells in detail on his own personal crises.[1]

The Split and the March

The incident that triggered Malcolm's split with the Nation was his comment on December 1, 1963, regarding the assassination of John F. Kennedy a week earlier. Elijah Muhammad, in keeping with his ban on political activity, had warned Malcolm X and all Black Muslim ministers to "teach the spiritual side" and to refrain from mentioning the assassination. Malcolm, perhaps because he was making every effort in these increasingly difficult times not to offend Elijah Muhammad, abandoned his usual note cards and extemporaneous speaking style and delivered the talk from a typed manuscript.[2] During the obligatory question-and-answer session that followed, a reporter asked Malcolm to comment on the assassination, and Malcolm was quoted in the *New York Times* as saying that he "never foresaw that the chickens would come home to roost so soon."[3]

Elijah Muhammad summoned Malcolm to Chicago, where he told him that his comments were "very bad" and that he would be silenced for ninety days.[4] At first the sentence seemed to mean only that Malcolm could not make public statements; then it became clear that he could not speak even inside his own Mosque #7; and then Muhammad stated that

Malcolm would be reinstated only "if he submits." During his "silencing," Malcolm traveled with his family to visit Cassius Clay in Florida on the eve of his bout with Sonny Liston—also the eve of Elijah Muhammad conferring upon Clay his "original name," Muhammad Ali. Malcolm sent his family back home to New York but stayed in Florida himself, eventually hosting the new champ's victory celebration—described by some as an "ice-cream social"—in his hotel room. Back in New York, it became clear that Elijah Muhammad intended for the silencing to be permanent, and Malcolm began hearing rumors that his life was in danger from loyal Black Muslims.[5] On March 12, 1964, Malcolm X held a press conference to announce that he was leaving the Nation of Islam.[6]

Though the "chickens coming home to roost" was the triggering incident, the tensions driving the split had been long in building. Historians and biographers generally agree on some combination of three factors: the jealousies and corruption of the Nation of Islam; Malcolm's chafing against the inertial confines of Elijah Muhammad's proscription against political action; and Malcolm's growing interest in orthodox Islam. Malcolm rarely mentioned any of the these things in his public addresses, but these three accounts of the split are significant because they illustrate the emphasis on Malcolm's heroic evolution that typifies approaches to his important last year.

Peter Goldman argues that the split ultimately was caused not by "the great debate over engagement vs. nonengagement but the tacky office politics of an organization corroded by its own prosperity."[7] Many of the Nation's ranking members resented Malcolm X—in part because of his fame, in part because of his pious lifestyle, and in part because of his close relationship with Elijah Muhammad.[8] "They knew Malcolm's high moral standards," reasons Benjamin Karim, and feared the "thorough housecleaning" that would follow if the ailing leader died and Malcolm X, the heir apparent, took control of the Nation.[9] Among the most irksome affronts to Malcolm's pious sensibilities was Elijah Muhammad's adultery and illegitimate children. In the early spring of 1963, Malcolm met with several of Elijah Muhammad's secretaries who alleged that Muhammad was the father of their children, and in April Malcolm flew to Phoenix to confront his mentor. Malcolm and Elijah's son Wallace had scoured biblical texts for references to adulterous prophets, so that these materials might be used to explain this behavior to the Nation of Islam faithful. As Malcolm remembers their meeting in Phoenix, his mentor embraced these biblical precedents: "I'm David," he said. "When you read about how David took another man's wife, I'm that David. You read about Noah, who got drunk—that's me. You read about Lot, who went and laid up with his own daughters. I have to fulfill all of those things." Malcolm's responses were varied, from fearing that he would seem a "dupe" for not believing Elijah Muhammad capable of such indiscretions to fearing that Allah might "burn his brain" if he allowed himself to believe them. In private, he shared Elijah Muhammad's "confession" with Louis X (later Farrakhan) and other close intimates; many of these associates told Malcolm that they already knew about the illegitimate children but nonetheless reported back to Nation of Islam headquarters that Malcolm was spreading vicious rumors. Publicly, Malcolm did not make explicit reference to these facets of Elijah Muhammad's personal life until after he left the Nation. Then, he used the information as ammunition in the escalating conflict between himself and his mentor.[10]

The second narrative is provided by George Breitman, who in contrast to Goldman argues that the split was motivated primarily by disagreements between Malcolm and Muhammad regarding political engagement. "The Black Muslims had been effective as a propaganda group," Breitman writes, "but the time had come [in 1963] for action as well as talk." Many ministers, he continues, "saw the danger of their movement being by-passed and isolated as growing numbers of black people moved into action."[11] Breitman quotes Malcolm from an interview with Louis Lomax: "But I will tell you this: The Messenger [Elijah Muhammad] has seen God. He was with Allah [W. D. Fard] and was given divine patience with the devil. He is willing to wait for Allah to deal with the devil. Well, sir, the rest of us Black Muslims have not seen God, we don't have this gift of divine patience with the devil. The younger Black Muslims want to see some action."[12] Breitman dismisses these references to Elijah Muhammad and Fard as "the religious garb of the movement" and declares that the meaning of this statement is "unmistakable," that Malcolm was seeking a way to become more politically active.[13] It should be kept in mind, however, that Malcolm X never engaged in or advocated any direct political action, even after he left the Nation of Islam.

Louis DeCaro provides the most thorough examination of the third major narrative concerning the split, that Malcolm X was gravitating toward orthodox Islam and away from the esoteric teachings of Elijah Muhammad. "Political historians have already noted that in the 1960s Malcolm X was moving steadily toward a progressive, activist stance that could not ultimately be reconciled to the nonpolitical, sectarian nature of the Nation," he writes, "but few have adequately appreciated the religious corollary to the same crisis in Malcolm X's career in the Nation." By mid-1963, DeCaro argues, "Malcolm's inclination toward traditional Islam was becoming more apparent," but Malcolm couldn't preach this new doctrine while a member of the Nation of Islam—neither, apparently, could Elijah Muhammad's own sons, since both Akbar and Wallace, Elijah Muhammad's two sons most well versed in orthodox Islam, were ex-communicated.[14] DeCaro suggests that, "Malcolm was experiencing the birth pangs of a new conversion and . . . his faith was constantly fluctuating between belief in Muhammad and belief in orthodox Islam."[15] Only after the split, then, could such a conversion be complete.

These three accounts of the split between Malcolm X and the Nation of Islam are intertwined, but none takes note of the central role played by Malcolm's rhetoric. Benjamin Karim frames the evolution of Malcolm's thought and his eventual split with the Nation of Islam in typically romantic terms: "Just as a baby moves into a larger world when it outgrows its mother's womb, Malcolm outgrew the Nation of Islam, and he had to move where his mind took him."[16] But as I argued in the first chapter, such heroic characterizations ignore Malcolm's most basic and fundamental identity—he was an *orator*. As such, Malcolm's exit from the Nation of Islam was not precipitated merely by an individual and isolated evolution but also by his public efforts to enact effective rhetorical performances before diverse audiences.[17]

Malcolm's split with the Nation of Islam overlapped some of the most memorable and significant events of the 1960s civil rights movement, most notably the desegregation campaign in Birmingham, Alabama, and the March on Washington. The two events aid our understanding of the rhetoric of Malcolm X because they present some of the elements of fragmentation to which he was responding, and they are closely related because momentum for the march built out of the successes in Birmingham.

In Albany, Georgia, the previous summer, a coalition of civil rights organizations working together under the leadership of Martin Luther King Jr. had not won anything like a decisive victory. Birmingham was carefully selected as a venue that offered both a more certain victory and more dramatic possibilities. In Albany, police chief Laurie Pritchett had proven to be a master of finesse and political acumen, rolling with the punches thrown by the movement and thus keeping the demonstrations from ever becoming viable media events. In contrast, Birmingham public safety commissioner Eugene "Bull" Connor was, as Goldman puts it, "a gravelly, one-eyed, central-casting seg" who could be expected to drive any confrontation between blacks and whites onto the front pages.[18]

The Birmingham campaign began on April 3 with a carefully orchestrated series of sit-ins at department-store lunch counters throughout downtown Birmingham. But the campaign eventually proved to be far more messy and improvisational than anyone originally planned. By early May, the movement had sputtered, the media were losing interest, and Bull Connor was promising not to leave office despite having lost an election. The movement leaders, running low on adult volunteers, decided to send hundreds of African American children out of the Sixteenth Avenue Baptist Church, into the streets, and, ultimately, into Birmingham's jails. This move was controversial, criticized by many outside the movement and by some within it, but the evening news carried horrific images of young African Americans being bowled over by high-pressure fire hoses and menaced by white policeman and their dogs. The outcry was global, and Birmingham became an international public relations crisis for the Kennedy administration. A series of political deals and concessions began to work quietly to resolve the conflict, but negotiations momentarily were set back when federal troops had to be mobilized to quell disorder instigated primarily by some African Americans not trained in King's nonviolent tactics. Finally, a list of desegregation concessions was agreed to, and the Birmingham movement largely was recognized as a success.

The high-profile success of Birmingham thrust King into a rarified stratum of celebrity, and the entire civil rights movement thus strode the international stage. The March on Washington was the realization of an idea that A. Philip Randolph had had in the 1940s, but it was King's celebrity and success that attracted the tremendous resources required to stage the event. The march was a highly scripted and orchestrated affair. It involved the logistics of bringing nearly 250,000 African Americans into the capital and then getting them safely back out again; the ego balancing required to organize an entire day's worth of high-profile entertainment, religious homilies, and political speeches; and the politicized ear required to manage the tone of the demonstration so that it was not so militant that it backfired but at the same time not so accommodating that it lost its edge. Images of the throngs crowding the reflecting pool, together with images of high-pressure fire hoses blasting demonstrators in Birmingham only a few months earlier, remain indelibly impressed upon our national consciousness as iconic representations of the 1960s civil rights movement.[19]

These two events played out against two emerging tensions that were significant both to the continued development of the civil rights movement and to Malcolm's biting criticisms of it. First, King seemed to be experiencing a slow estrangement from the Kennedy administration.[20] The Kennedys had been powerful, if sometimes reluctant, allies, but by 1963 Kennedy had repeatedly ignored King's pleas to commemorate the hundred-year anniversary of the Emancipation Proclamation, and King had snubbed Kennedy's invitation to a White House celebration of Lincoln's birthday.[21] The March on Washington originally was conceived to use the success of Birmingham to pressure Kennedy to issue an executive order ending segregation, but after Kennedy drafted a civil rights bill, the march was retooled to put pressure on Congress to pass some version of Kennedy's bill. For any Black Muslim, and perhaps especially for Malcolm X, this sort of collaboration with white power smacked of a sellout, and he repeatedly critiqued King and the nonviolent civil rights movement on this issue.

The nonviolent movement also had begun to face internal tensions that, in some ways, paralleled those inside the Nation of Islam. Many of the members of the Student Nonviolent Coordinating Committee (SNCC) were not only younger than King but also from the North, and friction between them and King would intensify over the next few years. As Branch puts it: "Resentment of King festered among young movement veterans who disapproved of his royal style or criticized him for harvesting attention that was built on their long sacrifice."[22] Eventually, these frictions would precipitate the birth of Black Power in 1967; in 1963, they were manifest in the censuring of a speech that John Lewis intended to deliver at the March on Washington. Washington archbishop Patrick O'Boyle declared that he would not deliver his planned opening benediction unless Lewis's criticisms of the Kennedy administration were toned down. They were, under the guidance of older movement leaders, and both O'Boyle and Lewis delivered their addresses.[23] Malcolm X, though actually a few years older than King, always identified himself with younger African Americans and exploited Lewis's censuring to argue that King's movement was suppressing a more militant youthful voice in favor of an older voice of compromise.

Three months later, Malcolm's assertions that King's brand of passive resistance was losing favor among an increasing number of African Americans seemed to be confirmed when an attempt to establish a northern, urban counterpart to the SCLC broke up in Detroit. The more militant participants walked out and organized their own convention, the center-piece of which was a two-day rally at King Solomon Baptist Church where Malcolm X was the featured speaker. His "Message to the Grass Roots," which I mentioned briefly in the previous chapter and which was widely available on an LP record, provides an alternate review of the key civil rights events of 1963. Malcolm characterizes Birmingham as a failure and critiques the March on Washington as a ruse by the "House Negroes" to keep the "Field Negroes" from starting a revolution. "When Martin Luther King failed to desegregate Albany, Georgia," Malcolm explains, "the civil-rights struggle in America reached its low point." King and other "Negro civil-rights leaders of so-called national stature became fallen idols," unable to inspire further action. In a compensatory move, "local leaders began to stir up our people at the grass-roots level. This was never done by these Negroes of national stature," who "have never incited you or excited you" but instead have only "kept you on the plantation."[24] Malcolm's version of the events may not be entirely accurate, but they are representative of the sorts of critiques that he leveled against the nonviolent civil rights leaders during his last months inside the Nation. He will craft a similar critique in his last official speech while a Black Muslim, which also offers a particu-larly vivid illustration of both Malcolm's growing interest in such critique and the confining limitations of Elijah Muhammad's prophetic vision.

The Chickens Coming Home to Roost

When Malcolm X faced the crowd of approximately seven hundred African Americans, and a very few white reporters, gathered at the Manhattan Center on December 1, 1963, he did not realize that he was delivering his last address as a member of the Nation of Islam.[25] Goldman dismisses the speech as "mostly standard Muslim stuff," and DeCaro describes it merely as a "prophetic-styled presentation." Perry summarizes its "principle theme" as "one he had reiterated countless times: God was wreaking, and would continue to wreak, his vengeance on white America until it let its black population go free."[26] But the speech deserves closer attention, not only because of the care that Malcolm clearly took in preparing it. Gold-man, DeCaro, and Perry are correct that this speech rehearses themes com-mon in Malcolm's Black Muslim rhetoric, but its significance is in the way that competing themes are *juxtaposed* within this single text. While its be-ginning and end do, indeed, offer a rather standard review of Black Mus-lim theology, its middle section presents the volatile abrasion of that theology against the politically engaged sensibilities that were emerging in Malcolm's speeches outside the mosque. This speech, then, vividly portrays the fundamental incompatibility between the two strands of his Black Muslim rhetoric—the tightly controlled prophetic narrative of "Black Man's History" and the more politically inflected prophecy of the speech at Michigan State University. It sets the stage for the radical innovations of Malcolm's later rhetoric by illustrating, at several levels within the text, the limitations and contradictions that Malcolm would seek to avoid, and equip his audiences to avoid, throughout his last year.

Muslim Review

The opening lines of Malcolm's speech provide a summary preview of the content and argument of the first third of the text. "The Honorable Elijah Muhammad teaches us," Malcolm begins:

> that as it was the evil sin of slavery that caused the downfall and destruction of ancient Egypt and Babylon, and of ancient Greece, as well as ancient Rome, so it was the evil sin of colonialism (slavery, nineteenth-century European style) that caused the collapse of the white nations in present-day Europe *as world powers*. . . . So we of this present generation are also witnessing how the enslavement of millions of black people in this country is now bringing White America to her hour of judgment, to her downfall as a respected nation.[27]

As in "Black Man's History," the duty of Elijah Muhammad in these last days is to warn of white America's impending doom, for the "time is past when the white world can exercise unilateral authority and control over the dark world" (130). African Americans are being given one last chance to separate from the whites. God has "prepared a refuge" in the form of the Nation of Islam, and therein might Malcolm's black audience be buffered from the divine destruction that is sure to come (131).

Malcolm's concluding remarks mirror these opening statements and also reiterate the Black Muslim prophetic style, in which biblical texts are understood as apocalyptic omens and concrete contemporary predictions. "History must repeat itself!" Malcolm warns. "Because of America's evil deeds against these twenty-two million 'Negroes,' like Egypt and Babylon before her, America herself now stands before the 'bar of justice.' White America is now facing her Day of Judgment, and she can't escape because today God himself is the judge" (146). There is some hope, however: "the only lasting or permanent solution is complete separation on some land that we can call our own." Most of the remainder of the speech consists of variations on this demand for land and on the promise of divine retribution if white America fails to offer this restitution.

Political Analysis

The strident tone of the introduction and conclusion is in marked contrast to the middle section of the speech, in which Malcolm presents almost scholarly analyses of the influence of white liberals on the civil rights movement, of the differences between integrationist and separatist politics, and of the March on Washington. He begins this section by arguing that his audience should not think in terms of Democrats and Republicans, because "white liberals from both parties cross party lines to work together toward the same goal, and white conservatives from both parties do likewise." But even "liberal" and "conservative" are not useful categories of analysis for African Americans, because neither is better than the other. The only difference is that conservatives are like wolves, showing their teeth "in a snarl that keeps the Negro always aware of where he stands with them. But the white liberals are foxes, who also show their teeth to the Negro but pretend they are smiling" (137). Malcolm is enacting for his audience a radical interpretive attitude, one that rejects the possibility of making any productive choice among these white options and instead suggests a radical critique of those very "choices" themselves.

Malcolm next differentiates between integrationist and separatist African Americans, using figures familiar from his "Message to the Grass Roots" and the speech at Michigan State. The nearly scholarly tone is reinforced by frequent oral footnotes, in which he cites several newspapers and "the late Howard University sociologist, E. Franklin Frazier." A curious contradiction is developed here and is allowed to stand. Malcolm gives the teachings of Elijah Muhammad an emancipatory potential that is unique in his discourse: Elijah Muhammed's teachings threaten the white power structure because they enable "the Negro . . . to think for himself" so that "he will no longer allow the white liberal to use him as a helpless football in the white man's crooked game of 'power politics'" (136). As I have argued in the previous chapter, however, the rhetoric of the Nation of Islam clearly does not encourage one to "think for himself." Certainly the teachings of Elijah Muhammad might insulate their audience from the vagaries of white power, but only because they isolate that audience within the bounds of esoteric doctrine and the unceasing commitment to internal purification. Political critique would be fruitless within the Nation of Islam, anyway, since Nation of Islam members were prohibited even from voting;

and such thinking for oneself could, as Malcolm was about to learn, be grounds for ostracism. Malcolm does not develop this point, instead explaining that while the "Negro 'revolution' is controlled by these foxy white liberals," the *black revolution* is controlled only by God" (137). Later in the speech, he asserts that the "government knows that The Honorable Elijah Muhammad is responsible only to God and can be controlled only by God" (140). Malcolm X makes no attempt to reconcile the implicit critique involved in thinking for oneself with the explicit lack of human agency (apparently, even Elijah Muhammad's) in a revolution controlled only by God; they are, perhaps, irreconcilable and exist in close juxtaposition here as a rhetorical testament to the conflicting discourses within which Malcolm was entrapped.

Malcolm finishes this middle section with a model critique of the March on Washington that puts into play the radical attitude he has described. The march, he says, began as a "grass roots level" plan to disrupt the Congress, the Senate, the White House, and even the airport but degenerated into a white-controlled exhibition signifying nothing. "In fact," says Malcolm, "it ceased to be a march. It became a picnic, an outing with a festive, circuslike atmosphere . . . CLOWNS AND ALL" (144). He mentions the censuring of John Lewis's speech and says that the marchers were told by the government "what signs to carry, what songs to sing, what speeches to make, and what speeches not to make" (145) and were "channeled . . . from the arrival point to the feet of a dead President, George Washington, and then [allowed to] march from there to the feet of another dead President, Abraham Lincoln" (144). Malcolm concludes that the march "would have to be classified as the best performance of the year; in fact it was the greatest performance of this century. It topped anything that Hollywood could have produced" (145). But now that "the show is over, the black masses are still without land, without jobs, and without homes . . . their Christian churches are still being bombed, and their innocent girls murdered. So what did the March on Washington accomplish? Nothing!" (146).

Symbolic Entrapment

Also in the middle section of this speech, Malcolm describes a "black revolution" that "swept white supremacy out of Africa" (137, 139) and is "sweeping down upon America like a raging forest fire" (138). But these potentially emancipatory images of disruption and rampage are overshadowed by the governing metaphor of entrapment. The civil rights movement is a "political football" being used in a game over which it has little control (133–34); the white liberals attempt to "harness" and "contain" the civil rights movement, thus keeping African Americans running "from the growling wolf . . . into the open jaws of the 'smiling' fox" (136, 137); the white government attempts to "get the rampaging Negroes back into the corral" (140); President Kennedy believed he needed to "hold the black masses in check, keep them in his grasp, and under his control" (139); and of course the marchers were allowed to march only "between the feet of two dead Presidents" (145). As I have noted, the arrangement or *disposition* of the speech further reinforces the entrapment metaphor—the middle section of the speech, in which Malcolm X offers his audience a model of engaged political analysis, is bounded on either end by the apocalyptic separatism of Elijah Muhammad.

In this speech, then, whatever emancipatory interpretive strategies that Malcolm X might offer his audience are tightly constrained by Elijah Muhammad's prophetic vision. His audience is encouraged to reject the interpretive categories imposed by the white dominant culture and to evaluate civil rights actions within a localized frame—both of which are hermeneutic practices central to Malcolm's later discourse. But these practices are rendered largely instrumental when they are subsumed within an apocalyptic vision and a demand for land. Malcolm's audience is encouraged to think of these potentially emancipatory strategies of critique as tools to be used in achieving political action, rather than *as* political action. The focus is not on cultivating a way of seeing the world that is itself potentially emancipatory but on making use of particular critiques as a means to fulfill a predetermined destiny. In short, this speech illustrates vividly the tendency for a rigid discourse of prophecy to negate even the potent emancipatory impulses in a critical rhetoric such as Malcolm's.

The Ballot or the Bullet

The speech that is widely recognized as one of Malcolm's best and most important, "The Ballot or the Bullet," is one version of his standard speech during the month between his split with the Nation and his trip to Mecca. Unlike most of his speeches, Malcolm himself gave this one its title. Given his extemporaneous speaking style, it is certain that this speech varied in its repetitions; the version included in *Malcolm X Speaks* and most often anthologized was delivered on April 3, 1964, to a predominantly black audience at the Cory Methodist Church in Cleveland, at a meeting sponsored

by the local chapter of the Congress of Racial Equality (CORE).[28] The
meeting Malcolm attended was in the form of a panel symposium, featuring Louis Lomax and Malcolm as lead speakers, and titled "The Negro
Revolt—What Comes Next?"

The speech differs significantly from Malcolm's Nation of Islam discourse. Unlike "Black Man's History," this speech is not an explanatory
narrative. Unlike his speech at Michigan State, there are no explicit markers to suggest that Malcolm is fulfilling a prophetic role. Unlike "God's
Judgment of White America," this speech is not crippled by explicit demands and material goals. Instead, "The Ballot or the Bullet" aims to alter
the frameworks through which its audience is to view the world. It invites
its audience to adopt a shifting critical perspective, not in an effort merely
to explain the world but in an effort to make possible a critical engagement
with it. Structurally, the first two-thirds of the speech push against boundaries that limit African American behavior and self-evaluation within the
dominant white culture. In a pattern common in his post-Nation of Islam
public address, Malcolm works first within a scene defined by the borders
of the United States and then expands to an international scene, drawing
parallels between the two. In this way, he widens the horizons of his audience, illustrating that their predicaments and their possible solutions prolif-
erate when viewed within a global frame. Then, in the final third of the
speech, working within the broadened circumference that he has established, Malcolm models a form of radical judgment.[29]

Voting or Violence

"Mr. Moderator," Malcolm begins, "Brother Lomax, brothers and sisters,
friends and enemies: I just can't believe everyone in here is a friend and I
don't want to leave anybody out."[30] It is "time for us to submerge our differences," he says. "If we have differences, let us differ in the closet; when
we come out in front, let us not have anything to argue about until we get
finished arguing with the man." "If the late President Kennedy could get
together with Khrushchev and exchange some wheat," he concludes, then
African Americans can get together because "we certainly have more in
common with each other than Kennedy and Khrushchev had with each
other" (25).

James Cone thinks that this speech represented Malcolm's bid for "black
unity," and these opening moments of the speech would seem to substan-
tiate this hypothesis.[31] But after these opening moments, this theme is
dropped almost entirely. And, more important, these comments on unity

are interspersed with other comments that repeatedly reject most sources
of identity that might form the underlying basis upon which unity might
develop.[32] Malcolm notes, for example, that "just as Adam Clayton Powell
is a Christian minister who heads the Abyssinian Baptist Church in New
York, but at the same time takes part in the political struggles to try to
bring about rights to the black people in this country," Malcolm himself is
"a Muslim minister" who believes "in action on all fronts by whatever
means necessary" (24). But a minister like Adam Clayton Powell—or the
other ministers he mentions, including King and Milton Galamison—
cannot endorse action "by whatever means necessary." They are constrained by the limitations of the doctrines that they preach, just as Malcolm X was constrained by the doctrines that he preached when he was
Black Muslim.

Further, though Malcolm professes still to be a "Muslim minister," he
also says that "I'm not here tonight to discuss my religion." He is true to his
word, for after these opening remarks, Islam almost completely vanishes
from the text. Indeed, Malcolm rarely mentioned Islam in any of his post-
Nation of Islam speeches, either before or after his journey to Mecca. Malcolm provides a lengthy list of other affiliations he rejects in favor of an
inclusive African American identity. It doesn't matter, he says, "whether
you're a Baptist, or a Methodist, or a Muslim, or a nationalist. Whether
you're educated or illiterate, whether you live on the boulevard or in the
alley, you're going to catch hell just like I am. We're all in the same boat
and we all are going to catch the same hell from the same man" (24). "I'm
not a Democrat, I'm not a Republican, and I don't even consider myself an
American," because "being born here in America doesn't make you an
American" (25). Having jettisoned all potential bases for identification,
Malcolm is a man from nowhere—a black man who has suffered under
white oppression but without any other definable commitment. This
speech works to develop a similar sort of grounded detachment in its audience, an attitude suspicious of commitment but yet dedicated to an overarching goal.

Malcolm warns that "time has run out! 1964 threatens to be the most
explosive year America has ever witnessed. The most explosive year.
Why?" Not because Allah is about to give the order to begin the racial Armageddon promised in Elijah Muhammad's speeches or in Malcolm's own
Black Muslim rhetoric. The threat now stems from the fact that 1964 is "a
political year," when "all of the white politicians will be back in the so-
called Negro community jiving you and me for some votes" (25). This

substitution of politics for prophecy extends to the recurring references to "sight." "I'm speaking as a victim of this American system," Malcolm declares. "And I see America through the eyes of the victim. I don't see any American dream; I see an American nightmare." African Americans, he declares, "are waking up. Their eyes are coming open" (26).

Unlike "Black Man's History," this speech does not encourage his audience to observe in awestruck passivity the "naked, undiluted truth" that he is displaying for them.[33] Rather, Malcolm is asking his audience to assume an active, critical perspective, as he makes clear in his distinction between seeing and looking: "[T]hey're beginning to see what they used to only look at. They're becoming politically mature." There may be "a few big Negroes," for example, getting jobs, Malcolm points out, but "those big Negroes didn't need big jobs, they already had jobs"; his audience must be able to see that that is "camouflage, that's trickery, that's treachery, window-dressing." "It's time," Malcolm continues, "for you and me to wake up and start looking at it like it is, and trying to understand it like it is; and then we can deal with it like it is" (28). Though the differentiation between looking and seeing does not remain stable—Malcolm frequently uses the two terms interchangeably—this speech does consistently emphasize seeing as a form of action; Malcolm is not presenting "truths" to be assimilated but patterns of interpretation to be emulated.

This speech depends for much of its development on exploring the "ballot" and the "bullet" in different contexts, with the meanings of these key terms shifting as the speech moves outward from within the confines of domestic U.S. politics. Malcolm indicates the potential power of the African American vote, explaining that "when white people are evenly divided, and black people have a bloc of votes of their own, it is left up to them to determine who's going to sit in the White House and who's going to be in the dog house" (26). But Malcolm is not, here, encouraging his audience to take action by voting; it is too soon for that, and indeed the sort of judgment he would have his audiences engage in is simply not possible within the narrow confines allotted to African Americans. "It was the black man's vote that put the present administration in Washington, D.C.," Malcolm assures his audience. "Your vote, your dumb vote, your ignorant vote, your wasted vote put in an administration in Washington, D.C., that has seen fit to pass every kind of legislation imaginable, saving you until last, then filibustering on top of that" (26–27).[34] Before he suggests any actions, Malcolm must provide for his audiences an effective model of analysis.

Echoing the argument embedded within "God's Judgment of White America," Malcolm argues that the filibuster on the Civil Rights Bill is "the same old giant con game" that proves that both of the political parties "are in cahoots together" (27). The Democrats have been successful in mobilizing the African American vote, Malcolm notes, but "after they get it, the Negro gets nothing in return." He explains that they could pass legislation if they wanted to, since "they have in the House of Representatives 257 Democrats to only 177 Republicans," and in the Senate "there are 67 senators who are of the Democratic Party. Only 33 of them are Republicans." "Why," he concludes, "the Democrats have got the government sewed up, and you're the one who sewed it up for them." The alleged division between the Democrats and the Dixiecrats, for Malcolm, is merely further evidence of the con. Ignoring long-standing political context as well as the tension between Lyndon Johnson and the southern Democrats, he declares that a "Dixiecrat is nothing but a Democrat in disguise." "Look at it the way it is," Malcolm urges his audience. "They have got a con game going on, a political con game, and you and I are in the middle" (28). "You just can't belong to that party," Malcolm urges, "without analyzing it" (30). But this analysis is intended as a form of action: "it's time in 1964 to wake up," so that "when you see them coming up with that kind of conspiracy" you can "let them know your eyes are wide open. And let them know you got something else that's wide open, too. It's got to be the ballot or the bullet. The ballot or the bullet" (28). When "the Negro awakens a little more and sees the vise that he's in, sees the bag that he's in, sees the real game that he's in," he promises, "then the Negro's going to develop a new tactic" (29).

Still, no such tactics are advocated. Malcolm instead continues to sharpen his audience's critical faculties, now turning their attention to the "bullet." This takes the form of street violence, as Malcolm warns that "now you're facing a situation where the young Negro's coming up," and "they don't want to hear that 'turn-the-other-cheek' stuff, no" (31). He cites approvingly a recent newspaper story about teenagers in Jacksonville, Florida, "throwing Molotov cocktails" as evidence that "there's new thinking coming in. . . . It'll be Molotov cocktails this month, hand grenades next month, and something else next month. It'll be ballots, or it'll be bullets. It'll be liberty, or it will be death." "The only difference about this kind of death," Malcolm continues, deftly subverting both American liberalism as well as this famous bit of American folklore, is that "it'll be reciprocal" (31–32). This sort of action is justified because African Americans are merely "trying to collect for our investment. . . . Three hundred and ten years we worked in this country without a dime in return—I mean without a *dime* in return." These slaves, whom Malcolm refers to as "your and my mother and father," "didn't work an eight-hour shift, but worked from 'can't see' in the morning until 'can't see' at night, and worked for nothing, making the white man rich, making Uncle Sam rich." But African Americans today must learn to "look at it like that," to see "how rich Uncle Sam had to become" through the unremunerated work of "millions of black people" (32). Malcolm does not tell his audience to throw Molotov cocktails at police officers. But he is presenting that vignette as a justifiable possibility, one that lies clearly beyond the limitations established by the dominant culture but that should be included within the possible actions contemplated by his audience. And it is an action that follows upon critical observation.

This logic of justified radicalism and startling reversal is repeated as Malcolm X ties African American injustice to a peculiarly limited threat of violence. Civil rights rightfully belong to African Americans, bought and paid for through their sacrifice, and "whenever you're going after something that belongs to you, anyone who's depriving you of the right to have it is a criminal." When African Americans protest against the white establishment, "the law is on your side. The Supreme Court is on your side." Because "the police department itself" is guilty of depriving African Americans of their rights, the officers therefore "are not representatives of the law." Again, Malcolm X does not offer an unambiguous call to action; where the domestic "ballot" was attenuated through a lesson in the intractable racial corruption of the U.S. political system, the "bullet" is blunted through metaphor: Malcolm tells his audience that if "a man has the audacity to put a police dog on you, kill that dog, kill him, I'm telling you, kill that dog. I say it, if they put me in jail tomorrow, kill—that—dog" (33).[35] This passage is as close as Malcolm X ever came to advocating violence in any of his speeches, but even here he carefully limits it. "I don't mean go out and get violent," he says, "but at the same time you should never be nonviolent unless you run into some nonviolence." Outrageously subverting the concept of nonviolence, he concludes: "I'm nonviolent with those who are nonviolent with me. But when you drop that violence on me, then you've made me go insane, and I'm not responsible for what I do. And that's the way every Negro should get" (34).[36]

This discourse opens up violence as a possibility for his audience, while at the same time it warns his audience not to initiate violence. It encourages a willingness to consider acting in ways that ignore the limits of the dominant culture but issues no command to take such action. Instead, the process of critical observation through which outrageous actions are justified—that process—is presented *as* a form of action. Urging the congregation gathered in the Cory Methodist Church to throw Molotov cocktails or kill police dogs would be imprudent. But expanding the boundaries of the possible so that they may include even these acts is an emancipatory rhetoric.

Representation or Warfare

In the next section of the speech, Malcolm directs his audience's attention to the "ballot," but now in an international context. The broader scope is evident as he makes his transition: "When we begin to get in this area, we need new friends, we need new allies. We need to expand the civil-rights struggle to a higher level—to the level of human rights" (34). The shift from "civil" to "human" rights places the particular case of U.S. race relations within an unfamiliar context and thus continues the effort to develop his audience's analytical range.[37] This shift also releases his audience from the confines of civility. "Whenever you are in a civil-rights struggle," Malcolm continues, "whether you know it or not, you are confining yourself to the jurisdiction of Uncle Sam," because "civil rights comes within the domestic affairs of this country" (34). Human rights do not follow from citizenship, so there is no obligation to continue to act in accordance with the expectations of any particular national government.

The international "ballot" entails taking "Uncle Sam before a world court" in the United Nations.[38] While this is not an uncivil action, it does represent an attempt to escape the oppressive "civility" of the white American justice system. Malcolm envisions an arena "where our African brothers can throw their weight on our side, where our Asian brothers can throw their weight on our side, where our Latin-American brothers can throw their weight on our side, and where 800 million Chinamen are sitting there waiting to throw their weight on our side." And, again, even when presenting this explicitly political plan, Malcolm does not offer any specific political action. There is no list of procedures that either Malcolm X or his audience might follow to convene this world court. Instead, he offers a model of outrageous behavior. "You'd get farther calling yourself African instead of Negro," he tells them, because "they don't have to pass civil-rights bills for Africans. . . . Just stop being a Negro. Change your name to Hoogagagooba." Malcolm tells about "a friend of mine who's very dark [who] put a turban on his head and went into a restaurant in Atlanta before they called themselves desegregated." He continues: "He went into a white restaurant, he sat down, they served him, and he said, 'What would happen if a Negro came in here?' And there he's sitting, black as night, but because he had his head wrapped up the waitress looked back at him and says, 'Why, there wouldn't no nigger dare come in here'" (36). Dressing in this way would not ensure the safety of the members of his audience in a segregated southern restaurant, and so the story does not serve the instrumental purpose of modeling a favored action. But the story does provide a vivid illustration of the sort of transgression that an expanded frame of reference might suggest—it strains against the definitional barriers erected by the dominant culture and illustrates the arbitrariness of those barriers.

The global reframing of the "bullet" follows this expansion of the "ballot," and instead of street fighting, we are presented with guerrilla warfare. "So, you're dealing with a man whose bias and prejudice are making him lose his mind, his intelligence, every day," Malcolm explains. "He's frightened. . . . Everywhere he's fighting, he's fighting someone your and my complexion.And they're beating him. He can't win any more" (36). America is "bad as long as she can use her hydrogen bomb, but she can't use hers for fear Russia might use hers. Russia can't use hers, for fear that [Uncle] Sam might use his." This means that "the only place where action can take place is on the ground," and "the white man can't win another war fighting on the ground. Those days are over. The black man knows it, the brown man knows it, the red man knows it, and the yellow man knows it." Like the coalition of people of color that Malcolm imagines in the United Nations, this more violent global coalition also seeks to use whites' own hubris against themselves. Malcolm invites his audience to identify with these dark soldiers, rather than with the "Americans" who were fighting against them: he describes the Japanese soldier during World War II, who would "wait until the sun went down" and then "take his little blade and slip from bush to bush, and from American to American. The white soldiers couldn't cope with that. Whenever you see a white soldier that fought in the Pacific, he has the shakes, he has a nervous condition, because they scared him to death." Similarly, "people who just a few years previously were rice farmers got together and ran the heavily-mechanized French army out of Indochina," and the "Algerians, who were nothing but Bedouins, took a rifle and sneaked off to the hills, and de Gaulle and all of his highfalutin' war machinery couldn't defeat those guerrillas. Nowhere on this earth does the white man win in a guerrilla warfare" (37).

Once again, in what by now is a recognizable pattern, it is clear that Malcolm X is not recommending to his audience that they fight a guerrilla war armed only with "a rifle, some sneakers and a bowl of rice" (37). But inviting his audience to identify with the Japanese rather than the U.S. soldiers and illustrating that the supposed might of the great white nations can successfully be challenged through guerrilla tactics certainly broaden his audience's horizon beyond the limitations imposed upon them by the white culture. Like the Jacksonville teens throwing Molotov cocktails, the U.N. trial, and the turban-wearing friend, the guerrillas that Malcolm presents as embodiments of the international "bullet" broaden the palate of identities and actions from which his audience might choose.

Ballots and Bullets

Malcolm has stretched the boundaries of the possible and thereby opened up some conceptual space that might allow analytical flexibility. He has not advocated or modeled any particular political action. The emphasis has been on enlarging the perceptual horizon of his audience, encouraging his listeners to become critical interpreters of their political environment. In the final third of the speech, Malcolm X begins to articulate some possible actions—but these, too, are not political actions of the sort with which he or his audience might be familiar. Malcolm does not advocate marches, or sit-ins, or demonstrations, or voter registration drives. He advocates, instead, a shift in attitude and perspective; that is, the *action* that Malcolm X finally advocates in this speech is an actualization of the nomadic shifts in perspective that he has demonstrated in the speech up to this point.

Malcolm marks his conclusion by mentioning Islam for the first time since his opening remarks, promising to say, "in closing, a few things concerning the Muslim Mosque, Inc., which we established recently in New York City." But, just as in the opening remarks, Malcolm suppresses religion as quickly as he introduces it. "[I]t's true we're Muslims and our religion is Islam," he says, "but we don't mix our religion with our politics and our economics and our social and civil activities—not any more. We keep our religion in our mosque" (38). Islam is not mentioned again in "The Ballot or the Bullet." What Malcolm does actually describe are the ideological foundations upon which he eventually would establish another organization, the Organization of Afro-American Unity (OAAU).

The OAAU would be characterized by a radical flexibility: "We become involved with anybody, anywhere, any time and in any manner that's designed to eliminate the evils, the political, economic and social evils that are afflicting the people of our community" (38). This is an organization that emphasizes judgment and observation, not a particular course of action determined by inflexible commitments or ideologies. The clear purpose linked with vague tactics—black liberation by whatever means necessary—allows a close analysis of particulars and a flexibility of response without losing sight of a fixed goal. Malcolm illustrates this balance between untethered critical observation and tightly focused objective in his three-part description of black nationalism.

"The political philosophy of black nationalism," Malcolm explains, "means that the black man should control the politics and the politicians in his own community." This form of inner-directed purification differs sharply from the political passivity of the Nation of Islam in that it entails an effort to develop critical faculties: "The black man in the black community has to be re-educated into the science of politics so he will know what politics is supposed to bring him in return." Malcolm's formulation of the relationship between ballots and bullets links critical perception and deliberative choice: "A ballot is like a bullet. You don't throw your ballots until you see a target, and if that target is not within your reach, keep your ballot in your pocket" (38).

"The economic philosophy of black nationalism is pure and simple," Malcolm continues. "It only means that we should control the economy of our community" (38). This, of course, recalls the economic self-sufficiency at the core of Booker T. Washington's program and, later, Marcus Garvey's Universal Negro Improvement Association (UNIA). But the solution really isn't so simple, because "the white man has got all our stores in the community tied up," so that "he's got us in a vise." While the Nation of Islam's innovation was to avoid engaging any large-scale, public economic projects, and thus to avoid overreaching the economic resources of its core audience, Malcolm's innovation is to change the meaning of "economic philosophy" from a fixed set of behaviors in which his audience is expected to engage into an educational program. Invoking again the metaphor of sight, Malcolm urges that "our people have to be made to see that any time you take your dollar out of your community and spend it in a community where you don't live, the community where you live will get poorer and poorer, and the community where you spend your money will get richer and richer." Economic black nationalism, then, as Malcolm describes it, emphasizes critical perception—Malcolm does not directly tell his audience members which businesses to patronize but instead urges them to learn to decode the intricacies involved in understanding the economics of ghetto life. He argues that "in every church, in every civic organization, in every fraternal order," people must "become conscious of the importance of controlling the economy of our community" and realize the need to "own the stores . . . operate the businesses [and] . . . try and establish some industry in our own community." Only then will the audience be able to avoid having "to picket and boycott and beg some cracker downtown for a job in his business" (39).

Finally, "the social philosophy of black nationalism only means that we have to get together and remove the evils, the vices, alcoholism, drug addiction, and other evils that are destroying the moral fiber of our community." African Americans must, Malcolm says, "make our own society beautiful so that we will be satisfied in our own social circles and won't be running around here trying to knock our way into a social circle where we're not wanted" (39). Malcolm revisits the themes of unity that were introduced in his opening remarks, but here it becomes clear that he is not talking about unity based upon any particular or stable substratum of identification and agreement but rather a unity based upon critical assessment. It is impossible to change whites' minds because "America's conscience is bankrupt" (40).[39] Thus, his program is "not designed to make the black man re-evaluate the white man—you know him already—but to make the black man re-evaluate himself" (39–40). African Americans have "got to change our own minds about each other. We have to see each other with new eyes. We have to see each other as brothers and sisters. We have to come together with warmth so we can develop unity and harmony that's necessary to get this problem solved ourselves" (40). The basis for this unity and harmony is not supplied by Malcolm but is something that his audience must invent for themselves.

The black nationalism that Malcolm describes is not a group or movement unto itself but a habit of thought and way of being that, once internalized, governs individual action. To illustrate this concept, he selects the unlikely figure of Christian evangelist Billy Graham, pointing out that if Graham "came in trying to start a church, all the churches would be against him." Instead, Graham "tells everybody who gets Christ to go to any church where Christ is. . . . So we're going to take a page from his book." "Our gospel is black nationalism," Malcolm continues. "We're not trying to threaten the existence of any organization, but we're spreading the gospel of black nationalism. Anywhere there's a church that is also preaching and practicing the gospel of black nationalism, join that church." Similarly, join the National Association for the Advancement of Colored

People (NAACP) or CORE if they are preaching black nationalism; but if you "get into it and see them pussyfooting or compromising, pull out of it because that's not black nationalism" (41).

George Breitman suggests that this "analogy with Billy Graham was badly flawed." Breitman is correct, but not because Graham "was not trying to establish a church of his own, either on a city-wide or a nation-wide level."[40] This is not merely a matter of scope. Rather, this analogy is flawed just as is Malcolm's opening analogy with other Christian ministers. A person who has been awakened in Christ might find relatively easy lodgment in any Christian church, but a person who has nurtured the critical habits of mind that characterize Malcolm's version of black nationalism would be difficult to contain within any traditionally organized, hierarchical movement. As we shall see, this inherently destabilizing effect of Malcolm's oratory, while at the core of its emancipatory potential, also contributes to some of the difficulties he had in establishing enduring political or religious organizations.

Malcolm calls in this speech for "a black nationalist convention," which never materialized. But his call emphasizes and clarifies the importance of discerning the resources available in particular situations, considering possible actions well beyond the bounds of white decorum. The convention "will consist of delegates from all over the country who are interested in the political, economic and social philosophy of black nationalism." Malcolm promises that "we will hold a seminar, we will hold discussions, we will listen to everyone," and "at that time, if we see fit then to form a black nationalist party, we'll form a black nationalist party. If it's necessary to form a black nationalist army, we'll form a black nationalist army. It'll be the ballot or the bullet" (41). The two key terms of this speech—the "ballot" and the "bullet"—mark the extremes of a wide range of options, most of which may be well outside the range accepted by the white dominant culture. Malcolm reinforces this wide circumference, promising that "we will work with anybody, anywhere, at any time, who is genuinely interested in tackling the problem head-on, nonviolently as long as the enemy is nonviolent, but violent when the enemy gets violent" (42). Anything is possible, governed on the one hand by an uncompromising commitment to racial uplift—in all its possible forms—and on the other by the shifting particulars of contingency.

Malcolm reminds his audience that they are justified in feeling outrage and betrayal "any time you and I sit around and read where they bomb a church and murder in cold blood, not some grownups, but four little girls while they were praying to the same god the white man taught them to pray to," and then hear the U.S. government declare that it cannot find the bomber when it "can find Eichmann hiding down in Argentina somewhere" (43–44). Further, if "a Negro in 1964 has to sit around and wait for some cracker senator to filibuster when it comes to the rights of black people, why, you and I should hang our heads in shame." Hanging one's head isn't what this speech advocates. Malcolm closes with this warning: "If he [the white man] waits too long, brothers and sisters, he will be responsible for letting a condition develop in this country which will create a climate that will bring seeds up out of the ground with vegetation on the end of them looking like something these people never dreamed of" (44). The contrast with Elijah Muhammad's vision is clear. Malcolm is not offering a prophetic vision of divine retribution to come from the skies at some preappointed time that is disconnected from worldly events; this is a grassroots revolution rising up from ground level in direct response to racial oppression.

Letters from Mecca

Malcolm X left the United States on April 13, 1964, ten days after delivering "The Ballot or the Bullet," and spent most of the remainder of 1964 out of the country on two extended visits to the Middle East and Africa. The first of these two trips is the best known, given detailed treatment in both the *Autobiography* and Spike Lee's film. Malcolm had learned that he could make the hajj, a pilgrimage to the holy city of Mecca that is required of all able-bodied Muslims who can afford the journey, only with a letter of introduction from Mahmoud Youssef Shawarbi. Shawarbi, a professor of soil science at the University of Cairo but on leave to serve as director of the Islamic Center of New York, met with Malcolm and wrote the letter. Malcolm was at first detained upon his arrival in Saudi Arabia, because Muslim officials were not convinced by his credentials. Then, through a fortuitous series of events, he eventually fell under the protective stewardship of Omar Azzam, an engineer who was a friend of Shawarbi's and a brother-in-law of Prince Faisal's. Malcolm completed the remainder of his hajj in the comfort of a private car provided him by the prince.[41] After his hajj, Malcolm spent several weeks visiting Ghana and its community of African American expatriates as well as a number of cities throughout Africa.[42]

While Malcolm was abroad, tensions with the Nation of Islam continued to escalate. On April 10, three days before Malcolm left for Mecca,

Muhammad Speaks featured a huge photograph of Muhammad Ali and Elijah Muhammad on the front page, signaling the heavyweight champion's role as the Nation of Islam's new most valued public asset. On page three of that same issue, under the headline "Malcolm: Exposed by his Brother," was the text of a statement prepared by John Ali, which had been read by Malcolm's brother Philbert at a press conference two weeks earlier. It warned that Malcolm's "reckless" actions threaten to cause "unnecessary loss of blood and life," for "Messenger Muhammad teaches that anyone who deviates from Islam is a hypocrite." That statement also had Philbert denouncing his brother for "falsely charging Mr. Muhammad's family and the officials of our headquarters with seeking his ouster."[43] Accompanying this article was another that reviewed the "prophesies concerning the fate of those who rejected and opposed God's prophets" and warning that "Malcolm disobeyed the Apostle of Allah." In that same issue was a cartoon, entitled "On His Own," which showed Malcolm's head tumbling toward the gates of hell, sprouting horns that grow longer with every bounce and muttering, "I split because no man wants to be number 2 man in nothing!" and "The officials at headquarters fear my public image!" and "The messenger's family was jealous of ME!" The first of a two-part essay denouncing Malcolm, written by Minister Louis X (Farrakhan) of the Boston Mosque, also appeared while Malcolm was abroad.[44]

There is some debate regarding the extent to which Malcolm's letters home from Mecca accurately reflect his reaction to his experiences there. He surely had seen the same multiracial hajj when he first visited Mecca, as Elijah Muhammad's emissary, in 1959. Goldman suggests that Malcolm may merely have "rejected the evidence of his senses" during the 1959 journey.[45] Shawna Maglangbayan thinks that it possible that, "in the face of Mecca, Malcolm X mistook the momentary, euphoric fervor unchained by religious belief, for a *permanent* state of amity among peoples of all colors."[46] Louis DeCaro discerns a "Muslim continuity" in Malcolm's experiences, so that his initial prison conversion and his later Mecca conversion are of a piece; he may have "stylized his presentation of the sacred pilgrimage and his experiences as a Hajji," but he did so because his agenda was the further propagation of Islam.[47] Kenneth Clark suggests that Malcolm's trip to Mecca was a calculated move to improve his public image.[48] And Bruce Perry offers perhaps the most cynical reading, portraying the journey to Mecca as an effort by a "gifted politician" to "shift political position without undermining his credibility" while perhaps attempting also to "refurbish his pocketbook" through endorsements by wealthy Saudi

Arabians.[49] But if we lay aside these ultimately unanswerable questions concerning Malcolm's sincerity, we can attend instead to the rhetorical work accomplished in the "Letter from Mecca." It is a remarkable document that works to broaden his audience's conceptual horizon and encourage the development of a faculty of radical judgment.

In the *Autobiography*, Malcolm X describes copying out "essentially the same letter" to a number of friends and associates in America, and all of the surviving letters are very similar in style, structure, and content.[50] The version that Mike Handler published in the *New York Times* initially received the most attention, and its wording only slightly differs from the version included in the anthology *Malcolm X Speaks*.[51] The version that over time has become the standard text, and the version upon which I focus, is the one included in the *Autobiography*.[52] This letter generally is summarized as portraying a softening attitude toward whites following Malcolm's apparent discovery that not all Muslims are black. But this letter also encourages its audience to participate in Malcolm's own rebirth out of a world governed by rigid prophecy and into a world characterized by the necessity of interpretive judgment. Goldman suggests that his experience of the multiracial hajj struck Malcolm "with something like the force of revelation—one of those sudden, impulsive, flare-in-the-night recognitions that he trusted and by which he had ordered and reordered his life," but this is not the way that Malcolm describes it.[53] Malcolm in Mecca is not like Paul on the road to Damascus—or even Marcus Garvey reading Booker T. Washington's memoirs and feeling his "doom" as a race leader descend upon him.[54] This is not a prophetic document.

The "Letter from Mecca" exhibits a balanced structure, beginning and ending with conversational narratives of Malcolm's experiences while in Saudi Arabia and in the middle describing his contact with white Muslims. The first section begins with Malcolm declaring that he had never before "witnessed such sincere hospitality and the overwhelming spirit of true brotherhood as is practiced by people of all colors and races here in this Ancient Holy Land, the home of Abraham, Muhammad, and all the other prophets of the Holy Scriptures." The "Muhammad" that Malcolm refers to is not, of course, Elijah Muhammad, which itself is significant. More so, however, is Malcolm's authorial position—he is at this point in the "Letter" a witness to these actions in the land of the prophets, not a participant. In fact, in the next sentence he describes himself as "utterly speechless and spellbound by the graciousness I see displayed all around me by people *of all colors*" (339). When he does describe his participation in the religious

rituals of the hajj, it is through peculiarly dispassionate sentences that display the actions before the reader but do not hint at Malcolm's emotional
or intellectual involvement: "I have made my seven circuits around the
Ka'ba. . . . I drank water from the well of Zem Zem. I ran seven times back
and forth between the hills of Mt. Al-Safa and Al-Marwah. I have prayed
in the ancient city of Mina, and I have prayed on Mt. Arafat" (339–40).
The prose comes to life again when Malcolm refocuses his reader's attention on the "tens of thousands of pilgrims, from all over the world. They
were of all colors, from blue-eyed blonds to black-skinned Africans." They
were "displaying a spirit of unity and brotherhood that my experiences in
America had led me to believe never could exist between the white and
the non-white" (340). Malcolm partakes in the hajj, but primarily as an
observer, seeing for his African American readers an exotic and unfamiliar
setting against which his revelations will be described.

The tone shifts as the text moves into its middle section, with Malcolm
no longer a participant-observer in a religious ritual but suddenly engaging
in direct address and modeling a self-reflexive willingness to change. "You
may be shocked by these words coming from me," Malcolm warns, but his
pilgrimage "has forced me to *re-arrange* much of my thought-patterns previously held, and to *toss aside* some of my previous conclusions." Still, the
change has not been "too difficult for me," since he has been "always a
man who tries to face facts, and to accept the reality of life as new experience and new knowledge unfolds it." "I have always kept an open mind,"
Malcolm continues, "which is necessary to the flexibility that must go hand
in hand with every form of intelligent search for truth" (340). Malcolm has
moved in this passage away from mere observation and ritualized participation toward an engaged critical stance that links observation to changes
in attitudes and behavior; judgment requires engagement.

What follows is among the most often quoted passages from any of Malcolm X's speeches and statements: "During the past eleven days here in the
Muslim world, I have eaten from the same plate, drunk from the same
glass, and slept in the same bed (or on the same rug)—while praying to the
same God—with fellow Muslims, whose eyes were the bluest of blue, whose
hair was the blondest of blond, and whose skin was the whitest of white."
Malcolm feels true brotherhood with these white Muslims, he says, "because their belief in one God had removed the 'white' from their *minds,* the
'white' from their *behavior,* and the 'white' from their *attitude*" (340). This is
at far remove from the rigid racial essentialism of Elijah Muhammad;

seeing these qualities of these particular white people requires situated observation.

These insights lie at the vertex of the symmetry of the "Letter"; the remainder of the text moves backward through the same topics—and sometimes the same language—that were presented in its first half. Islam, Malcolm repeats, might be the salvation of America if the nation could convert to this religion and "accept the Oneness of God" and therefore also "the Oneness of Man." "The whites of the younger generation," Malcolm thinks, especially might be agreeable to a conversion to this *"spiritual* path of *truth"* (341). Then the "Letter" ends as it began, describing some of Malcolm's activities in the Holy Land: Prince Faisal of Saudi Arabia allowed Malcolm X use of his air-conditioned hotel suite, a sheikh gave Malcolm two books on Islam, a car and driver were placed at his disposal, and the government provided "servants in each city" that he visited (341–42).

The "Letter," then, roughly describes three concentric circles: the outermost one of tourist activity, the middle one urging a mass American conversion to Islam, and the center concerning Malcolm's "discovery" that not all Muslims are black. Malcolm leads the reader from the outside circle, through the middle, to the center, and then back again to the outside. The symmetry is not perfect, and after the experience, the reader and Malcolm are not exactly where they began. But at the center of it all is a flexible interpretive attitude that cannot easily be reconciled with religious revelation.

Return and Interlude

Malcolm returned to the United States on May 21, 1964, staying only about six weeks before returning again to the Middle East and to Africa. His public discourse from this brief return from Mecca reinforces the fact that whatever softening of his racial attitudes may have occurred, this was a limited response to a unique situation and not a global or universal shift. What was appropriate in Mecca is not appropriate in America. Malcolm put it this way: "I kept being asked the question by some reporters, 'We heard you changed.' . . . I smiled and all. But I would say to myself: How in the world can a white man expect a black man to change before *he* has changed? . . . How do you expect us to change when the causes that made us as we are have not been removed?"[55]

In two key oratorical events from the interim between his two African journeys in 1964, Malcolm reiterates the emphasis on flexibility and observation that emerged as central themes in "The Ballot or the Bullet" and "Letter from Mecca." On May 29, 1964, one week after his return, Malcolm took part in a panel discussion organized in response to rumors of a Harlem "hate gang" that allegedly claimed allegiance to Malcolm and had threatened to kill some white store-owners. Hearing of the gang, Malcolm says, "didn't make me sad at all. And I don't see why anybody should be sad or regretful in any way, shape or form—if such does exist." After comparing this gang, called the "Blood Brothers," to the Black Muslims, he continues: "I am one person who believes that anything the black man in this country needs to get his freedom right now, that thing should exist." Malcolm describes a very different scene from what he observed in Mecca, saying that "a black man in America lives in a police state. He doesn't live in any democracy, he lives in a police state. That's what it is, that's what Harlem is." He compares Harlem to Algeria under occupation and then warns that "Afro-Americans . . . who live in these communities and in these conditions" are no longer "willing to continue to sit around nonviolently and patiently and peacefully looking for some good will to change the conditions that exist. No!"[56] Malcolm may have glimpsed a potential for racial brotherhood outside the domestic scene, but there is little evidence that he changed his perception of that scene itself. In the question-and-answer session that followed, someone asked Malcolm about the "Letter from Mecca." "Travel broadens one's scope," Malcolm replied, "It doesn't mean you change—you broaden. No religion will ever make me forget the condition of our people in this country." Asked about what sort of political and economic system he would prefer, Malcolm answered: "I don't know. But I'm flexible."[57]

A second key event was the founding of the OAAU. On June 28, 1964, at a press conference in Harlem, Malcolm read the "Statement of Basic Aims and Objectives of the Organization of Afro-American Unity," officially establishing the OAAU as a secular counterpart to the Muslim Mosque, Inc (MMI). The OAAU developed out of Malcolm's realization that the MMI limited his audience too much to serve his future purposes, out of his fascination with the Organization of African Unity, and out of late-night talks with expatriate African Americans in Ghana. As Goldman describes it, the "Statement of Basic Aims and Objectives" was written soon after Malcolm's return from Africa by "a brain trust of writers, academics, politicians, students, celebrities, professional people, Old Muslims and budding revolutionaries" that Malcolm assembled to work "secretly in a motel on the north fringe of Harlem."[58] A. Peter Bailey, a member of that brain trust and later editor of the OAAU's newsletter, remembers being "told to go to a motel on 153rd St. and 8th Ave. at 9 A.M. Approximately twelve other people were present including historian John Henrik Clark and author John O. Killens."[59]

The OAAU seems to have been an attempt to establish an organization along the rather disruptive lines presented in "The Ballot or the Bullet." During the June 28 press conference, Malcolm interrupts his reading of the "Statement of Basic Aims" with his own running commentary, framing and reconfiguring that document until it seems to describe more a profusion of possibilities than an organization with recognizable boundaries.[60] Malcolm's motto for the OAAU is predictably vague: "We want freedom by any means necessary. We want justice by any means necessary. We want equality by any means necessary" (37). The varied goals of the OAAU, likewise, spread over a rather wide and ill-defined territory. They included: realizing Pan-Africanist ideals—"to unite everyone in the Western Hemisphere of African descent into one united force" and to unite with "our brothers on the motherland" (38); bringing global pressure on U.S. racial injustice—the OAAU plans to take the United States to "the UN before a world body wherein we can indict Uncle Sam for the continued criminal injustices that our people experience in this government" (57); and promoting black nationalist self-determinism—"Instead of waiting for the white man to come and straighten out our neighborhood, we'll straighten it out ourselves" (48). Malcolm notes that the OAAU would even accept the nonfinancial support of whites, who "can form the White Friends of the Organization of Afro-American Unity and work in the white community on white people and change their attitude toward us" (58). On the other hand, Malcolm also acknowledges the separatist legacy of his organization by noting—inaccurately—that Marcus Garvey never asked whites for help and that therefore the OAAU would "try and follow his books" and charge a $2.00 initiation fee and dues of $1.00 a week (59). At the second OAAU rally, held a week later, the radical flexibility of the organization that Malcolm is imagining is clear: "Don't let the [white] man know what you're against or who you're against. It's tactical suicide." Malcolm puns: "A black man that's committed is out of his mind. Be uncommitted."[61]

Malcolm's return to the United States also precipitated further escalations in the hostilities between himself and the Nation of Islam. On June 8, Malcolm sat with Mike Wallace for an extensive interview concerning Elijah Muhammad's extramarital affairs, but Wallace's report the next day only made indirect reference to the allegations. Malcolm followed up by repeating the accusations on several radio shows, and the ensuing mood of impending violence was palpable enough that New York City police officers escorted him to a courtroom hearing on June 15. This hearing was intended to establish ownership of Malcolm's home in Queens. Malcolm contended that it had been a gift from the Nation of Islam in recognition of his years of hard work, but the Nation of Islam asserted that the house was a rectory and that since Malcolm X no longer was a minister, he was required to vacate the premises. Malcolm used the opportunity to repeat his allegations. On July 2, partially on Malcolm's urging, two of Elijah Muhammad's former secretaries filed paternity suits against Muhammad. The next day, an "Open Letter" from John Shabazz appeared in *Muhammad Speaks:* "I would have referred to you as 'Uncle Tom,' Malcolm," it began, "except that it would have been an insult to all the Uncle Toms on earth to class you with them."[62]

Malcolm left the United States again on July 9, 1964, and returned to the Middle East and Africa. His first destination was the second meeting of the Organization of African Unity in Cairo. Because he was not a national representative, Malcolm X was not allowed to address the conference. He did, however, gain official "observer" status and was able to circulate a memo, an "Appeal to African Heads of State," in which he addressed the African leaders as "long-lost brothers and sisters" and asked that European colonialism not be replaced by "American *dollarism.*" "Your problems will never be fully solved until and unless ours are solved," he argued. "We beseech the independent African states to help us bring our problem before the United Nations, on the grounds that the United States government is morally incapable of protecting the lives and the property of 22 million African Americans."[63] M. S. Handler, writing in the *New York Times,* reported that "after studying [this memo], officials said that if Malcolm succeeded in convincing just one African government to bring up the charge at the United Nations, the U.S. government would be faced with a touchy problem."[64] The assembled heads of state at the Cairo summit passed a carefully worded resolution that praised the United States for passing the Civil Rights Act of 1964 a few weeks earlier but at the same time expressed concern about continued American racial inequalities. This was not a clear-cut victory for Malcolm, but it was evidence that his presence there had some impact.[65]

Malcolm would stay abroad this time for nearly five months, visiting many of the same nations he had passed through on his earlier trip. The conflict with the Nation of Islam continued unabated. Elijah Muhammad himself contributed an article to the July 31 issue of *Muhammad Speaks* entitled "Beware of False Prophets," consisting mostly of quotations from the Quran on the subject of hypocrites. In the same issue, Louis X (Farrakhan) addressed Malcolm indirectly when he warned that "we, the true followers of the Honorable Elijah Muhammad, will not stand by and allow you or any one to attempt to destroy the greatest leader who has ever been among us."[66] Malcolm responded with a second letter from Mecca, which M. S. Handler published in the *New York Times* on October 4, calling Elijah Muhammad a "religious faker" and stating that for "twelve long years I lived within the narrow-minded confines of the 'straitjacket world' created by my strong belief that Elijah Muhammad was a messenger direct from God Himself and my faith in what I now see to be a pseudo-religious philosophy that he preaches." Malcolm also declares "emphatically that I am no longer in Elijah Muhammad's 'strait jacket' and I don't intend to replace his with one woven by someone else." He promised he would "never rest until I have undone the harm I did to so many well-meaning, innocent Negroes who through my own evangelistic zeal now believe in him [Elijah Muhammad] even more fanatically and more blindly than I did."[67]

Malcolm missed Freedom Summer. He was in Africa when the mass mobilization of northern white and African American students began and when Michael Schwerner, Andrew Goodman, and James Earl Chaney were brutally slain. He was abroad when Martin Luther King Jr. was engaged in a volatile effort to desegregate St. Augustine, Florida; when King spent a few weeks in mid-July rallying support for the voter registration drive in Mississippi; and when King went to New York to try to defuse the rioting that followed the shooting death of a fifteen-year-old boy. Malcolm wasn't there when, in response to this shooting, angry Harlemites marched on the same police station to which Malcolm had led his group of Black Muslims seven years earlier to demand hospital care for Hinton Johnson.

On July 13, in the racially charged atmosphere of the Republican national convention in San Francisco, Barry Goldwater was nominated for president. A few days later, civil rights leaders agreed to a moratorium on Birmingham-style demonstrations until after the election. A few weeks later, Johnson and Goldwater met in the White House and agreed to exclude civil rights and Vietnam from the presidential campaign. In August, the presence of members of the Mississippi Freedom Democratic Party (MFDP) at the Democratic national convention and their efforts to seat their delegates among, or instead of, the regular Mississippi Democrats drew from the party leadership a series of compromises, eventuating in the seating of two of the MFDP representatives as "at large" delegates. On October 13, Martin Luther King Jr. was awarded the Nobel Peace Prize. And in November, Lyndon Johnson was elected president in a record-setting landslide. Malcolm X commented on some of these events, calling his lawyer, Percy Sutton, from Africa to say that he would not have attempted to quell the Harlem riots and telling reporters in Cairo that the civil rights leaders had sold out and allowed themselves to "become campaign managers to the Negro community for Lyndon Johnson."[68] But for the most part, Malcolm looked in on the voter registration drives, the slayings, and the political compromises from the perspective of exile, able to locate the events upon a broad world stage but otherwise unable to participate.

Malcolm X returned from Africa on November 24, 1964, and immediately took up his typically crowded speaking schedule. He spoke almost weekly at the Audubon Ballroom in Harlem but also in a number of other northern U.S. cities; he addressed members of SNCC in Selma, Alabama, while King was in jail there; in London, he addressed both the Council of African Organizations and the London School of Economics; and he attempted to speak to the Federation of African Students in Paris, but after his plane landed he was not allowed to leave Orly Airport.[69] Back home, early in the morning of February 14, the house in Queens that had been the focus of so much acrimony between Malcolm and the Nation of Islam was firebombed, Molotov cocktails breaking through the windows while Malcolm and his family slept; after finding temporary lodgings for his wife and daughters, Malcolm kept a speaking engagement later that day at the Ford Auditorium in Detroit.

It is not accurate to describe the speeches from this period as a search for a program or platform or stable set of goals or methods; Malcolm repeatedly and explicitly disavows any such purpose. Such stability would be anathema to the emancipatory strategies of interpretation he was modeling and advocating. He disavows weaving a new "straitjacket" for himself or for anyone else. But three closely interrelated themes do emerge in his discourse from this period: an individualized judgment, characterized by a fundamental suspicion of leadership; a position of Pan-African exile, which extols the insights available from looking in from outside the race problems of the domestic United States; and a commitment to radical flexibility, which is a paradoxical commitment to the rejection of commitment.

For example, in a letter from Cairo apparently intended for the membership of the fledgling organizations he had left behind—the MMI and the OAAU—Malcolm sounds strongly individualist themes. He says that "none of us is qualified to judge each other, and that none of us should therefore have that authority." "I've never sought to be anyone's leader," he writes, though when he returns he promises to "work with anyone who thinks he can lead." Abdicating his own leadership almost entirely, he tells his followers that "you can make the Muslim Mosque and the OAAU a success, or you can destroy both organizations. It's up to you."[70] On December 20, at Harlem's Audubon Ballroom, he tells his audience that "I, for one, believe that if you give people a thorough understanding of what it is that confronts them, and the basic causes that produce it, they'll create their own program; and when the people create a program, you get action. When these 'leaders' create programs, you get no action." What is needed is to start people "thinking in a way that they should think," because "you can bet that when you write the script for yourself, you're always doing something different than you'd be doing if you followed somebody else's script."[71] In January, he told a group of high school students visiting Harlem from Mississippi that "one of the first things I think young people, especially nowadays, should learn how to do is see for yourself and listen for yourself and think for yourself. Then you can come to an intelligent decision for yourself." This takes the form of a habit of critical observation and analysis followed by individualized judgment: "It's good to keep wide-open ears and listen to what everybody else has to say, but when you come to make a decision, you have to weigh all of what you've heard on its own, and place it where it belongs, and then come to a decision for yourself."[72] But this individualist bias always is tempered with a conception of collective identity; Malcolm is not describing an atomistic fragmentation of African American culture but a constitution of it.

A Pan-Africanist perspective replaces, for the most part, the calls for "unity" with which Malcolm began "The Ballot or the Bullet." Perhaps as "The Ballot or the Bullet" was a rhetorical prefiguration of Malcolm's physical excursions beyond the borders of the United States, so Malcolm's rhetoric after his return attempts to offer his audiences a vicariously broadening experience. This is especially evident in a speech that Malcolm delivered at the Audubon Ballroom in November, in which he tells his audience that "you waste your time in this country, in any kind of strategy that you use, if you're not in direct contact with your brother on the African continent who has his independence." His "main theme" while traveling in Africa, he explains, "was to try and impress upon [the Africans] that 22 million of our people here in America consider ourselves inseparably linked with them."[73] This doesn't mean that African Americans should identify themselves as

Africans but that they cannot understand their own situation as long as they believe themselves to be isolated. A month later, again at the Audubon, Malcolm reminds his listeners that they think they are a "minority" in the world only because they have "been maneuvered out of a position where we could rightly know and understand where we fit into the scheme of things. . . . It's impossible for you and me to know where we stand until we look around on this entire earth." His audience members are being asked to position themselves where they can see from both the domestic and the global perspectives at the same time: "You don't know where you stand in America until you know where America stands in the world. We don't know where you and I stand in this context, known to us as America, until we know where America stands in the world context."[74]

Strategies of individualized judgment that suspend their practitioners betwixt and between stable categories of identity perhaps necessarily foster some degree of flexibility. On December 3, Malcolm participated in a debate at Oxford University on Barry Goldwater's proposition that "extremism in defense of liberty is no vice, moderation in the pursuit of justice is no virtue." Malcolm argued in support of the proposition and told the audience—to prolonged applause—that "any time you live in a society supposedly based upon law, and it doesn't enforce its own law because the color of a man's skin happens to be wrong, then I say those people are justified to resort to any means necessary to bring about justice where the government can't give them justice."[75] In a speech on December 12, Malcolm echoed his second letter from Mecca, saying that "I believe that the injustices that we have suffered and will continue to suffer will never be brought to a halt as long as we put ourselves in a straitjacket while fighting those injustices."[76] But Malcolm does limit this flexibility somewhat. On December 20, he explained to his audience at the Audubon Ballroom that "policies change, and programs change, according to time. But objective never changes. . . . The reason you change your method is that you have to change your method according to time and conditions that prevail."[77] Any means are appropriate, but only when they are responsive to immediate circumstances and contribute to achieving the ultimate goal. And he tells the students from Mississippi that although "[w]e reserve the right to use any means necessary to protect our humanity, or to make the world see that they respect us as human beings," he also emphasizes that "I don't mean anything illegal."[78]

A key term that recurs in Malcolm's speeches during this time period is "positive neutrality." He borrows the idea from the nonaligned movement among independent African states, following from the Bandung Conference of 1959, and modifies it to fit domestic American politics.[79] At the Audubon on December 20, he notes that this "is the position taken in African policy," manifest in their refusal to "line up either way." He explains "what this positive neutrality means:"

> If you want to help us, help us; we're still not with you. If you have a contribution to make to our development, do it. But that doesn't mean we're with you or against you. We're neutral. We're for ourselves. Whatever is good for us, that's what we're interested in. That doesn't mean we're against you. But it does mean we're for ourselves.[80]

The emphasis on individual judgment, the borderland perspective, and the radical flexibility all contribute to "positive neutrality." Malcolm's audience is being encouraged to think for themselves in ways beyond the limitations imposed by the dominant culture and to entertain a wide range of inventional possibilities always tempered by the need to stay focused on making positive contributions toward obtaining freedom.

Just as Malcolm developed "The Ballot or the Bullet" as a set speech during the weeks between his split from the Nation of Islam and his first journey to Mecca, he also evidently developed another set speech during the final weeks of his life. The speeches he delivered at the Audubon on and December 13 and 20, at the Harvard Law School Forum on December 16, at the London School of Economics on February 11, and in Detroit on February 14 all are structured around similar themes, allusions, and images, and all display the same concern with the ability of the white press to manipulate the truth in parallel ways at the domestic and international levels. Many of the same anecdotes recur, and even the wording of whole passages is sometimes repeated almost verbatim, suggesting that Malcolm X was working from the same set of inventional resources—perhaps from the same set of note cards. The speech on which I focus from this period, delivered in Rochester, New York, on February 16 is representative of Malcolm's rhetoric during this time and brings to coherence the themes he was developing.

The Final Speech

Malcolm addressed a racially mixed audience at the Corn Hill Methodist Church three months after returning from his second African visit and only five days before he was assassinated.[81] In this speech, Malcolm shifts his audience's perspective between domestic and international scenes in ways similar to "The Ballot or the Bullet." However, while that earlier text strove to broaden its audience's perspective to foster boons of critical observation and flexibility that might be brought to bear upon the domestic situation, this speech works to position its audience *between* the domestic and international scenes. Perhaps his experiences abroad had convinced Malcolm that the racial corruption that he believed characterized the dominant American culture reached to the places that he had once thought of as the potential antidote for that corruption. He had told students at the University of Ghana, for example, that whites are just as duplicitous in Africa as they are in America; they might seem friendly, but all they really want is "to integrate with the wealth they know is here."[82] In any case, Malcolm at Rochester understands the international scene to be very nearly as corrupt as the domestic one, so simple international identification offers no hope for liberation. Africa is not a virgin motherland, and African identity is corrupted by the presence of the white oppressor in the same way as African American identity. Merely becoming "African" instead of "American" seems, here, to offer little hope for emancipation. Rather, Malcolm invites his audience to join him at the border between the domestic and the global—between Africa and America—a site that resists the limitations of both while not wholly rejecting either. Positioned at this border, Malcolm and his audience can *see* the parallel manipulations of image through which white power is maintained.

While "The Ballot or the Bullet" traced the shifting referents for the "ballot" and the "bullet" as those terms were framed domestically and then globally, this speech stresses instead the unbending similarities between the domestic and the global perspectives. Malcolm's intention to draw parallels between these perspectives is clear in the opening remarks: "And my reason for being here is to discuss the Black revolution that's going on, that's taking place on this earth, the manner in which it's taking place on the African continent, and the impact that it's having in Black communities not only here in America, but in England and in France and in other of the former colonial powers today" (143–44). Malcolm warns his audience that "we have to not only know the various ingredients involved at the local level and national level, but also the ingredients that are involved at the international level," because racial oppression has "become a problem that is so complex . . . that you have to study it in its entire world, in the world context or in its international context, to really see it as it actually is" (144).

Malcolm illustrates the critical and productive attitude befitting this broader context. Since returning from Africa, he has "no desire whatsoever to get bogged down in any picayune argument with any birdbrained or small-minded people who happen to belong to organizations" (147). Further, he says that "I never like to be tied down to a formal method or procedure when talking to an audience," because "when people are discussing things based on race, they have a tendency to be very narrow-minded" (148). And Malcolm does not proceed through formal argument but rather by enacting juxtapositions between the domestic and international scenes, repeatedly laying out fundamental parallels and then drawing his audience's critical attention to them. His discussion of religion is representative of this mode of argument. "To straighten out my own position," Malcolm says, "I'm a Muslim, which only means that my religion is Islam. I believe in God, the Supreme Being, the creator of the universe. Which is a very simple form of religion, easy to understand." "But despite the fact that I believe in the brotherhood of man," he continues, "I have to be a realist and realize that here in America we're in a society that doesn't practice brotherhood" (149). Malcolm's "position," then, is one from which he can observe both the Islamic ideal and the American shortcomings with respect to that ideal.

This speech, like "The Ballot or the Bullet," also privileges sight. Malcolm tells his audience that they must learn to "see" the American race problem "in a different light," so they can "see it with more clarity" (144). The African Americans in the United States become empowered when they "awaken" and recognize the international connections to their struggle (146). "When you look at it in that context, you'll understand it. But if you only try and look at it in the local context, you'll never understand it. You have to see the trend that is taking place on this earth" (147). White people, he says, "are usually very intelligent, until you get them to talking about the race problem. Then they get blind as a bat and want you to see what they know is the exact opposite of the truth" (148). But the metaphor of "sight" in this speech becomes the basis of a theory of the way that racial oppression functions on a global scale. Most of the remainder of the speech is an extended effort to focus attention on seeing the ways that images of blacks are manipulated by whites. This theme is developed through two sets of parallel constructions in which the oppressive manipulation of images at the international level is used to underscore the similar manipulation at the local level, and vice versa.

Outward

In the first set of parallel constructions, Malcolm links together the images of black savagery that the dominant culture creates at home and abroad. The "racism practiced by America," he says, is the same racism that is involved in "a war against the dark-skinned people in Asia, . . . a war against the dark-skinned people in the Congo, the same as it involves a war against the dark-skinned people in Mississippi, Alabama, Georgia, and Rochester, New York" (150). It would be nearly another three years before Martin Luther King would publicly make similar connections;[83] but for Malcolm X, this essential connection between the racism practiced at home and that which informs international policy lays the groundwork for his larger point concerning its peculiar ocular fixation. In both the domestic and international scenes, Malcolm warns, the racism of the white dominant culture is manifested through "a science that's called image making" designed to make it "look like the victim is the criminal, and the criminal is the victim." This "science," as becomes clear, is Malcolm's phrase for the way that African American self-perception is rhetorically constructed by the dominant white culture. "Here's an example of how they do it. They take the press, and through the press they feed statistics . . . to the white public" to "make it appear that the rate of crime in the Black community is higher than it is anywhere else." This, Malcolm explains, "paints the Black community in the image of a criminal" and "paves the way to set up a police-type state in the Black community," so that a police officer can come in and "crush your skull, and then accuse you of attacking him" (150–51). Malcolm's speech works its emancipatory rhetoric by attempting to model and encourage in its audience the strategies of radical interpretation that will allow that audience to expose this "science."

Malcolm first illustrates this "science" in action with a domestic example: the press coverage of the Harlem riots of the previous summer. "During these riots," Malcolm notes, "the press, very skillfully, depicted the rioters as hoodlums, criminals, thieves, because they were busting up property." Malcolm admits that "it is true that property was destroyed," but he asks his audience to "look at it from another angle." "The Black man is not his own landlord," and as a result the African American "has no say-so in it whatsoever other than to live there, and pay the highest rent for the lowest-type boarding place." In this way, the inner-city African American is "a victim of economic exploitation, political exploitation, and every other kind." "Now . . . he would like to get at the one who's exploiting him," but "the one that he wants to get at isn't there." So, "when the Black man explodes . . . he's not trying to steal your cheap furniture or your cheap food. He wants to get at *you*, but you're not there" (152). The rioting is a symbolic act of retribution against "landlords who are nothing but thieves, merchants who are nothing but thieves, politicians who sit in the city hall and who are nothing but thieves in cahoots with the landlords and the merchants" (153). It is an attempt to manipulate images in response to a manipulation of images.

Malcolm marks his transition, noting that "just as this imagery is practiced at the local level, you can understand it better by an international example" (153). For a representative example, Malcolm turns to the bombing of rebels in the Congo.[84] When "planes were dropping bombs on African villages," Malcolm says, "I heard no outcry, no voice of compassion for these thousands of Black people who were slaughtered by planes." He again shows the "image making" at work, pointing out how the press gets the "white public to support whatever criminal action they're getting ready to involve the United States in." "They refer to the villages as 'rebel held,'" for example, "as if to say, because they are rebel-held villages, you can destroy the population, and it's okay" (153); the pilots were called "'Anti-Castro Cuban,' that makes them okay"; and "they're able to do all of this mass murder and get away with it by labeling it 'humanitarian,' 'an act of humanitarianism'" (154). This manipulation is effective, Malcolm explains, for it was only after the white press "referred to the hostages as 'white hostages'" that he heard an outcry among American whites (155). But the villagers in the Congo "only held a hostage in the village to keep the mercenaries from murdering on a mass scale the people of those villages" (156).

"So it's imagery," Malcolm reiterates. "They use their ability to create images, and then they use these images that they've created to mislead the people" (156). The border perspective that Malcolm is describing allows the domestic and international manifestations of the "science of image making" to come into view simultaneously and invites the audience to recognize the parallels between them. That is, Malcolm is encouraging his audiences to engage in a complex rhetorical critique: the manipulative practices of the dominant culture are exposed, and the looting in Harlem has been revealed as a strategic act; the holding of hostages in the Congo is not an act of savagery but a strategic act of self-preservation that must be understood in its proper context. Like the "landlords who are nothing but thieves," in Malcolm's broader context the American-trained pilots are exposed as murderers while the villagers are the victims. Neither the international nor the domestic scene is subsumed by the other, but both are rendered equally present to the audience; the audience is then in a position to engage in an act of interpretation and judgment that would be impossible if they were firmly rooted in either one or the other of these points of view.

Inward

Malcolm next presents another set of juxtaposed parallel anecdotes, this time beginning with an international perspective and then moving toward a domestic perspective. But he does not return his audience entirely back into the domestic sphere, instead suspending them *between* the domestic and the global. Malcolm explains that "back in '55 in Indonesia—Bandung—they had a conference of dark-skinned people" in which the "people of Africa and Asia came together for the first time in centuries" (158). They found they were bound together by a common oppressor: "a brother came from Kenya and called his oppressor Englishman; and another came from the Congo, he called his oppressor a Belgian; another came from Guinea, he called his oppressor French. But when you brought the oppressors together there's one thing they all had in common, they were all from Europe" (158). It was this "spirit of Bandung that fed the flames of nationalism and freedom not only in Asia, but especially on the African continent" (159). These "flames of nationalism, independence on the African continent, became so bright and so furious" that they couldn't be confined, so the colonial powers "passed the ball to the United States." Because the European powers could no longer oppress through colonialism, the United States developed a new program of oppression: "Instead of coming over there with gritted teeth, they started smiling at the Africans," a "friendly approach" that Malcolm calls "benevolent colonialism" or "philanthropic imperialism" (160). In other words, the United States used a tactic of symbolic manipulation, seeming to be benevolent while actually continuing the colonialist project.

These same tactics are used domestically. It was "the same desire for freedom that moved the Black man on the African continent [that] began to burn in the heart and the mind and the soul of the Black man here, in South America, Central America, and North America, showing us we were not separated. Though there was an ocean between us, we were still moved by the same heartbeat" (159). Malcolm believes that as "the Black man in Africa got independent" and became "master of making his own image," the "Black man throughout the Western Hemisphere, in his subconscious mind, began to identify with that emerging positive African image," and that identification "made him become filled with the desire also to take a stand" (161). This necessitated a new strategy of domestic oppression, for "just as [the Americans] had to change their approach with the people on the African continent, they also began to change their approach with our people on this continent. As they used tokenism and a whole lot of other friendly, benevolent, philanthropic approaches on the African continent . . . they began to do the same thing with us here in the States." The integration efforts at the University of Mississippi and the University of Georgia are examples of these token moves and case studies for the importance of decoding appearances. "They fooled the people in Mississippi by trying to make it appear that they were going to integrate the University of Mississippi" and "stuck two of them in the school in Georgia and said there's integration in Georgia." "Why," Malcolm continues, "you should be ashamed. Really, if I was white, I'd be so ashamed I'd crawl under a rug. And I'd feel so low while I was under that rug that I wouldn't even leave a hump" (162).

Forward

Malcolm's peroration consists primarily of an autobiographical narrative concerning his split from the Nation of Islam and his subsequent founding of the MMI and OAAU, and it culminates in the plea—familiar from "The Ballot or the Bullet" and other speeches—to take the United States before the United Nations on charges of human rights violations. Within this argument, the Nation of Islam and the United Nations represent two competing versions of marginality: the Nation of Islam is a dysfunctional version, isolationistic and disempowered, while the United Nations represents a productive arena conducive to judgment and action. As I have mentioned, Malcolm began this narrative much earlier in the speech, when he reminded his audience that, "as many of you know, I left the Black Muslim movement" and that he has spent much of his time since then on extended tours "in the Middle East and on the African continent" and that as a result he is not interested in "picayune argument" with "small-minded people" (147). When he takes it up again at the end of his speech, however, he supplies much greater detail and a more complex understanding of the broad-mindedness he is advocating; it is not merely an escape from the confines of the domestic scene but a middling position, modeled by the United Nations, that allows the local and the global to interact. Only from such a position can the oppressive imagery be recognized and critiqued.

The Black Muslim movement, Malcolm explains, offered a double constraint: because "the orthodox Muslim world would never accept the Black Muslim movement as a bona fide part of it, it put those of us who were in it in a sort of religious vacuum"; and "because we were never permitted to take part in politics we were in a vacuum politically." The Nation of Islam presents a negative model of marginalization, "a sort of a religious-political hybrid, all to ourselves. Not involved in anything but just standing on the sidelines condemning everything." "We were actually alienated, cut off from all type of activity with even the world that we were fighting against" (164). This form of marginalization is useless either as a position of insight or as the foundation for political action.

The antidote to this sort of mute marginalization is not assimilation but a productively multiperspectival position. Reframing the struggle as one for human rights, rather than civil rights, allows this sort of flexibility. "As long as you call it civil rights, it's a domestic problem within the jurisdiction of the United States government" (168), but if it is reframed as a human rights issue, then it can be taken before the United Nations. There, a two-way identification is possible, as Africans might identify with African Americans, and African Americans might identify with Africans. Malcolm recalls seeing "African diplomats at the UN crying out against the injustices that were being done to Black people in Mozambique, in Angola, the Congo, in South Africa," and wondering "how they could talk all that talk . . . and [then] see it happen right down the block and get up on the podium in the UN and not say anything about it" (169). He now understands that African diplomats cannot interfere with the American civil rights struggle because "[i]f any of them open up their mouths to say anything about it, it's considered a violation of the laws and rules of protocol." If the movement were redefined as one for human rights, then the Africans would not be barred from supporting it. Similarly, on the domestic side, Malcolm believes that "anyone who classifies his grievances under the label of human rights violations, those grievances can then be brought into the United Nations and be discussed by people all over the world" (170).

The United Nations, as Malcolm conceives it, presents a potentially emancipatory sort of marginalization, a liminal space where he and his audience might be able to glance between the limitations and possibilities of both the domestic and global perspectives. Victor Turner argues that individuals or groups occupying a liminal position are "betwixt and between all fixed points of classification" and therefore might "acquire a special kind of freedom" because their position "liberates them from structural obligations." Within this borderland to which Malcolm has invited his audience, they are free to "think hard, about cultural experiences they had hitherto taken for granted"—it is, in other words, a position particularly conducive to interpretation and judgment.[85] As bell hooks has noted, there is a way to claim marginalization as a "space of resistance," a space that because of its relationship to the dominant culture is a "central location for the production of a counter hegemonic discourse." There, one can avoid "estrangement, alienation, and, worse, assimilation and cooption" because terms of self-definition might flourish beyond the control of the dominant culture. "Understanding marginality as a position and place of resistance," hooks argues, "is crucial for oppressed, exploited, colonized people."[86] Molefi Asante writes that "the rhetoric of black revolution is isolationistic," that it "seeks to carve out an area that the Black audience can call its own," a "moral or psychological territory" that is "free of white intervention."[87] But Malcolm is not isolating his audience—unlike the dysfunctional isolation of the Black Muslims, the position Malcolm X describes is critically engaged and politically charged. In Malcolm's final remarks, he says that "we want to get into a body or conference with people who are in such positions that they can help us get some kind of adjustment for this situation before it gets so explosive that no one can handle it" (170).

This borderland position is marked by a telling rhetorical figure, chiasmus, which is characterized by paired phrases that turn back upon themselves. Perhaps the best-known contemporary example is from John F. Kennedy's inaugural address: "ask not what your country can do for you, but what you can do for your country."[88] In Malcolm's speech, the repeated chiasmus refers to the ability of the American press to make it "look like the victim is the criminal, and the criminal is the victim" (151, 152, 153, 156). As the speech develops, Malcolm moves from the domestic to the international and then from the international to the domestic, forming through the disposition of his speech chiasmus in large scale. Thus, the form of the speech itself is an amplified echo of this central, recurring statement. The figure, however, performs a more potent rhetorical function because of its close association with the "science of image making." This image manipulation is, like chiasmus, an antimetabolic trope—through it, the dominant culture has taught a people to turn back against themselves.

Attention to the manipulation of image as a potent resource of oppression permeates the entire speech, but it receives its most sustained attention precisely at the junction between the two arcs of the dispositional chiasmus—that is, between the first part of the speech in which Malcolm moves outward from the domestic to the international perspectives and the second part in which Malcolm moves inward from the international to the domestic. The "science of image making" is, then, literally and figurally at the center of this text: "We ended up with twenty-two million Black people here in America who hated everything about us that was African. We hated the African characteristics, the African characteristics. We hated our hair. We hated our nose, the shape of our nose, and the shape of our lips, the color of our skin. Yes we did. And it was you who taught us to hate ourselves simply by shrewdly maneuvering us into hating the land of our forefathers and the people on that continent." "When you teach a man to hate his lips, the lips that God gave him, the shape of the nose that God gave him, the texture of the hair that God gave him, the color of the skin that God gave him," Malcolm continues, "you've committed the worst crime that a race of people can commit" (157). "This," Malcolm argues, "is how you imprisoned us." He calls it, simply, "the worst form of slavery that has ever been invented by a so-called civilized race and a civilized nation since the beginning of the world" (158). In this speech, through the mobilization of his own chiastic tropology, Malcolm has taken control of this figure, fashioning it himself but this time developing it through carefully crafted parallelism, straightening out the confusion and untangling the Gordian knot of manipulated imagery through which the dominant culture constrains African American self-definition.

Emancipatory Interpretation

The key texts analyzed in this chapter do exhibit a trajectory of development, from the close confines of "God's Judgment of White America," to the outrageous characters portrayed in "The Ballot or the Bullet," to the delicate yet productive balance in the speech at Rochester. But they are not merely a trajectory, and the speech at Rochester is neither a self-sufficient fulfillment of Malcolm's rhetorical vision nor a pointer toward some later, imagined development. Rather, these texts, especially "The Ballot or the Bullet" and the speech at Rochester, work together in a dynamic model of rhetorical invention. "The Ballot or the Bullet" frees the thought patterns of its audience from within the limitations of white domination, while the speech at Rochester modulates that freedom into a middling position that resists coalescing into yet another confining codification of rules and expectations. This rhetoric is dynamic because its work is never done— African Americans *always* must work to free themselves from the confining ways of thinking prescribed by the dominant white culture and must *continuously* reposition themselves so that multiple perspectives always are available. Only then can these audiences enact the radical judgment that Malcolm models and advocates.

In "God's Judgment of White America," his last official public speech as a member of the Nation of Islam, Malcolm's burgeoning political critique remains encased within a prophetic worldview. The text is saturated with images of entrapment, in contrast to the tropes of expansion and transgression evident in his later speeches. This text presents the end point of Malcolm's rhetorical development within the Nation of Islam; it is a dysfunctional juxtaposition of the prophetic rhetorics he was developing inside and outside the mosque and illustrates their fundamental incompatibility. "The Ballot or the Bullet" offers Malcolm's initial rhetorical vision stripped of the prophetic voice. It offers no predetermined historical narratives, no prescriptive formulas, and no certain steps to follow. It is an emancipatory speech, drawing its audience simultaneously out of the confines of both Nation of Islam doctrine and the white dominant culture. It does not ask its audience to gaze upon revealed truths but instead to analyze the American political landscape—and to consider a wide range of possible actions and identities well beyond the horizons of that landscape. At the Corn Hill Methodist Church in Rochester, Malcolm establishes for himself and his audience a borderland position, a liminal perspective from which he and his audience can view both domestic U.S. white racism and global white-power colonialism at the same time. He thus models for his audience a mode of critique that does not require becoming implanted in either the domestic or the international perspective; it is a critique that depends upon flexibility and suspicion, not obstate allegiance. Remember: "A black man that's committed is out of his mind."[89]

Such a stance offers tremendous emancipatory potential. Suspended among stasis points of dangerous power and stability, it presents opportunities for judgment and critique that would not be otherwise available: the actions and ideologies of the dominant culture can be observed without the necessity for immediate political engagement; the categories that the dominant culture produces as a means to manage its own analysis can be rejected; options for response and intervention that fall well beyond the limitations imposed by the dominant culture can be considered; productive comparisons and parallels between local and global events can be drawn; and judgment becomes individualized and egalitarian rather than the purview of heroic orators or divine prophets. But it carries liabilities, most significantly that the very flexibility that makes it invulnerable to cooptation and calcification also makes it unsuitable as the basis for a recognizable "movement." Because these emancipatory interpretive strategies require a fundamental suspicion of hierarchy, they cannot be fostered within a traditionally structured organization. Because a part of the emancipatory potential of such strategies is their specific rejection of the possibility that a single voice might speak for all, they resist leadership.

In the final chapter, I explore some of these potentials and limitations in more detail. I provide a brief history of the Nation of Islam after Malcolm's assassination and of the two organizations that Malcolm founded in his last year, partly to conclude the historical narrative that has undergirded this project but, most important, to suggest some of the organizational limitations of a rhetorical stance of "positive neutrality." I also provide some theoretical density to Malcolm's incipient project by locating his stance and his discourse within some other relatively well developed concepts. Such an attempt is inherently risky; because Malcolm's position explicitly rejects any well-defined norms, an explanatory attempt that would enfold his discourse within some codified theoretical paradigm would immediately and irrevocably eviscerate its emancipatory potential. The libratory power of Malcolm's discourse lies in its refusal to be named. Thus, I will locate Malcolm's discourse through a mode of triangulation, utilizing theories of the *constitutive* potential of rhetorical discourse, the mythological figure of the *trickster* as representative of certain types of discourse, and the premodern virtue of *prudence*, or practical wisdom.

5

Context and Assessment

◇ ◇ ◇ ◇ ◇

Malcolm X was assassinated on February 21, 1965, at one of his regularly scheduled Sunday afternoon meetings at the Audubon Ballroom in Harlem. Longtime associate Benjamin Karim, one of the few who followed Malcolm out of the Nation of Islam, had "opened up" for him that day, and Malcolm had just begun to speak. A man in the middle of the audience created a diversion, shouting that someone was picking his pocket; another man charged the stage and fired a 12-gauge shotgun into Malcolm's chest. He was dead before he could be rushed to the medical center across the street.[1] One of Malcolm's assassins has admitted that a speaking engagement was selected because "it was the only place *we* knew he'd be there."[2]

Malcolm was fundamentally an orator, and in this concluding chapter I assess some aspects of his oratorical legacy. First, to conclude the historical and biographical narrative that has undergirded this project, I discuss briefly the fate of the Nation of Islam after Malcolm left and of his two independent organizations, the Muslim Mosque, Inc. (MMI) and the Organization of Afro-American Unity (OAAU), after his assassination. Then, to explore some of the emancipatory potentials of Malcolm's discourse, I approach his rhetoric from three different points of view—I describe his discourse as a *constitutive* rhetoric, a discourse that calls its audience into being through the act of address; I suggest that Malcolm's audiences specifically were being called to enact a form of consciousness that resembles closely that of the mythical figure of the *trickster;* and finally I suggest that the nomadic critical sensibilities that Malcolm would instill in his audience can be understood as a form of *prudence,* or practical wisdom. None of these concepts fully accounts for Malcolm's rhetoric either on its own or through some synthesis with the other two. Instead, these perspectives are useful because of their diversity: the constitutive dimensions of rhetoric involve the manner in which such discourse is addressed to an audience, the trickster figure embodies attitudes about culture, and prudence is a virtue that can be assimilated through careful attention to rhetorical performance. The concepts work together to bring particular aspects of Malcolm's rhetoric into relief, but they do not congeal into a single theoretical system. The emancipatory power of Malcolm's discourse lies in its refusal to be pinned down to any fixed formula. He and his audience are forever suspended among commitments, always keeping in play the widest possible range of action and identity and thus sustaining indefinitely the flexibility required for radical judgment. To codify such discourse, attempting to contain it within a single theoretical vocabulary, would be to deflate its cultural usefulness and, in short, to negate most of my argument up to this point. My aim in this chapter is to bring to light some of the potentials and limitations of Malcolm's rhetoric while still preserving its dynamic mobility.

The Nation of Islam after Malcolm X

The Nation of Islam both did and did not survive the deaths of Malcolm X and, in 1975, Elijah Muhammad. As the Nation of Islam was formed out of the shards of previously shattered religious and nationalist organizations, so the organization that is most widely recognized as the Nation of Islam today grew out of fragments of the organization that Malcolm X built for Elijah Muhammad. The various factions and splinter groups that trace their lineage to the Nation of Islam are too numerous to discuss in detail, but the two most important ones are those headed by Louis Farrakhan and by Elijah Muhammad's son, Wallace. As Steven Barboza describes them: "Those of Muhammad's disciples who believe in orthodox Islam support Warith [Wallace], while those who believe, as Muhammad preached, that the black man is the progenitor of all civilization and will inherit the earth, support Farrakhan."[3] In this way, Wallace's and Farrakhan's branches of the Nation of Islam represent and purify two elements of Malcolm's rhetoric.

Wallace Muhammad was the focal point of much of the disharmony within the Nation of Islam during the decade between the deaths of Malcolm X and Elijah Muhammad. He was recognized as one of Elijah Muhammad's more talented sons, and before Malcolm was "silenced" it was unclear whether Wallace or Malcolm was Elijah Muhammad's heir apparent. Wallace studied traditional Islam and had a long history of questioning his father's esoteric version of the faith.[4] Excommunicated soon after Malcolm, for the next several years he was repeatedly readmitted and ousted as various disagreements surfaced between his and his father's religious beliefs. At one point, Wallace founded his own organization, the Afro-Descendants Society of Upliftment, which seems to have been his attempt to pattern an organization on the model of Malcolm's MMI.[5] About a year before Elijah Muhammad's death, Wallace was firmly enough in his father's good graces to be awarded the ministry of the high-profile Chicago Mosque. Elijah Muhammad never publicly appointed an heir to the leadership of the Nation of Islam, but at the "Savior's Day" convention held a few days after his father's death, Wallace announced—amid ritual accolades from various high-ranking Nation of Islam officials, including Louis Farrakhan—that he was ascending to the most powerful position in the Nation.[6]

Almost immediately, Wallace began moving the Nation toward orthodox Islam. He relaxed the dress code, disbanded the Fruit of Islam paramilitary guard, divested the Nation of much of its business empire, and began to eliminate the black nationalist overtones from Nation of Islam doctrine. Wallace also announced that his father should be considered a great "teacher" rather than the last prophet of Muhammad, opened membership in the Nation of Islam to whites, and encouraged his followers to participate in the political process by voting.[7] He changed the name of the organization several times, and finally in the late 1980s he dissolved completely the remaining vestiges of the organizational structure of the original Nation of Islam. The membership was urged to enter fully into the international Islamic community, and, as is characteristic in Islam, leadership became vested in local and autonomous imams associated with each mosque rather than in a centralized hierarchy.[8]

While Wallace Muhammad was stripping the Nation of Islam of its prophetic voice and dismantling the organization, Louis Farrakhan was

assuming the mantle of prophecy and crafting a new Nation. After Malcolm X was "silenced" following his comments concerning the assassination of President Kennedy, Elijah Muhammad appointed Louis Farrakhan
minister of the important Harlem Mosque #7; soon after Malcolm left the
Nation, Elijah Muhammad established Farrakhan in Malcolm's place as his
national spokesman. After Wallace initiated his program of reforms, Farrakhan left the organization and began to preach the old Nation of Islam
doctrine, attracting followers, and in 1981 his resurrected Nation of Islam
held its first national convention.[9] This new Nation, as Martha F. Lee puts
it, "adopted the original doctrine of Elijah Muhammad, including its millenarian tenets. The myth of Yacub once again became a central tenet of
belief, Elijah Muhammad's original Muslim creed was emphasized, and the
eschatological vision of the Fall of America and Ezekiel's Wheel was revived."[10] Mattias Gardell notes that although "Farrakhan himself denies
being a prophet, he partly fulfills the function of a prophet." Farrakhan reveals truths to his followers, presenting his discourse as a conduit through
which explanatory codes and apocalyptic promises are delivered to his listeners: "under the right circumstances," he said in 1989, "things will come
out of my mouth that I have never thought of before. . . . [S]omething has
been put in me, not just for my immediate community, but for . . . the entire world."[11]

Wallace Muhammad's version of the Nation of Islam continues Malcolm's turn toward orthodox Islam near the end of his life. It also, in its
current form—or, more accurately, formlessness—embodies Malcolm's distrust of hierarchical organizations and charismatic leadership. Its members
now have been simply absorbed into the larger, traditional Islamic community, bringing to fruition one version of Malcolm's idealized Islamic brotherhood. But in the process of this transformation, Wallace's group lost their
distinctive political identity. His group was not constituted around any particular political agenda and in this sense was assimilationist. At one point,
before he disbanded the organization altogether, Wallace Muhammad de-
creed that both an Islamic flag and an American flag should fly over the
mosques.[12] Farrakhan, on the other hand, continues in the tradition of
Malcolm's role while a Nation of Islam minister. Farrakhan's speeches are
revelatory and prophetic, melding esoteric Nation of Islam doctrine with
sometimes astute political analysis. His ability to meld disparate ideologies
and vocabularies even more seamlessly than Malcolm X is evident in his
speech at the Million Man March on Washington, D.C., in 1995.[13] But Farrakhan's skill in this regard means that his rhetoric lacks much of the

curious tension so often evident in Malcolm's. His audiences are presented with rather limited options for interpretation and action, being urged primarily to pledge allegiance to a set body of ritualized discourse. Consistently, Farrakhan provides for his African American audiences a codified assembly of interpretive keys through which he unlocks the mysteries of contemporary life.

While Farrakhan's version of the Nation of Islam, founded on a revival of strict hierarchy and rigid prophecy, has been able not only to survive but even to thrive, Malcolm's own organizations, the OAAU and the MMI, conceptualized as flexible and decentralized from their beginnings, exist today mostly as memories. The inherent flexibility of Malcolm's discourse, together with its distrust of hierarchy, leadership, and formulas, mean that it is ill-suited as the foundation for a long-lived, traditionally conceived organization.[14] But the extent to which Malcolm X was attempting to establish such organizations is at best open to question. I have mentioned Malcolm's own deconstruction of the "Statement of Basic Aims and Objectives" of the OAAU as he read that document at the OAAU founding rally as a case in point.[15] At any rate, the weak foundation that Malcolm's rhetoric provides for the formation of these organizations was exacerbated by a number of other factors. The MMI never was given any particular identity, being intended primarily as a pulpit for Malcolm. Its fate may have been sealed by the fact that in 1964 the MMI was vying for membership with both the Nation of Islam and the splinter group that Wallace Muhammad was heading at that time.[16] The OAAU also was heavily dependent upon Malcolm, so much so that its members often were unable to make even minor decisions without telephoning him, wherever he was in the world. And, as was true of most black liberation organizations in the 1960s, the OAAU faced the obstacles constructed by the Federal Bureau of Investigation (FBI) informants and operatives who attempted either to destroy the organization or to use it for their own agendas.[17]

Even while Malcolm was alive, his MMI and OAAU fell to squabbling over definitional matters ranging from which organization should pay the overdue phone bill to whether an individual might be a member of both organizations at the same time.[18] After Malcolm's death, there was no one to resolve these conflicts. Since these organizations had no identity apart from their leader, they effectively ceased to exist.[19] Goldman reports that as early as 1973, membership had dwindled to a handful and that the OAAU's "most visible activities in Harlem were the annual commemorations of Malcolm's birth and death."[20] The post-Malcolm fate of the Nation of Islam reiterates the degree to which one of the most important distinguishing characteristics of Malcolm's rhetoric is its ability to hold multiple motives and ideologies in unresolved tension—allowed to purify themselves and develop in isolation, the elements represented by Farrakhan's and Wallace's groups lack the productive ambiguities in Malcolm's best rhetoric. The fate of Malcolm's own organizations after his death, on the other hand, illustrates the limitations of such rhetoric as the foundation of traditional organizations. The ability to balance multiple perspectives is a valuable resource for disrupting monolithic regimes, and it is one that Malcolm X would inculcate in his audiences; teaching such a skill, and obtaining it, *are* forms of political action. But they are forms of political action that culminate in habits of interpretation and judgment, not in traditional political organizations.

Triangulation

To highlight these habits of interpretation and judgment requires a shift in focus, from the careful reading of individual texts to describing the conceptual space and modes of critique that these texts, collectively, define. Again, though there is a developmental trajectory evident in the speeches and statements of Malcolm's last year, it is more important to understand that elements of Malcolm's discourse from this last year are components within a viable and generative rhetorical practice rather than merely indicators that point toward some imagined final destination. The goal here is not to conjecture about where Malcolm's rhetorical development might have led but to assess the cultural resources that can be located in the rhetoric that Malcolm produced. This requires a delicate touch; as we have seen, Malcolm's rhetoric has a tendency to conform to the contours of whatever theoretical container it may be forced into—socialist, Freudian, Aristotelian. Because the most important characteristics of his rhetoric include a flexible sensitivity to contingency and a rejection of rigid ideology, it can falsely reward efforts to impose an explanatory structure upon it.

In an effort to address this need for delicacy while yet providing a robust interpretive framework, the following argument is organized around three conceptual frameworks: constitutive rhetoric, trickster consciousness, and prudential performance. Any totalizing tendency of these perspectives is checked through a doubled argument, as Malcolm's rhetoric first is viewed as an exemplary illustration of each perspective but then is shown to exceed the limitations of that perspective. Through this sort of triangulation,

Malcolm's rhetoric is located as the object of a multifaceted understanding but retains its iconoclastic refusal to be constrained within definitive boundaries.

Constitutive Rhetoric

The first chapter began with an argument that a robust sense of rhetoric is needed to begin to account for the oratory of Malcolm X. An assessment informed by a conception of rhetoric as a tool to be used to accomplish some physical or political goal would judge Malcolm's rhetoric a failure—he left no organizations, no monuments, no buildings, no legal statutes. But a conception of rhetoric that allows public address itself to be empowering in its ability to model for its audiences a decolonized interpretive attitude suggests an altogether different assessment of Malcolm's legacy. This differentiation between the instrumental and consummatory functions of protest rhetoric has been noted by a number of rhetorical critics. Richard B. Gregg, as I have mentioned, defines an "ego-function" of protest discourse in which the speaker appeals primarily "to the protesters themselves, who feel the need for psychological refurbishing and affirmation." Such discourse can be understood as "*constituting* self-hood through expression"; in other words, as crafting an identity through the act of speaking.[21] Randall A. Lake extends this concept in his study of Native American protest discourse, arguing that in some cases its purpose is to promote the psychological well-being of the protesters themselves and not to create demonstrable change in the dominant culture. Lake cites, for example, "the performative declaration, made at Wounded Knee in 1973, that an Independent Oglala Nation had been constituted."[22] These protestors "*enacted* their sovereignty by *declaring* themselves the Independent Oglala Nation and by *acting* in a manner befitting this status."[23] Malcolm X, like these Native American rhetors, produces a discourse that forms his audience by declaring them to exist.

A number of rhetorical scholars have more specifically theorized rhetoric's constitutive potential. Edwin Black describes what he calls a "second persona" of rhetorical discourse, the implied ideal auditor who can be identified through attention to the discourse itself. Black provides the following illustration: "Let the rhetor, for example, who is talking about school integration use a pejorative term to refer to black people, and the auditor is confronted with more than a decision about school integration. He is confronted with a plexus of attitudes that may not at all be discussed in the discourse or even implied in any way other than the use of the

single term." The implied auditor of such a discourse would feel "the pull
of an ideology," as the auditor is invited to bring order to experience according to a recognizable "network of interconnected convictions" that
function "epistemically and that shapes his identity by determining how he
views the world."[24] Black identifies what he calls "stylistic tokens"—
rhetorical figures and tropes—which are condensed markers of ideology
that cue a particular *attitude* which, in turn, cues the auditor of rhetorical
discourse toward a preferred understanding of that discourse and of the
particular situation it was designed to address.

Michael McGee describes a more complex process in which a "people" is
offered as a rhetorical construct toward which individuals might be com-
pelled. This is a process through which "individuals must be seduced into
abandoning their individuality" and thus become a collective. Whereas
Black's second persona relies on the articulation of "stylistic tokens," the
constitution of McGee's "people" relies on advocates who, from time to
time, "organize dissociated ideological commitments into incipient political
myths." Such rhetoric, in other words, assembles into coherent form various bits of culture, and then an audience responds to this particular assem-
blage of narrative fragments and defines themselves and the world in its
terms. This is a people called forth by political myth. As McGee put it,
"Each political myth presupposes a 'people' who can legislate reality with
their collective belief."[25]

Maurice Charland, in an often-cited essay, has provided perhaps the
most productive recent description of constitutive rhetoric. Drawing on
both Black and McGee—and in some ways bridging the two—Charland describes the way that a particular rhetorical text, in his case a white paper issued by supporters of Quebec independence, has the potential to call forth
a "people." Charland incorporates Althusser's concept of "interpellation,"
reminding us that "the very act of *addressing* is rhetorical" in that it is
through this act that a people is formed. In other words, such discourse addresses a subject position as though it already were occupied by a physical
group of individuals, and through this addressing the individuals "hailed"
by such discourse come to occupy that subject position. "An interpellated
subject participates in the discourse that addresses him"; that is, when a
people is hailed by a discourse, that discourse then has the potential to
govern the collective identity and action of that people.[26] In Charland's
paradigm case, the white paper addressed a subject position that assumed a
right to a sovereign state, and the group of individuals who were thus interpellated were defined by this assumption.

Charland describes three specific "ideological effects" of a constitutive rhetoric that are relevant to understanding this concept in relation to the rhetoric of Malcolm X. In particular, they highlight the differing constitutive potentials of Malcolm's Black Muslim and post–Nation of Islam rhetoric; for this reason, I discuss first Malcolm's Nation of Islam rhetoric and then turn to the discourse of his last year.

The first of the ideological effects of constitutional rhetoric that Charland describes concerns the "process of constituting a collective subject." In contrast to Black's more individualist notion, Charland believes that constitutive rhetoric necessarily "renders the world of events understandable with respect to a transcendental collective interest that negates individual interest."[27] Malcolm's rhetoric while a Black Muslim minister exhibited this ideological effect—indeed, much of Malcolm's explicit purpose while preaching within the Nation of Islam was to invite his audience to understand themselves as a unified collectivity instead of as a mere collection of individuals. When Malcolm insists in "Black Man's History" that "if you're here at the Mosque you're black, because the only ticket you need to get into Muhammad's Mosque is to be black," he is establishing the term "black" as the marker of a "collective subject" in much the same way that the white paper established "Québécois" as a term available for nationalist identification.[28] Malcolm's Pan-Africanist arguments perform similar work, establishing a worldwide, dark-skinned, collective persona with which his audience is to identify.

The second ideological effect that Charland ascribes to constitutive rhetoric is the "positing of a transhistorical subject," by which he means the ability of such discourse to project an ideological bridge "between the dead and the living," providing continuity and identification across time.[29] When Malcolm tells his African American audience in "Black Man's History" that the "thing that has made the so-called Negro in America fail, more than any other thing, is your, my, lack of knowledge concerning history," he is working to provide precisely this sort of link.[30] In fact, the entirety of "Yacub's History" performs this function, explaining African American oppression, Anglo-American cruelty, and the promise of eventual African American redemption through a mythic precedent: whites in the present day are evil and blacks in the present day are noble because whites in the past were bred to be bad and blacks in the past were scientists. The peculiarly concrete nature of Black Muslim discourse itself reinforces this ideological effect, urging its audiences to identify with stories in the Bible because they are referring directly to events in the present day.

Similarly, a transhistorical subject is established by the set analogy that Malcolm rehearses in his speech at Michigan State, his "Message to the Grass Roots," and throughout his last year as a Black Muslim, which aligns the historical distinction between "House Negroes" and "Field Negroes" with the present-day distinction between the assimilationist "Old Negroes" and nationalist "New Negroes."

Charland describes the third "ideological effect" of constitutive rhetoric as the "illusion of freedom" enjoyed by rhetorically constituted peoples. Like McGee, Charland emphasizes the narrative elements of constitutive rhetoric: "In the telling of the story of a *peuple,* a *peuple* comes to be." And it is the centrality of this sense of narrative to Charland's definition of constitutive rhetoric that renders illusory the freedom felt by such peoples. "Subjects within narratives are not free," Charland points out, "they are *positioned* and so constrained. All narratives have power over the subjects they present."[31] These subjects may believe themselves to be free, but narratives are, by definition, teleological—they describe a series of events and actions intended to culminate in some recognizable resolution. The very existence of the people constituted through such discourse depends on their willingness *"to follow through"* with the dictates prescribed by a governing narrative. Of the three ideological effects described by Charland, this one may be the most self-evident with regards to Black Muslim rhetoric. The stories that Malcolm told while a Black Muslim minister were intended to implicate his audiences in just such a teleological narrative. The demand for land, for example, repeated even in Malcolm's very last speech while a Black Muslim, "God's Judgment of White America," provides one definite and determined end to that discourse. The apocalyptic destruction of the white race provides another. From the creation of the white race by an older race of black scientists to the inevitable destruction of the white race by divine black astronauts, "Yacub's History" presents a story into which Malcolm's audiences are invited to insert themselves. It is presented as the "natural" history of African Americans, forgotten because it has been suppressed by whites for thousands of years. It is the "naked, undiluted truth," the "clean glass of water" that need only be revealed to its audience for its authenticity to prevail.[32]

After he leaves the Nation of Islam, Malcolm's rhetoric continues to perform each of these three ideological effects, but it also exceeds them in significant ways. His rhetoric still exhibits appeals to collective unity, but these are leavened with appeals to individualized judgment; his rhetoric still mines the past as a resource through which to understand the present, but he also asks his audience to form identifications with others across *space* rather than across time; his rhetoric still presents narratives through which his audience is invited to make sense of themselves and the world, but these are fragmented narratives that do not cohere in a teleological alignment.

The theme of "unity" still is present in such speeches as "The Ballot or the Bullet," for example, but it is accompanied by an emphasis on individual perspective. Though Malcolm reminds his audience that "we're all in the same boat and we all are going to catch the same hell from the same man," he also refuses to suggest that his audience should join any particular organization.[33] Many of the actions that he does describe—throwing Molotov cocktails, engaging in guerrilla warfare—emphasize individual action as much as collective identity. The "Letter from Mecca," similarly, describes an Islamic brotherhood that Malcolm can perceive because he, personally—and in contradistinction to his critics—has "always kept an open mind, which is necessary to the flexibility that must go hand in hand with every form of intelligent search for truth."[34] Malcolm often included a vignette in his speeches during the last few months of his life that illustrated this commitment to individual judgment:

> I was flying on a plane from Algiers to Geneva about four weeks ago, with two other Americans. Both of them were white—one was a male, the other was a female. And after we had flown together for about forty minutes, the lady turned to me and asked me—she had looked at my briefcase and saw the initials *M* and *X*—and said, "I would like to ask you a question. What kind of last name could you have that begins with *X?*" So I told her, "That's it: *X.*" She was quiet for a little while. For about ten minutes she was quiet. And then finally she turned and she said, "Well, what's your first name?" I said, "Malcolm." She was quiet for about ten more minutes. Then she turned and she said, "Well, you're not *Malcolm X?*"

Malcolm's point, he explained after the laughter subsided, was that this woman had been too much influenced by what "she had gotten from the press, and from things that she had heard and read," so that she was "looking for something different" than what was right in front of her. She could not "see" Malcolm X as an individual, nor could she herself come to an individual judgment, as long as her vision was clouded by the judgments of others. When he told this story to the Mississippi high school students visiting Harlem on New Year's Day, 1965, he followed up by telling them that "the reason I take time to tell you this is, one of the first things I think

young people, especially nowadays, should learn how to do is see for yourself and listen for yourself and think for yourself."[35]

After Malcolm left the Nation of Islam, he still prized the importance of
studying history, but he did not so persistently insist on crafting transhistorical subjects who would recover their past as a primary resource for addressing the present. He did not ask his audience to identify with a mythic
narrative like "Yacub's History," of course, because after he left the Nation
such narratives were no longer either useful or available to him. But also,
nowhere in "The Ballot or the Bullet," or the "Letter from Mecca," or in
the speech at Rochester does Malcolm X offer a sustained invitation to his
audience to identify themselves with a representative people from the distant past; the "House Negro/Field Negro" analogy completely disappears
from Malcolm's discourse after he leaves the Nation of Islam.[36] The emphasis of his post–Nation of Islam rhetoric, instead, is on forming what
might be called trans*spatial* subjects, a people defined through their relationships to other peoples in distant locales. His frequent evocation of the
United Nations as a place where an international brotherhood of dark-
skinned peoples might be able to reverse the racial arithmetic at the base of
global oppression is one "stylistic token" through which this transspatial
subject might be hailed. In the speech at Rochester, this strategy is particularly pronounced, right from the opening remarks in which Malcolm tells
his audience that he is there "to discuss the Black revolution that's going
on . . . and the impact that it's having in Black communities not only here
in America, but in England and in France and in other of the former colonial powers today."[37] As I have argued, this text is representative of Malcolm's final speeches and statements in that it enacts a paratactic logic
whereby scenes of domestic and global oppression are repeatedly juxtaposed: whites manipulate images in racist ways in Harlem just as they do
in the Congo; the same revolutionary mood that has motivated Africans is
now motivating African Americans; white Americans use token integration
to steal Africa's wealth and to rob African Americans of real racial progress.

Finally, and perhaps most significant, Malcolm's rhetoric after he left the
Nation of Islam does not provide his audiences with a sustained, teleological narrative. In fact, Malcolm's discourse during his last months is replete
with both implicit and explicit rejections of the sort of "predetermined and
fixed ending" that characterizes the narrative structures of constitutional
rhetoric, according to Charland.[38] There are short stories in these speeches,
some drawn from Malcolm's own experiences and others featuring characters performing outrageously indecorous acts. But these do not present a

telos in the sense that Charland describes. Upon hearing these tales, Malcolm's audience is not invited to follow through. And these stories do not add up to one single teleological narrative. While "classical narratives have an ending," Charland argues, "constitutive rhetorics leave the task of narrative closure to their constituted subjects."[39] But those constituted in Malcolm's post–Nation of Islam discourse are not called upon to complete the story, because there is no single story for them to complete. His rhetoric does not present a "narrative without closure," like the white paper that Charland analyzes, but instead presents no sustained narrative at all.

In an address at the Audubon Ballroom in Harlem on December 29, 1964, Malcolm materializes this rejection of a rigid telos in his discussion of voter registration. He denounces the message of the mainstream civil rights movement, "Register and vote." His message, in contrast, is: "Don't register and vote—register!" Being registered means that his audience is perpetually poised for action but never obligated to follow through in any particular manner or indeed obligated to follow through at all. "'Register,'" Malcolm explains, "means being in a position to take political action any time, any place and in any manner that would be beneficial to you and me."[40] Through the brief narratives that populate Malcolm's discourse, his audiences are presented with multiple teloi that shift moment by moment in response to whatever options are perceived to inhere in each situation.[41] The overarching goal—black liberation—would remain unchanged, but the collective identity of Malcolm's audiences is constituted through alignment with any number of possible narratives.

Both while he was a minister of the Nation of Islam and afterward, Malcolm X was constituting subjects. In both cases, Malcolm's rhetoric exerted the "pull of an ideology" upon its audience through the deployment of "stylistic tokens" and actively "dangled" before individuals a "vision of mass man."[42] Discourses of nationalism are, perhaps by definition, constitutional rhetorics, and Malcolm's description of black nationalism is particularly so—he does not describe it in terms of actions to take or political goals to achieve but in terms that invite a transformation of consciousness very like that described by McGee in his discussion of the rhetorical invention of a "people." Malcolm is addressing an immediate, physical audience, but an audience that also exists only insofar as his auditors recognize themselves among those who are "beginning to see what they used to only look at."[43] His discourse after he left the Nation of Islam clearly was successful in interpellating this audience—and successfully continues to do so into the present day.

But after he left the Nation of Islam, Malcolm addressed quite different subjects. Rather than constituting a people who were collectively identified transhistorically and set upon a predetermined narrative trajectory, he instead addressed a people who valued individualized judgment, transspatial identification, and the rejection of a monolithic narrative telos. In other words, Malcolm's post–Nation of Islam constitutive rhetoric works differently than that described by Charland. Some of the differences between Charland's formulation and the constitutive potential enacted in Malcolm's post–Nation of Islam rhetoric may be traced to differences in access to power and social position. The white paper addresses a Québécois already confident of their individuality but lacking a collective identity; but audiences constituted through Malcolm's discourse had been treated as a homogenous collectivity for generations and as the victims of stereotype were seeking the affirmation of their individual capacities for judgment and action. And the Québécois had access to a libratory history of which the white paper needed only to remind them; Malcolm's audiences never had been allowed access to their own history, and to recover the libratory potential of that history required critiquing the oppressive narratives of passivity, laziness, and dysfunction with which they had been burdened.

Malcolm's discourse models and enacts a constitutive rhetoric of the weak. It has a doubled burden: he must not only call a "people" into existence, but he must also divest them of the oppressive discourses through which they already have been defined. As Benjamin Karim remembers Malcolm telling his "public speaking" students: "We had to be untaught before we could be taught."[44] These oppressive discourses not only persist but retain their dominant cultural voice, and thus they present the perpetual threat of reconstituting Malcolm's audience in problematic ways, undoing his unteaching. Malcolm therefore must perform the almost paradoxical work of constituting a people who would then be resistant to becoming constituted. Malcolm's audiences cannot afford blindly to commit to any single narrative telos or a single stable identity, because they must remain always vigilant. They must be flexible, always willing and able to dodge the ideological onslaught of the dominant culture. In becoming Malcolm's audience, his hearers are inoculated against becoming someone else's.

A conception of rhetoric as instrumental limits its useable lifespan—if discourse is understood merely as a tool through which some physical goal is to be achieved, then the achieving of that goal inters that rhetoric. Charland's conception of constitutive rhetoric retains something of this limitation because it is constrained by the dictates of a narrative that draws its audience toward a predetermined end. Malcolm's discourse, however, avoids this limitation. A "people" constituted through Malcolm's discourse would engage in shifting and uncodified strategies of interpretation. Such strategies retain their usefulness because they always direct their practitioners to attend carefully to particulars in the present. This is a mode of interpretation that refuses to become satisfied, continually enacting shifts in perspective and circumference so that no reading ever becomes permanently ensconced as authoritative. It is a mode of interpretation, in other words, that exhibits a nomadic restlessness often associated with mythological characters known collectively as tricksters.

Trickster Consciousness

Gloria Anzaldúa believes that "living in a state of psychic unrest, in a Borderland, is what makes poets write and artists create."[45] Anzaldúa's comment acknowledges the inventional animus of liminality, which Victor Turner describes as a state of unrest between two or more well-defined social categories. Liminal positions are generative places of experimentation and investigation wherein new individual and cultural identities are forged.[46] Such positions may foster "the liberation of human capacities of cognition, affect, volition, creativity, etc.," in ways that are impossible within more stable and well-defined social structures, so that always implicit in these positions are "the seeds of cultural transformation, discontent with the way things are culturally, and social criticism."[47] And because individuals occupying positions of liminality are outside of the stable social structures that make up the status quo, they pose a threat. Malcolm and his audience threaten the dominant culture because they reject the narratives and terminologies that allow that culture to cohere. "Revolutions," Turner suggests, "whether violent or non-violent," can be understood as manifestations of the threat of the liminal. But while individuals occupying liminal spaces are empowered because they are privy to insights unavailable to others, they also are "temporarily undefined" because they are "beyond the normative social structure. This weakens them," Turner points out, "since they have no rights over others."[48] A truly liminal position, then, despite its potential for insight and its implied threat, is problematic as a foundation for social change because it has the potential to render its occupants politically ineffective.

Trickster tales provide a useful place to investigate the potentials and limitations of liminality, because liminality is a trickster's native habitat.

These figures occupy the middle ground between heaven and earth, good and evil, predator and prey; in countless tales recounting the exploits of Coyote, Raven, Spider, or Brer Rabbit, the trickster is unwilling to pledge allegiance to the authority of anyone or anything—tricksters, like the audiences constituted through Malcolm's discourse, are notoriously uncommitted.[49] Unshackled by the limitations and expectations of binding orientations, the trickster has access to inventional materials otherwise unavailable. Like Malcolm X and his audiences, tricksters are perpetually "poised on the threshold," as Lewis Hyde puts it, existing in a "crepuscular, shady, mottled, ambiguous, androgynous, neither/nor space of Hermetic operation" from which they might "move in either direction or, more to the point, act as the agency by which others are led in either direction." Hyde offers three possible fates for the trickster: they might be "eaten" and thus become a part of the dominant culture; they might be "spit out," rejected and marginalized; or they might teeter perpetually at the threshold and thus successfully avoid either of these traps of culture. Malcolm's discourse invites its audience toward this last type of freedom.[50]

The tricksters' liminal position is fundamental to the sort of equipment for living they provide. Because tricksters are known for "manipulating the strong and reversing the normal structure of power and prestige," they employ their liminal positions to expose the arbitrary and sometimes self-contradictory rules laid down by the dominant culture. As Levine puts it, referring to the trickster tales told by African slaves in the United States, these stories often "taught the art of surviving and even triumphing in the face of a hostile environment" and "emphasized the necessity of comprehending the ways of the powerful, for only through such understanding could the weak endure." From this position of doubled perspective, able to observe both oneself and one's oppressors, tricksters are able to mount their characteristic "assault upon deeply ingrained and culturally sanctioned values."[51] Hyde terms this sort of trickster activity "*artus*-work," labor at the joints. Tricksters abhor arthritic cultural stiffness, so they attack those joints and press them to their limits, loosening them: "If a joint comes apart," Hyde tells us, "or if it moves from one place to another, or if it simply loosens up where it had begun to stick and stiffen, some trickster has probably been involved."[52] When Malcolm X repeatedly pushes his audience across the boundaries usually established for them until those boundaries become so destabilized that they might themselves become resources of empowerment, he is performing trickster work.

Other scholars have noted that Malcolm X plays the role of a trickster.[53] But my point is that Malcolm's rhetoric *constitutes* tricksters. His discourse schools his audience in tricksterish habits of mind by displaying a trickster consciousness and inviting his audience to habituate themselves into it. Wearing a turban in a segregated restaurant, and thus exposing the repressive mores of American culture as thin and arbitrary; threatening to try the United States before a global jury in the court of the United Nations, and thus to turn a creature of the U.S. political system back against itself; advocating that black folk should be both violent and nonviolent, depending on the situation; and even suggesting that America could only become non-racist if it also became non-Christian, thus upending a theology that likes to think of itself as inclusive—all of these are the work of a trickster, and each of them addresses an audience who would themselves do tricksterish work in the world. They may not engage in these particular trickster antics, but they would be defined by a willingness to include such antics among their inventional armamentarium.

Chiasmus may be the "stylistic token" most clearly associated with trickster consciousness. Henry Louis Gates Jr. has suggested that "chiasmus, perhaps the most commonly used rhetorical figure in the slave narratives and throughout the subsequent black literature, is figured in the black vernacular tradition by tropes of the crossroads, that liminal space where Esu [a Pan-African trickster figure] resides."[54] Chiasmus addresses an audience who might fold the logic of the dominant culture back upon itself. When Malcolm punctuates his speeches with chiasmus—and even arranges his discourse as large-scale enactments of this trope—he is inventing an audience who inhabits a trickster's world.

Chiasmus, as all tropes, marks the doubled activity of rhetorical invention. It entails interpretation and production as two elements within the same critical process. In his speech at Rochester, Malcolm X perceives the power of the "science of image making" to twist the truth back upon itself; the antidote is to fashion a chiasmus of his own, naming and demystifying this manipulation. For Malcolm, then, this trope offers a way of understanding the world *and* a way of articulating an appropriate response to it. The trickster, likewise, provides at once both a critical lens and a template for production; it suggests a way of *speaking*, and speaking always requires a way of critique. On the one hand, as Hyde memorably puts it, trickster tales might "cut open the third ear that hears the multiple meanings in every utterance."[55] On the other hand—or, better, on the other side of the same hand—Gates reminds us that tricksters such as

Esu and the Signifying Monkey exist "in the discourse of mythology not primarily as a character in a narrative but rather as a vehicle for narration itself."[56] Tricksters present "both the divine linguist and the divine interpreter," as Gates also notes: "As Hermes is to hermeneutics, so is Esu to the black art of interpretation, *Esu-'tufunaalo.*"[57] Among the realms that such liminal figures bridge, then, are the twin realms of interpretation and production.

Tricksters pass their advantages on to their audiences through imitation. This is not the sort of slavish copying generally referred to as imitation but rather a complex mode of critical observation and artful variation that is similar to the classical rhetorical practice of *imitatio,* a pedagogical technique that, Michael Leff argues, "marked the most obvious intersection between the reading of texts and the production of persuasive discourse."[58] *Imitatio* aims not to pass along to an audience the ability to produce merely a specific skill or product but to induce in the audience more generalizable skills that then might be called upon as resources for future production. The goal is not to learn how to produce this particular discourse or action but to become habituated into patterns of thought so that future, and perhaps dissimilar, discourses or actions might be produced.[59] The value of trickster tales is not that they show their audiences how to construct a tar baby, or how to get unstuck from one, but that they encourage ways of thinking so that attractive traps of various sorts might be recognized and dealt with when they are encountered. The value of Malcolm's story about his friend who wore a turban into a segregated southern restaurant is not that the audience should copy that action but that they might emulate the tricksterish modes of thought and critique that the story illustrates. It is in this way that the liminal position described in and through Malcolm's rhetoric is not a discourse of isolation or silence. It privileges interpretation, but as a mode of speech. Malcolm's audiences are not restrained from engaging in political action; rather, it is by learning to interpret the world in tricksterish ways that they are *engaged* in political action.[60]

But while the rhetoric of Malcolm X displays tricksterlike characteristics and models tricksterish attitudes for the emulation of its audiences, it also strains against even these flexible boundaries. Or, rather, it shies away from the utter rejection of all boundaries that characterizes a pure trickster consciousness. In particular, those constituted through Malcolm's rhetoric exhibit neither the recklessness nor the radical individualism of true tricksters. The tricksters' freewheeling, rootless, and opportunistic habits allow them to challenge and expose the codes of any culture they confront, but this liberating lack of moral vision also causes them often to bring harm down upon themselves. Tricksters are both impious and imprudent. Various trickster tales make this point: Raven is angered by the behavior of his own anus and burns it, thus burning himself; Coyote is given a magical cow that can feed him forever if he only takes a sliver of flesh at a time, but his overwhelming appetite gets the better of him and he kills the cow and magpies eat the meat before he does; Rabbit is granted a larger tail, greater wisdom, and bigger eyes, but God also gives him a bag and warns him not to open it until he reaches home, so of course Rabbit cannot wait and thirty bulldogs rush out and devour his new tail.[61] One of the most salient characteristics of Malcolm's audiences, in contrast, would be their reluctance to act until after all available options have been carefully evaluated. Malcolm's is not a discourse of rashness or impulse but a rhetoric of controlled vigilance. "A ballot is like a bullet," he tells his audience. "You don't throw your ballots until you see a target, and if that target is not within your reach, keep your ballot in your pocket."[62] At Rochester, he repeatedly warns his audience to avoid taking action until they have learned to look through the "tokenism" used against them and until they have learned to see it both locally and globally.

Just as tricksters are not able consistently to gain advantage for themselves individually without also doing themselves harm, they also are ill-equipped to consider the communal good. There is no allegiance among tricksters. The members of Malcolm's audiences, however, are affirmed in their individualism without losing sight of their collective identities. His audiences are urged to develop their own individuality as a defense against the collective oppression they have experienced for centuries but still are urged toward collective goals and to think of themselves as members of a community. In "The Ballot or the Bullet," for example, the political, economic, and social philosophies of black nationalism all necessarily entail some collective, communal commitment. He urges that he and his African American audience "should control the politics and the politicians "in their own community"; that they "should control the economy" of their community"; and, finally, that "we have to get together and remove the evils, the vices, alcoholism, drug addiction, and other evils that are destroying the moral fiber of our community."[63] The "Letter from Mecca" portrays a global Islamic brotherhood, and the repeated Pan-Africanist appeals that are found throughout Malcolm's discourse can be understood as attempts to define a "community" on a global scale. The United Nations, for Malcolm, presents the possibility for this sort of global, dark-skinned community to exert political influence, which is in contrast to the "alienated," insular, and solipsistic isolation of the Black Muslims.[64]

Trickster tales have the potential to develop communal identities by providing a locus of collective identification—the audiences for such tales are invited to recognize in the trickster a version of their collective selves, a "people" without access to power who must survive by their wits. But Malcolm's discourse is describing something rather more complex. He is not only asking that his audience collectively identify with him as a trickster figure or to see in him some more purified version of themselves. He also is asking them individually to embody trickster consciousness while yet always collectively seeking a common goal. Malcolm and his audience can never allow themselves to be *merely* free, in a radically individualistic sense, because that would leave them vulnerable to the old strategy of "divide and conquer" that Yacub taught his white creations so many millennia ago.[65]

Prudential Performance

The complex rhetorical action of Malcolm's discourse, then, entails both the communal identity entailed by its constitutional impulses *and* the individualist impulses associated with the trickster figure. Malcolm must describe and address a people who do not otherwise exist, but this must be a people suspicious of subsuming their identity into a collective whole while at the same time recognizing the necessity of collective identification. Recognizing these mixed motives is essential background for understanding the particular interpretive habits of mind that Malcolm models for his audience as a species of prudence, or practical wisdom.

Prudence "was given systematic articulation by Aristotle (as *phronesis*), received additional emphasis and wide dissemination by Cicero (as *prudentia* . . .), and became a central concept (*prudenza*) for Renaissance political theorists such as Machiavelli."[66] Aristotle's most thorough discussion of prudence comes in Book VI of his *Nicomachean Ethics,* in which he describes prudence as the ability of a citizen "to be able to deliberate finely about things that are good and beneficial for himself, not about some restricted area—about what sorts of things promote health or strength, for instance— but about what sorts of things promote living well in general."[67] Aristotle also articulates three key components of prudence, describing it as "a state grasping the truth, involving reason, and concerned with action about human goods" (1140b21–22). Robert Hariman casts this definition into modern language, calling prudence "the mode of reasoning about contingent matters in order to select the best course of action."[68] This is a faculty enabling judgment in rhetorical situations, relying on situated critique rather than codified knowledge and on an effort to balance individual gain and communal interest rather than a simple commitment to either. Malcolm's discourse constitutes audiences defined by their embodiment of this faculty—they are to attend with care to the particulars in a given situation and are then to consider actions that balance their individual interests with the interests of their community.

Becoming prudent, like becoming a trickster, requires a form of imitation. This is partly because prudence is manifest as a performance of judgment—it cannot be codified or abstracted but must be vivified at the moment of interaction between a rhetor and an audience. Prudence can only be studied, in other words, when it is witnessed. This relationship between prudence and performance is evident in Aristotle, who notes that "to grasp what prudence is, we should first study the sort of people we call prudent" (1140a25–26). Because prudence is "acting well itself" (1140b8), it signifies a process, shape-shifting and constantly in motion because it flies low to the ground of contingency. Malcolm's audiences are invited to attend to the patterns of thought displayed in his discourse and then to appropriate those patterns into their own habits of mind. Victoria Kahn describes this sense of rhetoric as performed judgment, noting that rhetorical texts are thus "seen less as an object than as reflecting a certain process or activity of judgment."[69] Rhetorical performance becomes the means through which prudence is disseminated to audiences. As Ronald Beiner puts it, "We ourselves are schooled in the exercise of this faculty [prudence] by observing the exemplary performances of others. We learn by example." By observing Malcolm make decisions regarding "language, style, and means of persuasion" at the moment of his rhetorical performance, his audiences are schooled in the faculty through which they might make similar judgments.[70]

A fundamental characteristic of prudence is discernment, as Aristotle points out when he calls prudence "a faculty of discerning what things are good [for oneself] and for mankind."[71] I have mentioned that the recurring theme of "sight" in Malcolm's discourse shifted in meaning, so that prior to his exit from the Nation of Islam, "seeing" meant beholding the truth of Elijah Muhammad's revelations, while after the split "sight" refers to an ability to judge, observing a thing from multiple perspectives and weighing alternative interpretations. Beiner refers to this perceptual ability as "imagination," the making and interpreting of images, and emphasizes the fundamental flexibility of perspective that it entails. To become prudent, he argues, requires that "I must project myself, imaginatively, into a position I do not actually occupy, in order to enlarge my perspective and thereby open up an awareness of new possibilities, to broaden the range of alternatives from which my judgment then makes its selection."[72] This is precisely the sort of work that Malcolm's rhetoric encourages his audiences to perform—seeing the situation from unaccustomed perspectives, thus encouraging the imaginative invention of new possibilities for action.

The border position toward which Malcolm calls his audiences in his last speeches and statements requires a balancing of perspectives, an ability to see two ways at once and to weigh the local and the global against one another. Malcolm's audiences must also, as I have mentioned, balance collective identity against the need for individual agency, making use of the latter to resist complete absorption into the former. They are to manage, perpetually, the basic paradox at the heart of Malcolm's description of "positive neutrality": "We're neutral. We're for ourselves."[73] These emphases on balance and duality are reflected in prudence generally as "that form of reasoning that manages the incommensurability of goods . . . it is how one thinks when trying to achieve both security and freedom, human rights and prosperity, foreign markets and domestic revenues, democratic values and reliable allies, etc."[74] The prudent person that Malcolm would constitute would exhibit this ability to sustain a dynamic balance between individual advance and universal good, particular cases and global rules, action and thought, praxis and theory, in an ongoing effort "to determine action consistently advantageous to the individual and the community."[75] This emphasis on balance also provides the historical and theoretical link between prudence and decorum, a flexible principle "that unifies the elements of a discourse even as it adjusts them to the fluid ethical and political contexts in which it appears."[76] Decorum is a notoriously slippery subject, signifying a menagerie of rhetorical concepts and sensitivities that all cycle around the ideas of fittingness or appropriateness. For my purposes, I concentrate on a mode of decorum that Hariman terms "humanist decorum."[77]

This conception of decorum finds its most thorough description in the works of Cicero, for whom it becomes the central axis upon which all other aspects of rhetorical invention turn: "The universal rule, in oratory as in life, is to consider propriety."[78] This brief passage references two senses of decorum that Cicero develops at length and which are of particular relevance for my argument.[79] One is decorum—or, more accurately, the ability to perceive the decorous—as a life skill. Being able to discern the contours of a particular situation, and then fashion a fitting response to that situation, is the fundamental faculty of both the rhetorician and the effective citizen. In this sense, decorum refers to the degree of propriety achieved between a discursive performance and the external expectations it was fashioned to address. Decorum, then, helps to position rhetorical invention as equipment for living, because those able to produce decorous discourses also will be those most able to gain access to power. And as in life, so in oratory: the other sense of decorum implied in Cicero's formulation refers to the internal textual residues of the ways that a text was crafted to fit a situation, audience, speaker, and topic. Any number of specific textual attributes may be the locus of this sense of the decorous—metaphor, arrangement, tone, style, genre—but generally the emphasis is on the internal consistency of a discourse and the way in which the elements of a speech interact and cohere to form a unified and apparently finished product.[80] Decorum, in both of these senses, is the manifest performance of practical wisdom, the "dramatic realization" of the virtue of prudence.[81] An individual who displays a well-developed faculty of perceiving the decorous would be said to be a prudent person; an oration exhibiting decorous composition would be a product of prudent thinking. Decorum, as a result, is the specific medium through which prudence is transmitted to an audience, for just as prudential wisdom constitutes decorous texts, an audience constituted through such texts is instructed in prudential habits of mind. A decorous discourse, Eugene Garver reminds us, "teaches prudence by presenting its own argument as an example of prudent action."[82]

For a protest rhetor, and particularly one like Malcolm X who willfully claims a marginalized position, this link between prudence and decorum is problematic. Indeed, Malcolm often seems to reject the possibility of acting in accordance with *any* set of norms, fearing that to do so would reinscribe Elijah Muhammad's "straitjacket" onto himself and his audiences.[83] Because decorum requires fitting speech and action to external expectations, it threatens to squelch the commitment to individual agency, which in Malcolm's thought is the essential counterbalance to the pull of debilitating ideology. That is, the tension between individualism and collectivity makes possible the productive border position where Malcolm would have his audiences reside, and to allow the reverence for social order that is entailed by traditional senses of decorum to exert too strong an influence would be to negate Malcolm's essential oppositional stance. Still, it seems that he would constitute audiences characterized by some form of rhetorical judgment, a flexible, praxis-centered, multiperspectival, exigence-specific form of practical wisdom very similar to the classical faculty of *phronesis*. And yet a prudence cut loose completely from the bounds of decorum would not be recognizable as prudence at all.

Malcolm's rhetoric addresses these dilemmas by disrupting the continuity between the two senses of decorum that are most prominent in Cicero's formulation—decorum as a performance tuned to external norms and expectations, and decorum as a textual manifestation of internal coherence. Traditionally, these two senses of decorum are unified, and exemplars of rhetorical artistry display this continuity. Leff's assessment of Abraham Lincoln's "House Divided" speech as a rhetorical masterwork, for example, depends explicitly upon this internal/external, formal/functional interplay of decorum. The great achievement of Lincoln's speech, Leff demonstrates, is its "translation of a complex vision into a coherent rhetorical form, blending both the internal and external requirements of rhetorical performance. Internally the speech displays an aesthetic unity," while at the same time its "structure develops from and remains attached to public experience."[84] In contrast, Malcolm's task as an orator is to *separate* his audience from their public experience, because that experience itself is the source of oppression. At the same time, of course, Malcolm was obligated to produce coherent rhetorical statements fitted to the expectations of his audience and of his position as an *orator*—his audiences came to hear him, or invited him to speak on their campuses, because they expected him to produce coherent rhetoric. Much more importantly, as I have demonstrated through my analyses of his speeches, it was through the form of his address that he was able to give form to the situation as he would have his audiences understand it and to the identities he would have his audience inhabit.

Malcolm X negotiates these dual goals—rhetorical resistance and rhetorical coherence—by jettisoning the normative expectations of *external* decorum while retaining the expectations of *internal* decorum; his speeches are internally coherent while at the same time refusing to "fit" the expectations of the dominant culture. Dividing decorum in this way allows Malcolm to constitute individuals who possess a variation of the faculty of practical wisdom; they would balance their individual self-interests against a set of communal goods that are defined within a specific community.

Malcolm refuses to respect the bonds of external decorum by consistently saying outrageous things and refusing to be contained within the logic of the dominant culture: a "Dixiecrat is nothing but a Democrat in disguise"; "Change your name to Hoogagagooba"; America might be saved through a mass conversion to Islam as a *"spiritual* path of *truth"*; Harlem landlords "are nothing but thieves"; police officers "are not representatives of the law"; and the integration of southern schools is not a triumph but a disgrace.[85] Malcolm's most notorious rejection of decorum, of course, concerns the recurrent, though always carefully controlled, threat of violence: "It'll be Molotov cocktails this month, hand grenades next month, and something else next month. It'll be ballots, or it'll be bullets"; "I don't mean go out and get violent, but at the same time you should never be nonviolent unless you run into some nonviolence."[86] The interpretive judgments to be made by an audience constituted through such discourse would be cut free from the expectations and constraints of the dominant culture, able to engage logics and possibilities that outstrip that culture's limitations.

Malcolm's treatment of the other variation of decorum, that which names the relationship among the various internal elements of a discourse, is more complex. In short, my argument is that the internally coherent nature of Malcolm's rhetoric is responsible for defining an audience that is responsive to its own communal needs. As Black, McGee, and Charland make clear, the aspects of a rhetorical text that perform its constitutive function are its internal, formal elements—figures, tropes, arrangement, "stylistic tokens," or perhaps even something as minute as the manipulation of pronouns. It is primarily a text's internal coherence, in other words, that is responsible for its ability to address a "people." Malcolm's discourse is able to perform a constitutive function because it exhibits some degree of internal decorum. And this internal coherence is a manifestation of the mode of rhetorical judgment that Malcolm would have his audience emulate. Thus, Malcolm's rhetoric connects this mode of judgment with the "people" he addresses, making them interdependent. Malcolm's audience would balance their individual self-interests against localized communal goods, which would be communal only with respect to this very audience.

In summary, Malcolm was faced with a number of parallel dilemmas. He needed to school his audiences in habits of independent thinking, but he also needed them to recognize themselves as part of a collective identity. They needed to attend carefully to the shifting particulars of specific situations, but they needed always and simultaneously to be focused on relatively stable and far-reaching goals. Malcolm's audiences required the prudential faculty of judgment through which sometimes incommensurable individual and collective needs are balanced against one another, but their own needs were sometimes violently opposed to the perceived needs of the dominant culture and, at any rate, had been denied validity for centuries. Malcolm manages these dilemmas by dissociating two senses of decorum that traditionally are linked in rhetorical performance. He refuses to abide by the decorous constraints of the dominant culture, reserving a right to consider possibilities for thought and action that lie well beyond its bounds and that indeed pose a threat to some of its fundamental assumptions. This frees his audience to engage in individualized interpretation. But Malcolm also refuses to neglect the decorous internal coherence of his own rhetorical texts, crafting them so that they may serve as a model of prudential judgment, a field of action that constitutes audiences defined by their internalization of this mode of judgment. His audience is directed to perceive themselves as a "people" with certain and identifiable goods that must be weighed against individual affirmation, and they are directed to witness the composition of Malcolm's discourses as a model performance of this sort of balance.

Garver reminds us that Aristotle formulated his ideas about prudence in a context far different from our contemporary social world, that we lack anything that Aristotle would recognize as a "polis," and that in Aristotle's eyes, our lives would be "unnatural." "Therefore *phronesis*," he concludes, "has to be something different for us than it was for Aristotle."[87] Similarly, Robert W. Cape Jr. suggests that in "the current climate of intellectual relativism and skepticism, augmented by renewed religious fundamentalism and political conservatism, the conditions may exist for recovering a new version of prudence for our times and achieving a synthesis of prudential reasoning and rhetorical-political practice."[88] And Beiner warns that we need a conception of contemporary citizenship, informed by phronesis, "that will allow us to reclaim our capacity of judgment from those who presume to exercise it on our behalf."[89] Malcolm's rhetoric illustrates one model for the revivification of prudence in contemporary life. It does not transport intact a premodern concept and drop it into contemporary culture. Rather, Malcolm presents an updated prudence, one freed from its normative limitations but not entirely loosed from its moorings. He presents his auditors, regardless of their race, with an invention of prudence that takes contingency into account while escaping both radical relativism and prophetic prescription.[90]

Again, it is not my purpose, through this theoretical triangulation, to construct a comprehensive theory of Malcolm's rhetoric. More theoretical constructs could be added, or those that I have presented could be replaced. The resulting perspective would highlight aspects of Malcolm's rhetoric that would differ from—and perhaps even contradict—those that I have chosen to emphasize. No matter the quantity or quality of the theoretical approaches employed, however, Malcolm's rhetoric always will exceed their limitations. This is true, of course, for all public discourse; but the libratory potential of Malcolm's rhetoric consists in its presentation of a restless mode of thought and critique that resists attempts at thorough codification.

Still, it may be useful to suggest an analogy that brings into focus the perspectives on Malcolm's rhetoric that I have described. John Poulakos has suggested a "sophistic" definition of rhetoric, based on the ideas of itinerant teachers of rhetoric in Greece in the fifth century BC. As Edward Schiappa has argued in fine detail, the Sophists were not a unified group teaching a homogenous body of theory.[91] Much about what they did teach, and how they taught it, remains in dispute. Poulakos's hypotheses about sophistic rhetoric, however, can suggest one view of rhetoric that entails key aspects of the theoretical perspectives that I have emphasized. Such a rhetoric, he argues, would be conceived as *the art which seeks to capture in opportune moments that which is appropriate and attempts to suggest that which is possible.*[92] This would signify an important divergence from an Aristotelian conception of rhetoric as the art of discerning the *probable.* Sophistic rhetoric, by Poulakos's definition, would be characterized not by "an abstract absolutism created in the spirit of *a priori* truths" but instead by "a relativism of concrete rhetorical situations to which situationally derived truths are the only opportune and appropriate responses." Such a rhetorician would understand her or his task as refusing "to keep people in their actual situation" and as attempting to "lift them from the vicissitudes of custom and habit and take them into a new place where new discoveries and new conquests can be made."[93] The terms I have been engaging do not account for this definition of rhetoric additively so that conceptions of rhetoric as constitutive, tricksterish, and as a medium of prudence exhaust the possibilities inherent in a sophistic definition of rhetoric. And Malcolm certainly wasn't a sophist; he could not have been, in any proper sense of the word, and to term him such would be a reductive anachronism that would obscure more than it could reveal. But Poulakos's conception of sophistic rhetoric can be understood as entailing constitutive, tricksterish, and prudential notions about the possibilities for public discourse and as opposed to an instrumental view of such discourse merely as a means to an end. It also helps to emphasize and consolidate the most salient and innovative aspects of Malcolm's discourse after he left the Nation of Islam: Malcolm was a teacher of rhetoric, schooling his audiences in the critique and interpretation of discourse; he taught primarily through example, by modeling the patterns of judgment that he would have his audiences assimilate; and the particular sort of rhetoric in which he schooled his audiences was inherently, in and through its very form, suspicious of naturalized, hierarchical, and codified cultural formations.

Summary and Implications

When Malcolm X was a minister in the Nation of Islam, his rhetoric consisted of a particularly rigid strain of African American prophetic protest. It required a lockstep allegiance to a clearly articulated ideology; it invited its audience to define themselves according to an essentialized, quasi-scientific conception of race; and it advocated a stifling political isolation. This was a discourse that incorporated diverse and sometimes contradictory elements from across a spectrum of African American protest, encouraging its audiences toward frenetic activity within narrow boundaries and directing their attention toward collective self-help and the effacement of individual expression or judgment. The form of Malcolm's rhetoric itself was severely constrained by his position as spokesperson for Elijah Muhammad, for he was merely a conduit through which Muhammad spoke. As a result, he could model for his audiences only a relatively narrow and limited form of rhetorical invention. Malcolm's own interpretive activities were limited to translating Elijah Muhammad's statements, and the interpretive activities of his audiences were limited to finding omens in the world and the Bible that reinforced Elijah Muhammad's predictions. The productive side of rhetorical invention was similarly narrowed for both Malcolm and his Black Muslim audiences, who all were reduced to sounding variations on the praise of Elijah Muhammad's wisdom and on the expectation of Allah's eventual act of racial redemption.

This sort of prophecy, despite its unusual rigidity, offers potential for empowerment. It provides an alternative mythical framework that rivals those available in the dominant culture in both reach and coherence, a mechanism through which long-neglected African American egos might find resources for self-respect, and a prescription for action that may be, in some ways, well suited to survival in the often abject and isolated world of the black urban ghetto. But the hermetically sealed rhetoric of Black Muslim prophecy offers a rather severe set of limitations. It may encourage a suspicion of the dominant culture, but those suspicions themselves are structured and articulated by Elijah Muhammad and merely mimed by the membership. Such liberation requires bringing thought and action into alignment with norms that appear to be freed from the confines of the dominant culture but requires also that these norms themselves must be immune from interrogation. In other words, the rhetoric of the Nation of Islam provides only a freedom *from* the oppressive practices of the dominant culture, not a freedom *to* engage in radical critique.[94]

After Malcolm left the Nation of Islam, his rhetoric was characterized by repeated efforts to broaden the palate of possibilities for his audience, by a suspicion of commitment and constraint, by an emphasis on individualized judgment, and by a demonstration of radical flexibility. Perhaps he wished to avoid reinscribing the limitations that had been imposed upon him and his audiences by the Nation of Islam; perhaps his experiences addressing audiences outside the Nation of Islam and, eventually, outside the United States impressed upon him the shape-shifting nature of global race politics. In any case, and for whatever reason, Malcolm's post–Nation of Islam rhetoric presents a sustained effort to avoid the limitations of stable commitments and formulas and instead to foster an ability within his audiences for attending to the particulars of a situation, coming to a judgment based on those particulars, and then speaking or acting—or not—in a manner designed to benefit themselves individually and as members of a group. The middling or border position toward which Malcolm invites his audiences allows them to attend simultaneously to the domestic and to the global, the individual and the collective, the contingent and the persistent. They are to avoid a calcified commitment to either side of any of these dichotomies yet always to keep both in view; they are to remain always flexible but also steadfastly focused on attaining African American liberation.

The attitude is encapsulated in Malcolm's most-often repeated catch phrase, "by any means necessary." *By any means:* untethered by oppressive expectations and limitations, free to roam widely over myriad and diverse cultural resources, his audiences are invited to engage in interpretive practices with unusual emancipatory potential. *Necessary:* this wide-ranging interpretive consciousness is tightly focused on a specific problem, one that shows itself in the multiple local outrages of contemporary life, and one that may be ultimately intractable because it is systemic, but still a problem against which the value of each particular reading must be measured.

Such a stance is not without limitations—the post-Malcolm histories of his OAAU and MMI serve as concrete reminders that this sort of radical critique cannot easily sustain a traditionally defined political movement. The collective boundaries of the "people" Malcolm would constitute are defined by a willful exclusion from dominant white Christian culture of the United States but otherwise are amorphous. This "people" is to be suspicious of any form of hierarchy and leadership, and as a result its outlines never can be defined with any final certainty. But for Malcolm X, and for his audiences, these liabilities may be outweighed by the emancipatory potential that is offered through his rhetoric. After centuries of having their faculties of judgment dismissed and of having their individual identities subsumed within a maligned collective stereotype, they may be unusually receptive to a rhetoric that resists these forms of oppression. A rhetoric that enacts resistance by modeling interpretive strategies and ways of speaking, which are insolubly linked together into a single radical attitude of cultural production, presents an invaluable resource for an emancipatory rhetorical invention.

To close, I offer two implications, one that frames these innovations of Malcolm's post–Nation of Islam rhetoric specifically as a contribution to discourse on race in America and another that situates this rhetoric within a broader cultural and interpretive context.

Malcolm's rhetoric provides a way to avoid two dangers of contemporary racial discourse, which might be termed "racial complicity" and "depoliticized individualism." Rhetorics of complicity and individualism are particular manifestations of the general tension present in many social movements between the needs to recognize individual and group identities. Aaron Gresson refers to this tension as *"the paradox of liberation"* and calls on Kenneth Burke to describe this phenomenon with regards to African Americans: "Striving for freedom as a human being generically, he must do so as a Negro specifically. But to do so as a Negro is, by the same token, to prevent oneself from doing so in the generic sense; for a Negro could not be free generically except in a situation where the color of the skin had no more social meaning than the color of the eyes."[95] W. E. B. Du Bois's famous formulation, in *The Souls of Black Folk*, of "double consciousness" as fundamental to the African American experience, marks out a similar paradox:

> It is a peculiar sensation, this double-consciousness, this sense of always looking at one's self through the eyes of others, of measuring one's soul by the tape of a world that looks on in amused contempt and pity. One ever feels his two-ness,—an American, a Negro; two souls, two thoughts, two unreconciled strivings; two warring ideals in one dark body, whose dogged strength alone keeps it from being torn asunder.

"The history of the American Negro," Du Bois continues, "is the history of this strife—this longing to attain self-conscious manhood, to merge his double self into a better and truer self." The African American experience, for Du Bois, entails a persistent wish "to make it possible for a man to be both a Negro and an American, without being cursed and spit upon by his fellows, without having the doors of Opportunity closed roughly in his face."[96]

Malcolm's rhetoric while a minister in the Nation of Islam did not confront such paradoxes. By suppressing individual expression and differentiation within a united and homogenous organization, Nation of Islam discourse described a people untroubled by double consciousness. The only question was whether to submit fully and completely to the teachings of The Honorable Elijah Muhammad. If one did so, then one was a member of the Nation of Islam, and questions of individual recognition simply were moot (except for some of the top bureaucrats within the Nation, who enjoyed considerable autonomy). If one did not do so, then she or he was not a member of the Nation of Islam and instead was one of the "dead ones" who had not yet been awakened in the faith. This is a rhetoric of simple table-turning, establishing an exclusive black nation as a mirror image of the white one.[97]

Such discourse, by avoiding the paradox of liberation, reiterates the Manichaean logic of the oppressor as a rhetorical equivalent of the infamous "one-drop" rule of racial identity. Mark McPhail describes the rhetorical action of such discourse as a form of "complicity," which he describes as "any oppositional discourse that uncritically accepts the underlying assumptions of foundationist or essentialist classification" of the dominant culture.[98] Such discourse limits its own libratory potential by offering an oppositional stance that is still defined within the terms of the system it is opposing. Not only does this rhetoric undermine "the possibility of collective emancipatory action across racial lines," but it also "silences voices within a race in a manner that simply replaces one oppressive discourse for another."[99] I have noted, for example, that Louis Farrakhan has revived many of the central tenets of Elijah Muhammad's Nation of Islam, and in McPhail's analysis this resurrection has included Elijah Muhammad's complicitous rhetoric: "though ostensibly aimed at achieving symbolic realignment, [Farrakhan's rhetoric] also perpetuates the worst tendencies of the 'system' it calls into question by embracing the same essentialized and antagonistic justificatory tactics and conceptions of identity sustained by the dominant order."[100] McPhail has argued that rhetorics of black conservatism and Afrocentricity are similarly complicitous, and Cornel West has noted a parallel phenomenon he calls "racial reasoning."[101]

Malcolm's rhetoric after he left the Nation of Islam does not engage in this sort of table-turning and thus avoids complicity.[102] It casts identities as constituted through discourse, it is suspicious of collective commitment, and it finds its telos in performative judgment rather than in codified precepts. As such, it presents not an inverted mirror image of the dominant culture but instead the resources through which the essential dichotomies of that culture might be critiqued. The surest way to resist forming, or becoming aligned with, rhetorics that merely reproduce the essentialist assumptions of the dominant culture would be to reject all such assumptions. This sort of rhetoric would hold little complicitous potential, but through an extreme individualism it also would forfeit much of its potential to foster collective political action. Gresson describes a rhetoric of "personal choice" that has become prominent in some contemporary African American discourse and that preempts efforts to mobilize an audience constituted collectively. Such a rhetoric recognizes, Gresson argues, that race is a social and discursive construction, but it then encourages an isolationist withdrawal. Race is understood as *merely* a social construction, one that need not impinge on personal, private life. Such a rhetoric has great appeal, Gresson acknowledges, to a people "whose lives once found definition almost totally through a 'master's definitions of reality'"; it rejects all collective or publicly discursive definitions, privileging only personalized definitions that allow maximum individual freedom. African Americans, Gresson worries, "have had to share a common plight and have used this plight, in part, to forge a racial liberation agenda," but "many Blacks try to ignore their racial status and pursue the recovery of their 'inalienable rights' purely in terms of their status as human beings." While there is much to be gained through such an effort, there also is much to be lost through a rhetoric that has "exploded the historical race myth that American Blacks had forged during and after the journey from Africa."[103] This sort of rhetoric renders success, failure, and opportunity all matters of individual concern.[104]

The Nation of Islam, then as now, and like many other successful organizations, finds its strength in homogeneity and in a collective assent to a well-defined system of beliefs and actions. These rigidly collective racial views began to recede from Malcolm's rhetoric after he left the Nation. But never does Malcolm suggest that the members of his audience abandon fully either their individual or their collective identities; they must always be both individuals free to think for themselves *and* members of a group united in an effort to counter the pervasive power of white domination. Malcolm's African American audience is encouraged to privilege individual autonomy but also is caught up in a collective purpose; their tricksterish attitudes are uncommitted but always are turned toward collective liberation; and the practical wisdom they would display is grounded always in a sense of the good for a particular community. Suspended in this way between these two extremes, Malcolm's African American audience might enjoy some of the potential advantages of both while at the same time avoiding most of the dangers of either. Maintaining such a stance, however, requires constant vigilance, for both the ego-inflation of radical individualism and the arithmetic empowerment of collective identification offer significant seductions. Malcolm's audience can never come fully to rest.

This nomadic quality provides a link to the second implication I would like to draw for Malcolm's rhetoric: its potential usefulness to a broader audience as a model for a practice of rhetorical critique and production that is well suited to contemporary public culture. Robert L. Ivie has suggested that a trickster presence may be required in order to regain the productive agonistic quality necessary for the healthy functioning of American political discourse. Trickster figures present "the trope of cultural fluidity and ambiguity that yields humility as the antidote to hubris and excessive fear of the other." Such figures help to grease the wheels of democratic practice, encouraging an agonistic flexibility and discouraging a calcified ideological reification. "Were Americans a bit more like Coyote and thus less rhetorically inhibited," Ivie concludes, the nation might avoid some of the dysfunctional characteristics of a "distempered democracy."[105] Malcolm X, through the exemplars of his public address, models one way that a trickster attitude might productively be employed toward this sort of political revitalization. Because Malcolm's rhetoric constitutes tricksters, it encourages the members of its audiences—regardless of hue—to become "a bit more like Coyote" and thus willing to muddy the clear categories that often lead to stagnation and distemper. A nation of Coyotes would be, of course, no nation at all. But because the tricksters constituted through Malcolm's rhetoric are schooled in a sort of practical wisdom and thus are attuned to matters pertaining to a communal good, they provide an effective counterweight to the centrifugal individualist forces that would soon disintegrate a too-tricksterish culture.

The radical attitudes of interpretation and judgment that are presented in Malcolm's rhetoric are the locus of this revitalizing form of equipment for contemporary life. He invented the rhetoric of his last year through his rejection of a rigid narrative paradigm and because of his desire to disable the formation of any further such paradigms. Any number of contemporary scholars have reminded us that we live in an age characterized by a similar distrust of rigid definitions, categories, and "metanarratives."[106] Within the field of rhetorical studies, perhaps no such pronouncement has been more influential than Michael Calvin McGee's argument that "it is time to stop whining about the so-called 'post-modern' condition and to develop realistic strategies to cope with it as a fact of human life, perhaps in the present, certainly in the not-too-distant twenty-first century."[107] As McGee describes it, the fragmentation of culture is manifest at the level of the text, so that analysts of contemporary discourse do not have access to "finished" texts in the way that analysts of historical discourse might. New strategies of interpretation are needed, and the first step toward developing such strategies would be to realize that, in the present, "nothing . . . is complete enough, finished enough, to analyze—and the fragments that present themselves to us do not stand still long enough to analyze."[108] Fragments of discourse are made to congeal temporarily in response to specific contingencies but then break apart to be reassembled by other critics/rhetors in response to other contingencies. The most skilled critic, in such circumstances, is the one who is able to produce discourse through the assembly of fragments. McGee concludes that the best way to proceed "in our fractured culture is to provide readers/audiences with dense, truncated fragments that cue *them* to produce a finished discourse in their minds. In short, *text construction is now something done more by the consumers than by the producers of discourse.*"[109] A skill in the doubled logic of rhetorical invention, in which instrumental divisions between production and criticism cannot be sustained, emerges as a most constructive adaptation to contemporary fragmentation.

Malcolm's rhetoric schools its audiences in just such a species of rhetorical invention. It presents the interpretive/productive work required to assemble fragments into temporarily finished wholes, so that there is no final product but only a series of provisional constructions perpetually open to change in response to contingency. And yet, at the same time, these provisional wholes *do* exhibit an internal coherence capable of constituting audiences and sustaining critical analysis. They must, for otherwise Malcolm's rhetorical project fails to achieve political potency, and he leaves his audiences uprooted but ill-equipped. Malcolm demonstrates an ability to assemble momentarily coherent texts as an exhibition of practical wisdom and would have his audiences assemble similarly coherent texts, motives, and identities. Producing discourse that quickly solidifies and thus loses its adaptive qualities is a most dysfunctional response to contemporary fragmentation, but the ability to produce rhetorical texts whose coherence is situational and shifting is a most potent equipment for living.[110]

Malcolm is making his audience into rhetoricians, and he is doing so in the only way that it can be done—he is offering them models of critical interpretation that they themselves must critically interpret. His African American audiences were silenced through oppressive discourses that closed off the possibility of individualized critical practice, and his white audiences were blinded by discourses that framed African American identity as monolithic; he invented a practice of radical judgment that invited these audiences to breach the boundaries of those discourses. Malcolm's rhetoric was crafted in response to particular situations, as all rhetoric is, but it offers ways of interpretation and judgment with broader possible appeal. The significance of his discourse lies not in the rhetorical invention that it displays but in the faculties of rhetorical invention that it would foster in his audiences. Its import lies not in its own products but in the potential or incipient products that follow from the patterns of thought into which it would habituate its hearers. It is a catalytic rhetoric, designed not to accomplish concrete objectives but to incite its audiences toward libratory practices. As such, it is a self-propagating discourse, disseminated through culture by imitation—those who have been schooled in its faculties engage in action by critiquing and producing discourses that then become models for imitation. It is potent equipment for living, and only by reading discourses such as Malcolm's can we gain access to such equipment. Malcolm's radical judgment is a species of rhetorical invention, and invention achieves performative density only within the dynamics of situated rhetorical discourse. Malcolm's example suggests, therefore, that the challenge of contemporary life calls not for a more systematic theoretical complexity but for a more finely grained practice of critical reading.

Notes

Chapter 1

1. See Abdul Alkalimat, "Malcolm X in Cyberspace," in *The Malcolm X Encyclopedia*, ed. Robert L. Jenkins and Mfanya Donald Tryman (Westport, Conn.: Greenwood Press, 2002), 46–50. Alkalimat reports 150 sites and over 25,000 Web pages devoted to Malcolm X.
2. Peter Goldman, "Malcolm X: Witness for the Prosecution," in *Black Leaders of the Twentieth Century*, ed. J. H. Franklin and A. Meier (Urbana: University of Illinois Press, 1982).
3. Kenyatta quoted in Peter Goldman, *The Death and Life of Malcolm X* (Urbana: University of Illinois Press, 1979), 93; Young paraphrased in Goldman, *Death and Life*, 8; Marshall quoted in Joe Wood, "Malcolm X and the New Blackness," in *Malcolm X: In Our Own Image*, ed. J. Wood (New York: Anchor Books, 1992), 15.
4. Michael Eric Dyson, *Making Malcolm: The Myth and Meaning of Malcolm X* (Oxford: Oxford University Press, 1995), 15.
5. Rustin quoted in Goldman, *Death and Life*, 395; Wood, "New Blackness," 15; Bailey quoted in L. C. Jones, "Talking Book: Oral History of a Movement," *Village Voice*, February 26, 1985, 18.
6. Louis A. DeCaro Jr., *On the Side of My People: A Religious Life of Malcolm X* (New York: New York University Press, 1996), 2.
7. Cornel West, *Race Matters* (New York: Vintage Books, 1994), 135–51. In other variations on this theme, Mark Bernard White argues that "Malcolm's life was a series of abrupt and pivotal transformations, thrust upon him in his youth, chosen by him as an adult" ("Malcolm X," in *African-American Orators: A Bio-Critical Sourcebook*, ed. R. W. Leeman [Westport, Conn.: Greenwood Press, 1996], 410); Thomas W. Benson notes that "Malcolm's life is the story of a series of conversions, to which he gave witness in his rhetoric as a process of change impelled by a consistent motive: to break the bonds of racism" ("Malcolm X," in *American Orators of the Twentieth Century: Critical Studies and Sources*, ed. B. K. Duffy and H. R. Ryan [Westport, Conn.: Greenwood Press, 1987], 317).

8. Celeste Michelle Condit and John Louis Lucaites, "Malcolm X and the Limits of the Rhetoric of Revolutionary Dissent," *Journal of Black Studies* 23 (1993): 294–96.

9. Eugene Victor Wolfenstein, *The Victims of Democracy: Malcolm X and the Black Revolution* (1981; reprint, New York: Guilford, 1993), 213.

10. Malcolm X and Alex Haley, *The Autobiography of Malcolm X* (New York: Grove Press, 1965), 155, 158, 170.

11. Bruce Perry, *Malcolm: The Life of a Man Who Changed Black America* (Barrytown, N.Y.: Station Hill Press, 1990), 117.

12. Louis E. Lomax, *When the Word Is Given: A Report on Elijah Muhammad, Malcolm X, and the Black Muslim World* (New York: Signet Books, 1964), 15.

13. Malcolm X and Haley, *Autobiography,* 163. DeCaro provides a thoughtful commentary on Malcolm's Pauline associations (*On the Side of My People,* 33–37).

14. The members of the Nation of Islam refer to themselves as "Muslims." As Malcolm X explained during a question-and-answer session at Michigan State University in 1963: "We call ourselves Muslim—we don't call ourselves Black Muslims. This is what the newspapers call us. This is what Dr. Eric Lincoln calls us. We are Muslims. Black, brown, red, and yellow" (Malcolm X, "Twenty Million Black People in a Political, Economic, and Mental Prison," in *Malcolm X: The Last Speeches,* ed. B. Perry [New York: Pathfinder Press, 1989], 55). But Malcolm does sometimes refer to himself as a "Black Muslim." I also will refer to him that way when other locutions would be awkward.

15. Malcolm X and Haley, *Autobiography,* 304. According to Perry, Malcolm even sought medical attention for the physical symptoms brought on by his anguish over the split (*Malcolm,* 243–44).

16. Wolfenstein, *Victims of Democracy,* 307.

17. Malcolm X and Haley, *Autobiography,* 345.

18. Goldman, *Death and Life,* 182.

19. Spike Lee and Ralph Wiley, *By Any Means Necessary: The Trials and Tribulations of the Making of Malcolm X* (New York: Hyperion, 1992).

20. Goldman, "Malcolm X," 306.

21. Condit and Lucaites, "Limits of the Rhetoric of Revolutionary Dissent," 304. Condit and Lucaites also offer a fourth phase, which they call "a dissenting rhetoric," characterized by Malcolm's call for black nationalism and occurring during the time after he split from the Nation of Islam and before his journey to Mecca. I discuss the differences

between his pre-Mecca and post-Mecca rhetoric in later chapters, but in general I find much more similarity than difference.

22. Respectively: Marcus H. Boulware, "Minister Malcolm: Orator Profundo," *Negro History Bulletin* 30 (1967): 12–14; Karlyn Kohrs Campbell, "The Rhetoric of Radical Black Nationalism: A Case Study in Self-Conscious Criticism," *Central States Speech Journal* 22 (1971): 150; and reported in John Illo, "The Rhetoric of Malcolm X," *Columbia University Forum* 9 (1966): 12.

23. Although Malcolm X did not sit at a desk and "write" his autobiography, most people who discuss *The Autobiography of Malcolm X* refer to it as though he did. Because there does not seem to be an efficient way of describing Haley's role in the process of composing the text, I will follow this convention.

24. Goldman, *Death and Life*, 13.

25. Benjamin Karim, *Remembering Malcolm* (New York: Carroll and Graf, 1992), 97–98.

26. The species of rhetorical invention that I am describing bears strong resemblance to that which James Jasinski aligns with *imitation* (*Sourcebook on Rhetoric* [Thousand Oaks, Calif.: Sage, 2001], 327–31). The connection between imitation and rhetorical invention is implicit here and more explicit in my final chapter. See also Michael Leff, "The Idea of Rhetoric as Interpretive Practice: A Humanist's Response to Gaonkar," in *Rhetorical Hermeneutics: Invention and Interpretation in the Age of Science*, ed. A. G. Gross and W. M. Keith (Albany: State University of New York Press, 1997), 89–100; Sharon Crowley, *The Methodical Memory: Invention in Current-Traditional Rhetoric* (Carbondale: Southern Illinois University Press, 1990); Walter Watson, "Invention," in *Encyclopedia of Rhetoric*, ed. T. O. Sloane (Oxford: Oxford University Press, 2001), 389–404; Karen B. LeFevre, *Invention as a Social Act* (Carbondale: Southern Illinois University Press, 1987). Jasinski and Watson provide excellent bibliographies.

27. Condit and Lucaites, "Limits of the Rhetoric of Revolutionary Dissent," 308.

28. Perry, *Malcolm*, 380.

29. Dyson, *Making Malcolm*, xv.

30. West, *Race Matters*, 136.

31. Alex Haley includes Davis's eulogy in his epilogue to Malcolm's autobiography (Malcolm X and Haley, *Autobiography*, 454).

32. Kenneth Burke, *The Philosophy of Literary Form* (Berkeley: University of California Press, 1967), 293–304.

33. Karim, *Remembering Malcolm,* 128. The Nation of Islam referred to its places of worship as "temples" until 1961, when Elijah Muhammad ordered that they should be referred to as "mosques."

34. Goldman, *Death and Life,* 71; Karim, *Remembering Malcolm,* 128.

35. Archie Epps, ed., *Malcolm X and the American Negro Revolution: The Speeches of Malcolm X* (London: Peter Owen, 1968), 32.

36. See Robert L. Scott, "The Conservative Voice in Radical Rhetoric: A Common Response to Division," *Communication Monographs* 40 (1973): 123–35.

37. Near the end of his life, Malcolm X reported that in December 1960, he had been ordered by Elijah Muhammad to meet representatives of the Ku Klux Klan (KKK) in Atlanta to investigate their offer to Muhammad of a tract of land "so that his program of separation would sound more feasible to Negroes and therefore lessen the pressure that the integrationists were putting upon the white man" (Malcolm X, "There's a Worldwide Revolution Going On," in Perry, *Malcolm X: The Last Speeches,* 123). Interestingly, in 1922 Marcus Garvey met with the KKK's "Imperial Kleagle," Edward Young Clarke, and secured support for a "Back-to-Africa" program (C. Eric Lincoln, *The Black Muslims in America,* 3rd ed. [Grand Rapids, Mich.: William B. Eerdmans, 1994], 88).

38. Taylor Branch, *Parting the Waters: America in the King Years, 1954–63* (New York: Simon and Schuster, 1988), 272.

39. John H. Cone, *Martin & Malcolm & America: A Dream or a Nightmare* (Maryknoll, N.Y.: Orbis Books, 1991). See also Celeste Michelle Condit and John Louis Lucaites, *Crafting Equality: America's Anglo-African Word* (Chicago: Chicago University Press, 1993), 191–97. Akinyele O. Umoja provides a detailed account of the shifts in emphasis and leadership styles in SNCC and CORE; see his "The Ballot and the Bullet," *Journal of Black Studies* 29 (1999): 558–79. On the shift from civil rights to Black Power, see also Sean Dennis Cashman, *African-Americans and the Quest for Civil Rights, 1900–1990* (New York: New York University Press, 1991), 184–215.

40. Wilson Jeremiah Moses, *Black Messiahs and Uncle Toms: Social and Literary Manipulations of a Religious Myth* (University Park: Pennsylvania State University Press, 1982), 15.

41. Dyson, *Making Malcolm,* 55, 134.

42. Arnold Rampersad, "The Color of His Eyes: Bruce Perry's *Malcolm* and Malcolm's Malcolm," in Wood, *Malcolm X: In Our Own Image,* 120.

43. Hakim A. Jamal, *From the Dead Level: Malcolm X and Me* (New York: Random House, 1971); Karim, *Remembering Malcolm.*

44. Dyson offers an extended and insightful critique of these two biographies (*Making Malcolm,* 51–63).

45. Dyson, *Making Malcolm,* 56. See also Rampersad, "Color of His Eyes."

46. Perry, *Malcolm,* 9–11, 351–56.

47. Wolfenstein, *Victims of Democracy,* ix.

48. Ibid., 92, 118.

49. George Breitman, *The Last Year of Malcolm X: The Evolution of a Revolutionary* (New York: Pathfinder Press, 1967), 30, 69. Similarly, E. U. and Ruby Essien-Udom claim that "a logical extension of Malcolm's basic concept of the Black Revolution is revolutionary socialism" ("Malcolm X: An International Man," in *Malcolm X: The Man and His Times,* ed. J. H. Clarke [New York: Macmillan, 1969], 266).

50. Goldman, *Death and Life,* 189; John White, *Black Leadership in America: From Booker T. Washington to Jesse Jackson,* 3rd ed. (New York: Longman, 1990), 158.

51. White, "Malcolm X," 419.

52. Dyson, *Making Malcolm,* 82, 85, 108, 90–94.

53. West, *Race Matters,* 149.

54. Adolph Reed Jr., "The Allure of Malcolm X and the Changing Character of Black Politics," in Wood, *Malcolm X: In our Own Image,* 207, 224.

55. Dyson, *Making Malcolm,* 72.

56. Pathfinder Press proposed such a project and issued the first volume, *February 1965: The Final Speeches,* edited by Steve Clark, in 1992. The plan was to move backward through Malcolm's life, issuing definitive versions of all of his key speeches and statements, organized month by month. But the proposed second volume, covering January 1965, was never issued.

57. Malcolm X, "The Harvard Law School Forum of March 24, 1961," in *Malcolm X: Speeches at Harvard,* ed. A. Epps (New York: Paragon House, 1991), 188. Epps's disregard for the formal integrity of Malcolm's speeches is representative of attitudes about the rhetoric of Malcolm X. Imagine how outrageous it would be for an editor to "reorganize the paragraphs" of, for example, King's "I Have a Dream" speech.

58. Malcolm X, "Malcolm X at Harvard," in Lomax, *When the Word Is Given,* 119.

59. Malcolm X, "Harvard Law School Forum of March 24, 1961," 122.

60. Malcolm X, "The Black Revolution," in *Malcolm X Speaks,* ed. G. Breitman (New York: Pathfinder Press, 1965); Malcolm X, "Speech on

'Black Revolution,'" in *Two Speeches by Malcolm X* (New York: Pathfinder Press, 1965). The pamphlet version also is available in *The Voice of Black Rhetoric: Selections,* ed. A. L. Smith [Molefi Asante] and S. Robb (Boston: Allyn and Bacon, 1971).

61. Bruce Perry describes at length his efforts to track down cassette tapes of some of Malcolm's speeches, a tale that involves the murder of one of his informants, a journey to Guyana where one of Malcolm's former associates was living on a farm in the rain forest, and a near arrest (*Malcolm X: The Last Speeches,* 7–10). Perry's adventures suggest some of the difficulty that would be involved in editing a definitive collection of Malcolm's works.

62. Illo, "Rhetoric of Malcolm X," 5–6.

63. Ibid., 6.

64. Ibid., 6, 7, 9.

65. Ibid., 9, 7.

66. Thomas W. Benson, "Rhetoric and Autobiography: The Case of Malcolm X," *Quarterly Journal of Speech* 60 (1974): 3; Goldman, *Death and Life,* 396.

67. Illo, "Rhetoric of Malcolm X," 7.

68. Ibid., 9.

69. This is one of the central points made by Edwin Black in his indictment of neo-Aristotelian criticism; the misguided effort to reduce Aristotle's theory of rhetoric to a set of absolute categories caused this criticism to be muted through self-contradiction. See Edwin Black, *Rhetorical Criticism: A Study in Method* (1965; reprint, Madison: University of Wisconsin Press, 1978).

70. Campbell, "Rhetoric of Radical Black Nationalism," 151–60; Richard B. Gregg, "The Ego-Function of the Rhetoric of Protest," *Philosophy & Rhetoric* 4 (1971): 71–91. I choose these two essays both because they contribute to my later analysis and because they are representative of rhetorical critics attempting to analyze the rhetoric of Malcolm X during this time period. See also Finley C. Campbell, "Voices of Thunder, Voices of Rage: A Symbolic Analysis of a Selection from Malcolm X's Speech, 'Message to the Grass Roots,'" *Speech Teacher* 19 (1970): 101–10; Robert L. Scott, "Justifying Violence—The Rhetoric of Militant Black Power," *Central States Speech Journal,* 19 (1968): 96–104; Marilyn Van Graber, "Functional Criticism: A Rhetoric of Black Power," in *Explorations in Rhetorical Criticism,* ed. by G. P. Mohrmann (University Park: Pennsylvania State University Press, 1973), 207–22; Robert L. Heath, "Dialectical Confrontation: A Strategy of Black

Radicalism," *Central States Speech Journal* 24 (1973): 168–77; Aaron D. Gresson, "Minority Epistemology and the Rhetoric of Creation," *Philosophy & Rhetoric* 10 (1977): 244–62.

71. Campbell, "Radical Black Nationalism," 154.

72. Ibid., 157, 159.

73. Gregg, "Ego-Function," 73, 74. See also Randall A. Lake, "Enacting Red Power: The Consummatory Function in Native American Protest Rhetoric," *Quarterly Journal of Speech* 69 (1983): 127–42; Maurice Charland, "Constitutive Rhetoric: The Case of the *Peuple Québécois*," *Quarterly Journal of Speech* 73 (1987): 133–50.

74. John Louis Lucaites and Celeste Michelle Condit, "Reconstructing <Equality>: Culturetypal and Counter-Cultural Rhetorics in the Martyred Black Vision," *Communication Monographs* 57 (1990): 6.

75. Condit and Lucaites, "Limits of the Rhetoric of Revolutionary Dissent," 309. Both of these studies were elements within a larger project that culminated in their award-winning book, *Crafting Equality: America's Anglo-African Word*.

76. The connection between attitude and rhetorical form has a long history in rhetorical theory, stemming from the standard comparison between an oration and a human body. Tzvetan Todorov shows Quintilian, for example, repeating this common comparison, defining the rhetorical term "figure" as "applied to any form in which thought is expressed, just as it is to bodies which, whatever the composition, must have some shape (*Institutio Oratoria*, IX, 1, 10)"; "the name is to be applied to certain attitudes, or I might say gestures of language (IX, 1, 13)" (Tzvetan Todorov, *Theories of the Symbol*, trans. C. Porter [Ithaca, N.Y.: Cornell University Press, 1982], 65–66. See also Kenneth Burke's analogy between "mental *attitude*" and "bodily *posture*" (*A Grammar of Motives* [Berkeley: University of California Press, 1969], 242) and his argument that understanding rhetoric as "persuasion to *attitude* would permit the application of rhetorical terms to purely *poetic* [formal] structures" (*A Rhetoric of Motives* [Berkeley: University of California Press, 1969], 50).

77. Vito Signorile, "Ratios and Causes: The Pentad as an Etiological Scheme in Sociological Explanation," in *The Legacy of Kenneth Burke*, ed. H. W. Simons and T. Melia (Madison: University of Wisconsin Press, 1989), 89.

78. Burke, *Grammar of Motives*, 443.

79. Burke, *Rhetoric of Motives*, 50.

80. Quoted in Goldman, *Death and Life*, 10.

81. Michael Leff, "Cicero's *Pro Murena* and the Strong Case for Rhetoric," *Rhetoric and Public Affairs* 1 (1998): 63. Lanham discusses the "weak" and "strong" cases for rhetoric in *The Electronic Word: Democracy, Technology, and the Arts* (Chicago: University of Chicago Press, 1993), 155–56.

82. Michael Leff, "Things Made by Words: Reflections on Textual Criticism," *Quarterly Journal of Speech* 78 (1992): 228.

83. David Howard-Pitney, *The Afro-American Jeremiad: Appeals for Justice in America* (Philadelphia: Temple University Press, 1990), 12.

Chapter 2

1. Howard-Pitney, *Afro-American Jeremiad*, 26.

2. James Darsey, *The Prophetic Tradition and Radical Rhetoric in America* (New York: New York University Press, 1997), 16.

3. William S. McFeely, *Frederick Douglass* (New York: W. W. Norton, 1991), 173.

4. In David B. Chesebrough, *Frederick Douglass: Oratory from Slavery* (Westport, Conn.: Greenwood Press, 1998), 19.

5. See Kurt Müller, "Anti-Slavery Rhetoric on the Fourth of July: William Lloyd Garrison," in *The Fourth of July: Political Oratory and Literary Reactions, 1776–1876*, ed. P. Goetsch and G. Hurm (Tübingen, Germany: Gunter Narr Verlag, 1992), 121–38.

6. Ronald H. Carpenter, "The Historical Jeremiad as Rhetorical Genre," in *Form and Genre: Shaping Rhetorical Action*, ed. Karlyn Kohrs Campbell and Kathleen Hall Jamieson (Falls Church, Va.: Speech Communication Association, 1978), 104.

7. Sacvan Bercovitch, *The American Jeremiad* (Madison: University of Wisconsin Press, 1978), 93–94. Bercovitch offers a detailed history of the shift from Puritan to secular jeremiad in America (*American Jeremiad*, 93–131); Howard-Pitney offers a much more condensed version (*Afro-American Jeremiad*, 8–11).

8. Perry Miller, *Errand into the Wilderness* (Cambridge: Harvard University Press, 1984), 15.

9. Howard-Pitney provides an extensive and detailed argument concerning Douglass's use of the jeremiad in his discourse (*Afro-American Jeremiad*, 17–52).

10. Moses, *Black Messiahs*, 30–31.

11. Though Douglass generally spoke extemporaneously from minimal notes, this speech was written out and read from manuscript. See

Gerald Fulkerson, "Frederick Douglass," in Leeman, *African-American Orators,* 91.

12. Fulkerson, "Frederick Douglass," 91–92.

13. Bernard W. Bell, "The African-American Jeremiad and Frederick Douglass' Fourth of July 1852 Speech," in Goetsch and Hurm, *Fourth of July,* 139–53.

14. Howard-Pitney, *Afro-American Jeremiad,* 8.

15. See Len Travers, *Celebrating the Fourth: Independence Day and the Rites of Nationalism in the Early Republic* (Amherst: University of Massachusetts Press, 1997), 49–50.

16. Frederick Douglass, "What to the Slave Is the Fourth of July?: An Address Delivered in Rochester, New York, on 5 July 1852," in *The Frederick Douglass Papers,* vol. 2, ed. J. W. Blassingame (New Haven, Conn.: Yale University Press, 1982), 361. Subsequent references to this text will be by parenthetical page numbers, except when reference would not be clear.

17. Jim Jasinski notes that by the middle of the nineteenth century the revolutionary tradition had been constructed as "rational, inevitable, natural, orderly, and conservative; the Revolution had become, in a word, domesticated." See Jim Jasinski, "Rearticulating History in Epideictic Discourse: Frederick Douglass's 'The Meaning of the Fourth of July to the Negro,'" in *Rhetoric and Political Culture in Nineteenth-Century America,* ed. T. W. Benson (East Lansing: Michigan State University Press, 1997), 78. Similarly, Russ Castronovo argues that the post-Revolutionary generation, "sensing its own belatedness to national glory . . . charged itself with a custodial duty of preservation." See Russ Castronovo, *Fathering the Nation: American Genealogies of Slavery and Freedom* (Berkeley: University of California Press, 1995), 7. Both Jasinski and Castronovo aptly note that Douglass is critiquing this conservative custodialism, pointing out to his white listeners that the promise of America lies not in the preservation of the calcified memory of the Founding Fathers but rather in an enactment of their dynamic attitudes.

18. Fulkerson, "Frederick Douglass," 91.

19. Neil Leroux, "Frederick Douglass and the Attention Shift," *Rhetoric Society Quarterly* 21 (1991): 40.

20. Eric J. Sundquist, "Frederick Douglass: Literacy and Paternalism," in *Critical Essays on Frederick Douglass,* ed. W. L. Andrews (Boston: G. K. Hall, 1991), 129. Gregory Stephens offers a compelling argument concerning Douglass's "bi-racial" rhetoric in *On Racial Frontiers: The New*

Culture of Frederick Douglass, Ralph Ellison, and Bob Marley (Cambridge: Cambridge University Press, 1999), 54–113.

21. Burke, *Rhetoric of Motives*, 19–23.

22. Darsey, *Prophetic Tradition*, 202.

23. Ibid., 203.

24. Irony asks its auditors to see two—or more—ways at once. As Linda Hutcheon puts it, "ironic meaning is *simultaneously* double (or multiple), . . . you don't actually have to reject a 'literal' meaning in order to get at what is usually called the 'ironic' or 'real' meaning of the utterance." The judgment encouraged by irony must always be, or be made to seem, a result of the audience's own powers of observation. See Linda Hutcheon, *Irony's Edge: The Theory and Politics of Irony* (New York: Routledge, 1994), 60.

25. Leroux, "Frederick Douglass," 42. Ellipses as in Leroux's text.

26. Douglass closes with a poem by William Lloyd Garrison that promises the coming day of jubilee. The poem seems a curious choice. It suggests that the day of jubilee is coming, inevitably, and cannot be hastened by human action. Douglass's argument in the speech up to this point, however, has been to suggest that there is work to be done and that his white audience is too complacent and cautious to contemplate the actions necessary. Perhaps this poem by his former mentor is to be taken ironically? Or perhaps it reiterates the warning that time does progress inevitably and that these necessary actions cannot be infinitely postponed.

27. Howard-Pitney, *Afro-American Jeremiad*, 13. John Murphy goes so far as to argue that "the jeremiad cannot serve as a vehicle for social criticism," though this may be overstating the case somewhat ("'A time of shame and sorrow': Robert F. Kennedy and the American Jeremiad," *Quarterly Journal of Speech* 76 [1990]: 404).

28. Howard-Pitney, *Afro-American Jeremiad*, 15. Such orations often excoriated present behaviors that in any way might impede the progress of the race; Douglass, for example, when addressing black audiences, often criticized them "for their dismal failure to do those things necessary to advance," urging on them that economic success depended on their ability "to be thrifty, industrious, and frugal; they had to accumulate property, pursue education, and display in every way praiseworthy behavior" (ibid., 22).

29. Ibid., 14.

30. Edwin S. Redkey, *Black Exodus: Black Nationalist and Back-to-Africa Movements, 1890–1910* (New Haven, Conn.: Yale University Press,

1969), 24. Redkey offers a thorough history of separatist and emigrationist thought during this time period.

31. Henry McNeal Turner, "Emigration to Africa," in *Respect Black: The Writings and Speeches of Henry McNeal Turner*, ed. E. S. Redkey (June 21, 1883; reprint, New York: Arno Press, 1971), 52–59.

32. Redkey, *Black Exodus*, 177, 181.

33. Ibid., 39.

34. Ibid., 37.

35. W. E. B. Du Bois, "A Negro Nation within the Nation," in *W. E. B. Du Bois Speaks: Speeches and Addresses*, ed. P. S. Foner (New York: Pathfinder Press, 1970), 77–86.

36. W. E. B., Du Bois, *The Conservation of Races* (Washington, D.C.: American Negro Academy, 1897). Subsequent references to this text will be by parenthetical page reference to the version included in *W. E. B. Du Bois Speaks: Speeches and Addresses, 1890–1919*, ed. Philip S. Foner (New York: Pathfinder Press, 1966), 73–85.

37. David Levering Lewis argues that "The Conservation of Races" owes much to Crummell's protonationalist thought. See David Levering Lewis, *W. E. B. Du Bois, Biography of a Race* (New York: Henry Holt, 1993), 168–74.

38. Kirt H. Wilson, "Towards a Discursive Theory of Racial Identity: *The Souls of Black Folk* as a Response to Nineteenth-Century Biological Determinism," *Western Journal of Communication* 63 (1999): 196. Wilson provides an excellent brief overview of nineteenth-century racial science.

39. See, for example, Anthony Appiah, "The Uncompleted Argument: Du Bois and the Illusion of Race," *Critical Inquiry* 12 (1985); Lucius Outlaw, "'Conserve' Races? In Defense of W. E. B. Du Bois," in *W. E. B. Du Bois on Race and Culture: Philosophy, Politics, and Poetics*, ed. B. W. Bell, E. Grosholz, and J. B. Stewart (New York: Routledge, 1996); Robert Gooding-Williams, "Outlaw, Appiah, and Du Bois's 'The Conservation of Races,'" in Bell, Grosholz, and Stewart, *W. E. B. Du Bois on Race and Culture*.

40. Booker T. Washington, "Cotton States Exposition Address," in *Three Centuries of American Rhetorical Discourse: An Anthology and a Review*, ed. R. F. Reid (Prospect Heights, Ill.: Waveland Press, 1988), 523.

41. The first paragraph of Du Bois's *The Souls of Black Folk* reads: "Herein lie buried many things which if read with patience may show the strange meaning of being black here in the dawning of the Twentieth Century. This meaning is not without interest to you, Gentle Reader;

for the problem of the Twentieth Century is the problem of the color-line" (*The Souls of Black Folk* [New York: Penguin Books, 1989], 1).

42. Appiah, "Uncompleted Argument," 25.

43. Darsey, *Prophetic Tradition*, 16.

44. Moses, *Black Messiahs*, 6.

45. Redkey, *Black Exodus*, 55–56.

46. Peter B. Hinks, *To Awaken My Afflicted Brethren: David Walker and the Problem of Antebellum Slave Resistance* (University Park: Pennsylvania State University Press, 1997), xiv.

47. A brief but thorough history of the Missouri Compromise is provided by David Potter, *The Impending Crisis: 1848–1861* (New York: Harper and Row, 1976), 55–60.

48. Herbert Aptheker, *American Negro Slave Revolts* (New York: Columbia University Press, 1943), 81.

49. Daniel Wojcik, *The End of the World As We Know It: Faith, Fatalism, and Apocalypse in America* (New York: New York University Press, 1997), 12.

50. David Walker, *David Walker's Appeal, in Four Articles; Together with a Preamble, to the Coloured Citizens of the World, but in Particular, and Very Expressly, to Those of the United States of America*, rev. Sean Wilentz (New York: Hill and Wang, 1995). Subsequent references to this text will be by parenthetical page numbers. I use "pessimism" guardedly, since apocalyptic rhetoric could be described as an optimistic faith in a divine redemptive power.

51. Hinks provides a review of the historical evidence that Walker was in Charleston while Vesey's revolution was being planned and discovered, as well as a comparative textual analysis that locates some similarities between Vesey's words as recorded at his trial and Walker's language in the *Appeal* (*Awaken my Afflicted Brethren*, 30–40).

52. Hinks, *Awaken My Afflicted Brethren*, 105.

53. The pamphlet probably was stitched into garments and smuggled aboard ships by the sailors wearing them, and it probably was read aloud by literate slaves to those who could not read. Sean Wilentz gives August 3, 1830, as the date of Walker's death; Vincent Harding suggests June 28; Hinks cites the Boston Index of Deaths in support of August 6. All sources agree, however, on the suddenness of Walker's death. There does not seem to be any firm evidence of foul play, but various theories abounded at the time and continue to this day. See, particularly, Hinks, *Awaken My Afflicted Brethren*, 267–71.

54. Hinks, *Awaken My Afflicted Brethren*, 180. Hinks offers a thorough review of the sources that may have influenced Walker and an exegesis of the *Appeal* that traces these influences.

55. Sean Wilentz, "Introduction: The Mysteries of David Walker," in *David Walker's Appeal*, xix.

56. These notes appear on an unnumbered page before the preamble to Walker's *Appeal*. Subsequent references to this text will be by parenthetical page numbers, except when reference would not be clear.

57. Moses, *Black Messiahs*, 40, 38; Howard-Pitney, *Afro-American Jeremiad*, 13.

58. Wojcik, *End of the World*, 35.

59. Ibid., 34.

60. Stephen D. O'Leary, *Arguing the Apocalypse: A Theory of Millennial Rhetoric* (Oxford: Oxford University Press, 1994), 85.

61. Barry Brummett, *Contemporary Apocalyptic Rhetoric* (New York: Praeger, 1991), 58.

62. The *Appeal* actually closes with a version of Psalm 10 first published in 1696 by Nahum Tate and Nicholas Brady, followed by an excerpt from John Wesley's 1889 collection of Methodist hymns.

63. Wilson Moses notes that black jeremiads often referenced slave revolts but that "the rhetorical threat of violence was not based on any real desire for a racial Armageddon. Black jeremiads were warnings of evils to be avoided, not prescriptions for revolution" (*Black Messiahs*, 32). It is important to note, however, that pamphlets such as Walker's *Appeal* were seen by whites throughout the South as very real threats to Southern culture (Hinks, *Awaken My Afflicted Brethren*, 237–39).

64. Moses, *Black Messiahs*, 41.

65. Hinks provides an analysis of the ACS in the 1820s and of Walker's critique of it (*Awaken My Afflicted Brethren*), 202–4.

66. Vincent Harding, *There Is a River: The Black Struggle for Freedom in America* (New York: Vintage Books, 1983), 94. See also Hinks, *Awaken My Afflicted Brethren*, 169–70.

67. Actually, Nat Turner was the legal property of his deceased owner's nine-year-old son. When the boy's mother married Joseph Travis, Travis became Turner's de facto master.

68. A narrative description of the revolt is found in Stephen B. Oates, *The Fires of Jubilee: Nat Turner's Fierce Rebellion* (New York: Harper and Row, 1975).

69. Stephen H. Browne, "The Unparalleled and Inhuman Massacre": The Gothic, the Sacred, and the Meaning of Nat Turner," *Rhetoric & Public*

Affairs 3 (2000), 309–31. On the importance of narrative structure to apocalyptic rhetoric, see Stephen D. O'Leary, "A Dramatistic Theory of Apocalyptic Rhetoric," *Quarterly Journal of Speech* 79 (1993): 388.

70. Nat Turner, *The Confessions of Nat Turner*, ed. Kenneth S. Greenburg (Boston: Bedford Books of St. Martin's Press, 1996), 44. Subsequent references to this text will be by parenthetical page numbers, except when reference would not be clear. Though it is of course impossible to tell if these are Turner's actual words, in the interests of textual economy I will discuss them as though they are.

71. On the other hand, Gray substantiates Turner's claim to have experimented with making paper, gunpowder, and many other things. Gray writes in a footnote: "When questioned as to the manner of manufacturing those different articles, he was found well informed on the subject" (45).

72. O'Leary, *Arguing the Apocalypse*, 13. See also Brummett, *Contemporary Apocalyptic*, 95.

73. O'Leary, *Arguing the Apocalypse*, 77.

74. Brummett, *Contemporary Apocalyptic*, 101.

75. Ibid.

76. Oates, *Fires of Jubilee*, 56.

77. Harding, *There Is a River*, 96.

78. Ibid., 97.

79. Oates reports that fifty blacks stood trial in connection with Turner's insurrection and that twenty-one were hanged. Others were sold into the deeper South, perhaps into Georgia or Alabama, and still others were deported. Of course, many of Turner's recruits were killed either during the insurrection or soon after (Oates, *Fires of Jubilee*, 125–26). Kenneth S. Greenberg offers this macabre observation concerning Turner's dissection: "Apparently unaware of the bizarre mixture of horror and irony in their actions, Southampton whites consumed the body and the blood of the back rebel who likened himself to Christ" ("*The Confessions of Nat Turner:* Text and Context," in Turner, *The Confessions of Nat Turner*, ed. Kenneth S. Greenburg (Boston: Bedford Books of St. Martin's Press, 1996), 20.)

80. Browne, "The Gothic," 328. Greenberg offers a similar, though not as detailed, analysis of the different voices evident in the *Confessions* ("*Confessions of Nat Turner:* Text and Context," 7–10).

81. These biblical passages are quoted here as they appear in the *Confessions*, at page 46.

Chapter 3

1. The relationship between "nationalism" and "separatism" is complex. Raymond Hall insists that "black separatism is a subcategory of black nationalism" (*Black Separatism in the United States* [Hanover, N.H.: University Press of New England, 1978], 1). But John L. Golden and Richard D. Rieke describe precisely the opposite relationship between the terms, arguing that "separatism seems to be a more universal term, within which the nationalistic aspects can be included as well as other phases of rhetorical behaviors that are properly related" (*The Rhetoric of Black Americans* [Columbus, Ohio: Charles E. Merrill, 1971], 282). E. U. Essien-Udom's definition of "nationalism" indicates its intimate association with separatism: "The concept of nationalism . . . may be thought of as the belief of a group that it possesses, or ought to possess, a country; that it shares, or ought to share, a common heritage of language, culture, and religion; and that its heritage, way of life, and ethnic identity are distinct from those of other groups. Nationalists believe that they ought to rule themselves and shape their own destinies, and they should therefore be in control of their social, economic, and political institutions" (*Black Nationalism: A Search for an Identity in America* [Chicago: University of Chicago Press, 1962], 6). Hall admits that "black separatism is an elusive and subtle phenomenon. At times blacks embrace some form of it because they are denied access to what most other Americans take for granted; at other times they aggressively pursue separatism as an end in itself; and at still others they endorse separatist ideology as a mechanism for fostering integration. There is still another aspect: at times black separatism seems to become anything that articulate leaders of small groups say it is" (*Black Separatism*, 85). In this chapter, and throughout the remainder of this book, I use the two terms interchangeably, except when a distinction between them is required.

2. E. David Cronon, *Black Moses: The Story of Marcus Garvey and the Universal Negro Improvement Association* (Madison: University of Wisconsin Press, 1955), 27.

3. Ibid., 36.

4. Erdmann Doane Beynon, "The Voodoo Cult among Negro Migrants in Detroit," *American Journal of Sociology* 43 (1938): 897.

5. The story of the founding of the Nation of Islam is retold in almost every other book about the Nation of Islam or Malcolm X. See Malcolm X and Haley, *Autobiography*, 205–10; Essien-Udom, *Black*

Nationalism, 63–82; Lomax, *When the Word Is Given*, 41–49; Goldman, *Death and Life*, 35–40.

6. Marcus M. Garvey, *Philosophy and Opinions of Marcus Garvey*, 3rd ed., ed. A. J. Garvey (1925; reprint, Totowa, N.J.: Frank Cass, 1989), 2:126. Most of Garvey's important speeches and statements have been collected by his widow, Amy Jacques Garvey, in the two volumes of *Philosophy and Opinions*. The first volume was published in 1923, and the second followed in 1925, but most often today these two volumes are bound together as a single volume, though retaining the original pagination. Here, as in subsequent references, I refer to these two volumes as though they were published in separate bindings. Most of the speeches and statements contained in these volumes are culled from Garvey's editorials in the *Negro World*, but many are undated and lack other references to their original place of publication.

7. Cronon, *Black Moses*, 20. Garvey was unable immediately to adapt his ideas, honed in Jamaica, to the northern urban setting; after initial failure in Harlem, he toured the United States to study American race relations before returning to Harlem in 1917. See Cronon, *Black Moses*, 40–41.

8. Manning Marable, *W. E. B. Du Bois: Black Radical Democrat* (Boston: Twayne, 1986), 114.

9. Lincoln, *Black Muslims*, 248.

10. Malcolm X and Alex Haley, *Autobiography*, 6–7. Malcolm's version of the story of his father's death has been disputed; see Perry, *Malcolm*, 12–14. Louis A. DeCaro Jr. notes that Malcolm's mother contributed articles to Garvey's newspaper, the *Negro World* (*On the Side of My People*, 41).

11. DeCaro, *On the Side of My People*, 16. DeCaro also argues that Elijah Muhammad was a member of Garvey's UNIA. Edwin S. Redkey notes that Bishop Henry McNeal Turner, during a visit to Liberia, "praised the well-educated Muslim teachers who were active throughout West Africa," but Turner does not seem to have been an important portal to Islamic sympathies among his African American followers. The Muslim teachers in Africa were, for Turner, merely "preparing the way for Christianity" (Redkey, *Black Exodus*, 44).

12. Harold Cruse, *Rebellion or Revolution?* (New York: Morrow, 1968), 208; Manning Marable, *Through the Prism of Race and Class: Modern Black Nationalism in the U.S.* (Dayton, Ohio: Black Research Associates, 1980), 6.

13. Garvey, *Philosophy and Opinions,* 1:41.
14. Cary D. Wintz, "Introduction," in *African American Political Thought, 1890–1930: Washington, Du Bois, Garvey, and Randolph,* ed. C. D. Wintz (Armonk, N.Y.: M. E. Sharpe, 1996), 11.
15. Douglass's rhetoric when addressing black audiences *does* bear some resemblance to Garvey's discourse, in that in these situations Douglass often urged the importance of self-help and race improvement (Howard-Pitney, *Afro-American Jeremiad,* 22).
16. Garvey, *Philosophy and Opinions,* 2:1, 5. Garvey's discourse is a necessary anomaly among those rhetors discussed in this book, because his *Philosophy and Opinions* is comprised of a great number of relatively brief speeches and statements rather than a single, continuous oration.
17. Ibid., 1:64; 2:13.
18. Ibid., 1:31.
19. Ibid., 1:18, 20.
20. Theodore Vincent has noted that "in Black American history there are two personal feuds which stand out beyond all others, W. E. B. Du Bois vs. Booker T. Washington and W. E. B. Du Bois vs. Marcus Garvey." Quoted in Marable, *W. E. B. Du Bois,* 113.
21. A letter Du Bois published in the *New York Age* in June 1921 is a symptom of his frustration at continually having to differentiate himself from Garvey. In it, he warns that it is a "grave mistake" to confuse "the Pan-African Congress and the Garvey movement as practically one idea" (W. E. B. Du Bois, *Writings by W. E. B. Du Bois in Periodicals Edited by Others,* vol. 2 [Millwood, N.Y.: Kraus-Thomson, 1982], 147).
22. Wilson Jeremiah Moses, *The Golden Age of Black Nationalism, 1850–1925* (Hamden, Conn.: Archon Books, 1978), 267.
23. "As one would have expected, . . . many white journalists could see little difference between the Pan-African ideas of Du Bois and Garvey's UNIA" (Elliot P. Skinner, *African Americans and U.S. Policy toward Africa, 1850–1924: In Defense of Black Nationality* [Washington, D.C.: Howard University Press, 1992], 459). Garvey: "If Europe is for the white man, if Asia is for brown and yellow men, then surely Africa is for the black man" (*Philosophy and Opinions,* 1:25); Du Bois: "Africa should be administered for the Africans and, as soon as may be, by the Africans. [I do] not mean by this that Africa should be administered by West Indians or American Negroes. They have no more right to administer Africa for the native Africans than native Africans have to administer America" (*Writings in Periodicals Edited by W. E. B. Du*

Bois: Selections from the Crisis, vol. 1 [Millwood, N.Y.: Kraus-Thomson, 1983], 331).

24. Arnold Rampersad, *The Art and Imagination of W. E. B. Du Bois* (Cambridge: Harvard University Press, 1976), 149. While Du Bois grew increasingly frustrated with Garvey's program, Garvey himself seemed to revel in the similarities. "Much to the amusement of his followers who had gathered at Liberty Hall," Elliot P. Skinner reports, "Garvey remarked: 'We had two conventions this year. We had one in New York and we had one in Europe, and we sent Dr. Du Bois over to Europe to take care of the one we held there while we were busy with the one we had here'" (*African Americans and U.S. Policy toward Africa*, 461).

25. Garvey, *Philosophy and Opinions*, 1:35.

26. Ibid., 2:40.

27. Ibid., 2:56, 301. Garvey's conception of the class differences among African Americans was intrinsically tied to differences in complexion, a connection explicit in Jamaica but only implicit in the United States, where the so-called one-drop rule legally grouped all individuals with African blood together.

28. Elwood Watson, "Marcus Garvey's Garveyism: Message from a Forefather," *Journal of Religious Thought* 51 (1995): 93.

29. "Outsiders might laugh or scoff at some of the antics of the various Garvey organizations, their serious members ludicrous with high-toned titles and elaborate uniforms, but the importance of this aspect of the movement in restoring the all but shattered Negro self-confidence should not be overlooked" (Cronon, *Black Moses*, 174).

30. Redkey, *Black Exodus*, 294. Redkey also notes that Turner had proposed a steamship line to transport African Americans to Africa, a precursor to Garvey's ill-fated Black Star Line.

31. Ibid., 177; B. L. Ware and Wil A. Linkugel, "The Rhetorical *Persona*: Marcus Garvey as Black Moses," *Communication Monographs* 49 (1982): 50–62.

32. Garvey became affiliated with the African Orthodox Church, for example, which "functioned as the spiritual mouthpiece of Garveyism" (Watson, "Marcus Garvey's Garveyism," 81).

33. Garvey, *Philosophy and Opinions*, 1:34. Louis A. DeCaro Jr. suggests also that Garvey "seems to have personally minimized the differences between Christianity and Islam" and that he "provided Muslim missionaries in the United States with a friendly platform" (*On the Side of My People*, 16).

34. Cronon, *Black Moses*, 182.

35. Lincoln reports the date of Ali's birth as 1866 (Lincoln, *Black Muslims*, 48).

36. Some sources suggest that Ali resisted others' attempts to exploit his followers, but some suggest that Ali himself lived a rather lavish lifestyle on the backs of his converts.

37. My brief history of Noble Drew Ali and the Moorish Science Temple of America is based upon Arthur H. Fauset, "Moorish Science Temple of America," in *Religion, Society, and the Individual: An Introduction to the Sociology of Religion*, ed. John M. Yinger (New York: Macmillan, 1957); Mattias Gardell, *In the Name of Elijah Muhammad: Louis Farrakhan and the Nation of Islam* (Durham, N.C.: Duke University Press, 1996), 37–45; Lincoln, *Black Muslims*, 47–62; Karl Evanzz, *The Messenger: The Rise and Fall of Elijah Muhammad* (New York: Pantheon Books, 1999), 62–71. Of these, Fauset is the foundational study upon which the others, at least in part, rely; Evanzz provides the most recent and most thoroughly researched narrative; Gardell provides the best information about more recent Moorish history.

38. Gardell notes that a number of these splinter groups survive into the present day (*In the Name of Elijah Muhammad*, 45–46).

39. Arna Bontemps and Jack Conroy, *They Seek a City* (Garden City, N.Y.: Doubleday, Doran, 1945), 177–78. But Essien-Udom pointed out in 1962 that "Malcolm X and other leaders of the Nation of Islam have emphatically denied any past connection whatsoever of Elijah Muhammad, Master Wallace Fard Muhammad, or their movement" with the Moorish Science temples (*Black Nationalism*, 35–36).

40. Gardell offers an extended comparison between Drew Ali's *Holy Koran*, Dowling's *Gospel*, and various elements of Masonic ritual (*In the Name of Elijah Muhammad*, 40–45).

41. Noble Drew Ali's *Holy Koran* is available in multiple locations online, such as Noble Drew Ali, "The Holy Koran of The Moorish Science Temple of America," <http://www.geocities.com/Heartland/Woods/4623/frontspiece.html> (September 19, 2002). The text is divided into thirty-eight chapters identified by roman numerals. This quotation is from chapter XVI. Subsequent references will be by parenthetical citation of these roman numerals.

42. Du Bois, "Conservation of Races," in Foner, *W. E. B. Du Bois Speaks*, 81–82.

43. Fauset, "Moorish Science Temple," 499.

44. Quoted in Gardell, *In the Name of Elijah Muhammad*, 43.

45. Fauset, "Moorish Science Temple," 499.

46. Claude Andrew Clegg III, *An Original Man: The Life and Times of Elijah Muhammad* (New York: St. Martin's Press, 1997), 36.

47. Lincoln, *Black Muslims*, 22.

48. Ibid., 115; Branch, *Parting the Waters*, 915.

49. Lincoln, *Black Muslims*, 72.

50. In instructing Elijah Muhammad to tone down Fard's deification, Fard reportedly instructed him to "[g]ive them a little milk. . . . You cannot give babies meat!" (quoted in Clegg, *Original Man*, 26).

51. Clegg, *Original Man*, 35.

52. Quoted in Gardell, *In the Name of Elijah Muhammad*, 58.

53. Barbara Ann Norman, "The Black Muslims: A Rhetorical Analysis" (Ph.D. diss., University of Oklahoma, 1985), 161. Hakim A. Jamal provides a vivid description of an Nation of Islam meeting in Boston in which he heard "Lewis X" (Louis Farrakhan), Elijah Muhammad, and Malcolm X—he remembers being interested in Lewis X primarily because he recognized him as a former singer called "The Charmer," being deeply disappointed after hearing Elijah Muhammad, and being riveted by Malcolm X (*From the Dead Level*, 96–115). The spelling of Louis Farrakhan's first name varies in some sources. Here, and throughout, spelling is consistent with the source being cited.

54. Quoted in Lomax, *When the Word Is Given*, 81.

55. Jamal, *From the Dead Level*, 169.

56. The Fruit of Islam actually consists of every able-bodied man in the Nation of Islam. In the early days of the Nation of Islam, they were trained in military discipline and martial arts techniques.

57. For discussions of the Hinton Johnson incident, see Malcolm X and Haley, *Autobiography*, 233–35; Goldman, *Death and Life*, 55–59; Karim, *Remembering Malcolm*, 47–49; Lomax, *When the Word Is Given*, 28–29. In the *Autobiography*, Malcolm X seems to indicate that the incident took place in 1959; Lomax reports it as 1958; it is Goldman who places it in 1957.

58. Malcolm X and Haley, *Autobiography*, 215. Precise membership numbers for the Nation of Islam are difficult to obtain. Archie Epps supplies the estimate of 40,000 (*Malcolm X and the American Negro Revolution*, 29). Writing in 1962, E. U. Essien-Udom estimates the membership at close to 250,000 (*Black Nationalism*, 4). The actual numbers undoubtedly lie somewhere between these two estimates.

59. Goldman, *Death and Life*, 42.

60. Karim, *Remembering Malcolm*, 54–55.

61. Lomax tells of some "Moslems from Persia" who once attempted to enter an Nation of Islam mosque and were turned away (*When the Word Is Given*, 58).

62. Essien-Udom describes these "fishing" expeditions in some detail (*Black Nationalism*, 186–87).

63. Lomax, *When the Word Is Given*, 16.

64. On the search and questioning procedure for entering the mosque, see Karim, *Remembering Malcolm*, 50–51; Lomax, *When the Word Is Given*, 17–18; Jamal, *From the Dead Level*, 92–95.

65. Karim, *Remembering Malcolm*, 51–52. See also Lomax, *When the Word Is Given*, 19; Jamal, *From the Dead Level*, 134–35.

66. "Whey they heard someone talk too loudly or laugh foolishly they moved in unison and approached whoever it was, and one of them would beckon with his finger at the man playing games" (Jamal, *From the Dead Level*, 96).

67. Benjamin Karim, "Introduction," in *The End of White World Supremacy: Four Speeches by Malcolm X*, ed. B. Karim (New York: Little, Brown, 1971), 13–14.

68. Karim describes Malcolm's speech preparation: "Once he had determined where he wanted his words and ideas to take him, he would search the library in his mind as well as the bookshelves in his study, which was in the attic of his home in Queens, for the information that would help him accomplish his objective. As he selected each piece of information pertinent to his premises he would write down a cue to it on a three-by-five index card. . . . At the same time he was accumulating his cue cards he was continually arranging and re-arranging them until he settled finally upon the pattern for his thoughts" (*Remembering Malcolm*, 123; see also Goldman, *Death and Life*, 85–86).

69. Malcolm X, "Black Man's History," in Karim, *End of White World Supremacy*, 24. Subsequent references to this text will be by parenthetical page numbers.

70. Jamal, *From the Dead Level*, 106.

71. Garvey, *Philosophy and Opinions*, 2:310.

72. Compare this, from the prologue to Noble Drew Ali's *Holy Koran:* "The reason these lessons have not been known is because the Moslems of India, Egypt and Palestine had these secrets and kept them back from the outside world, and when the time appointed by Allah they loosened the keys and freed the secrets, and for the first time in ages have these secrets been delivered in the hands of the Moslems of America."

73. DeCaro, *Malcolm and the Cross,* 87; DeCaro, *On the Side of My People,* 104.

74. DeCaro, *Malcolm and the Cross,* 13, 45.

75. Michael Walzer, *Exodus and Revolution* (New York: Basic Books, 1985), 4; Howard-Pitney, *Afro-American Jeremiad,* 12. See also Walzer, *Exodus and Revolution,* 31–32.

76. Here, and throughout, biblical passages are quoted as they appear in Malcolm's speeches, according to the source text being cited. Malcolm refers to the King James version of the Bible, but occasionally makes slight changes.

77. In this speech, Malcolm X tells his audience: "You have to put a white man on the square. But the black is born on the square" (62). Compare this passage in Drew Ali's *Holy Koran,* in which he is borrowing heavily from Dowling's *Aquarian Gospels* to explain the symbolic significance of the mason's tools: "These tools remind me of the ones we handle in the workshop of the mind where things were made of thought and where we build up character. We use the square to measure all our lines, to straighten out the crooked places of the way, and make the corners of our conduct square" (V).

78. Malcolm X, "Malcolm X at Harvard," 114.

79. Malcolm X, "The Black Revolution," in Karim, *End of White World Supremacy,* 70.

80. Muhammad, "Muhammad at Atlanta," 102, 103.

81. Elijah Muhammad, *Message to the Blackman in America* (Chicago: Muhammad's Temple No. 2, 1965), 110–22. See also Elijah Muhammad, "Muhammad at Atlanta," in Lomax, *When the Word Is Given,* 99–111.

82. Compare Elijah Muhammad, speaking in Atlanta in 1961, concerning the creation of the moon: "We ourselves (the black nation) are a people who can never be destroyed. . . . So don't talk about getting rid of the Black Man, because you cannot do it" ("Muhammad at Atlanta," 99). Also, for the sake of comparison, this is Malcolm from "Black Man's History": "The Honorable Elijah Muhammad told us that this piece, that the Earth, that we remained on, shifted, dropped thirty-six thousand miles in the pocket that we remained in" (45). Elijah Muhammad: "That part of the planet which we call 'moon' today was blasted 12,000 miles from its original pocket that it had been rotating in at the time of the explosion, and this part that we call 'earth' today dropped 36,000 miles from that pocket and found another pocket and started rotating again" ("Muhammad at Atlanta," 99).

83. Muhammad, *Message to the Blackman,* 273–74. The parenthetical comments are included in the printed text and presumably are an attempt to transcribe Muhammad's habit of repeatedly interrupting himself with asides and explanations.

84. Ibid., 274–75, 281.

85. Ibid., 281.

86. Ibid., 291, 293, 304.

87. Ibid., 292.

88. Ibid., 298.

89. Archie Epps, "The Paradoxes of Malcolm X," in *The Speeches of Malcolm X at Harvard,* ed. A Epps (New York: William Morrow, 1969), 83; Malcolm X, "Malcolm X at Harvard," 116.

90. Malcolm X, "Malcolm X at Harvard," 117, 118.

91. Ibid., 123, 127. Compare this passage from *David Walker's Appeal,* as mentioned in Chapter 2: "Perhaps they will laugh at or make light of this; but I tell you Americans ! [*sic*] that unless you speedily alter your course, *you* and your *Country are gone! ! ! ! ! !*" (39).

92. Condit and Lucaites, "Limits of the Rhetoric of Revolutionary Dissent," 297.

93. Branch, *Parting the Waters,* 562, 659.

94. Goldman, *Death and Life,* 93.

95. Malcolm X and Haley, *Autobiography,* 289.

96. Lomax, *When the Word Is Given,* 79.

97. I refer to Kenneth Burke's differentiation between "action" and "motion" (*A Grammar of Motives* [Berkeley: University of California Press, 1969], 14–15).

98. Goldman, *Death and Life,* 81. Goldman lists many of the activities that filled the busy days and evenings of Nation of Islam members.

99. Malcolm X started *Muhammad Speaks* in his early days in the Nation of Islam. He did the writing, photography, and page layout all by himself. Each member of the Fruit of Islam was required to purchase $44 worth of papers each week at face value and thus had to sell them all just to break even. Later, sales of the newspaper were shifted to a commission basis, but even then it was expected that a prescribed number of papers would be sold. See Malcolm X and Haley, *Autobiography,* 237–38; Goldman, *Death and Life,* 82.

100. Taylor Branch opens his *Pillar of Fire* with an unusually detailed retelling of the Ronald Stokes incident (*Pillar of Fire: America in the King Years, 1963–1965* [New York: Simon and Schuster, 1998], 3–20). See also Goldman, *Death and Life,* 97–101.

101. Jamal, *From the Dead Level*, 196.
102. Ibid., 198. Benjamin Karim reports that the mayor of Los Angeles, fearing that Malcolm might incite further violence, telephoned Elijah Muhammad and asked that Malcolm be restrained (*Remembering Malcolm*, 135).
103. Karim, *Remembering Malcolm*, 136.
104. Malcolm X, "See for Yourself, Listen for Yourself, Think for Yourself: A Discussion with Young Civil Rights Fighters from Mississippi," in *Malcolm X Talks to Young People*, ed. S. Clark (New York: Pathfinder Press, 1991), 73.
105. Jamal, *From the Dead Level*, 199.
106. Quoted in Goldman, *Death and Life*, 99. Also quoted in Jamal, *From the Dead Level*, 200–201. On the Stokes incident, see also Breitman, *Last Year of Malcolm X*, 15–18. The July 1962 issue of *Muhammad Speaks* is devoted to the Stokes incident. Curiously, there is no mention of the event in the *Autobiography*.
107. Malcolm X, "Twenty Million Black People," 25–57. Like many of his speeches, this speech was never given a title by Malcolm X.
108. "Malcolm X Scores U.S. and Kennedy: Likens Slaying to 'Chickens Coming Home to Roost,'" *New York Times*, December 2, 1963.
109. Karim, *Remembering Malcolm*, 126.
110. Malcolm X, "Harvard Law School Forum," 115–31. As Epps acknowledges, this text is nearly identical to that included in Lomax's *When the Word Is Given* (112–27), where it is described as a "1960 speech." C. Eric Lincoln claims to have been instrumental in setting up this speaking engagement but does not clearly date the speech (*Black Muslims in America*, 262).
111. Malcolm X, "Malcolm X at Yale," in Lomax, *When the Word Is Given*, 155.
112. Malcolm X, "Black Man's History," 28.
113. Malcolm X, "The Old Negro and the New Negro," in Karim, *End of White World Supremacy*, 81–120.
114. Malcolm X, "America's Gravest Crisis since the Civil War," in Perry, *Malcolm X: The Last Speeches*, 68.
115. Malcolm X, "Message to the Grass Roots," in Breitman, *Malcolm X Speaks*, 12. This speech was delivered to an African American audience in Detroit. When the Detroit Council for Human Rights excluded nationalists from its Northern Negro Leadership Conference, Reverend Albert B. Cleage Jr. and other leaders organized a competing conference, the Northern Negro Grass Roots Leadership Conference.

Malcolm delivered this address on the last day of the conference. It is one of his last speeches as a member of the Nation of Islam.

116. Walker, *David Walker's Appeal*, 9; Garvey, *Philosophy and Opinions*, 2: 86.

117. Norman, "Black Muslims," 6.

118. Essien-Udom, *Black Nationalism*, 94.

119. C. Eric Lincoln, *The Black Muslims in America*, 3rd ed. (Grand Rapids, Mich.: William B. Eerdmans, 1994), 104.

120. Du Bois, "Conservation of Races," 75–76.

121. Malcolm X and Haley, *Autobiography*, 205.

122. Darsey, *Prophetic Tradition*, 20, 203.

123. In this, Malcolm's critique of King and of the mainstream civil rights movement echoes strongly Du Bois's critique of the monolithic leadership of Booker T. Washington. See Robert Terrill and Michael Leff, "The Polemicist as Artist: Du Bois's Response to Booker T. Washington," in *Argumentation and Values: Proceedings of the Ninth SCA/AFA Conference on Argumentation*, ed. Sally Jackson (Annandale, Va.: Speech Communication Association, 1995), 230–36.

124. Darsey, *Prophetic Tradition*, 16.

125. Robert L. Scott describes the difference between a relatively narrow conception of invention and a more constitutive view, which he labels "epistemic": "rhetoric may be viewed not as a matter of giving effectiveness to truth but of creating truth," a truth that the rhetor has "created moment by moment in the circumstances in which he finds himself and with which he must cope" ("On Viewing Rhetoric as Epistemic," *Central States Speech Journal* 18 [1967]: 13, 17).

Chapter 4

1. Alex Haley, in his epilogue to the *Autobiography*, describes at length how difficult it was to get Malcolm X to talk about himself (Malcolm X and Haley, *Autobiography*, 383–456).

2. Peter Goldman suggests that Malcolm may even have submitted the manuscript to Elijah Muhammad for approval (*Death and Life*, 118).

3. "Malcolm X Scores U.S. and Kennedy." The text of the speech is in Karim, *End of White World Supremacy*, 121–48. But Karim does not include the question-and-answer session in which Malcolm made the famous comment. In the *Autobiography*, Malcolm explained that he was merely observing that the atmosphere of hatred and violence fostered by the American government ultimately was responsible for the

assassination. He did not mention, however, that after the initial "chickens" comment got a rise from the crowd he added a cutting coda: "Being an old farm boy myself, chickens coming home to roost never did make me sad; they've always made me glad." See Malcolm X and Haley, *Autobiography*, 301; Goldman, *Death and Life*, 118–19.

4. In the *Autobiography*, Malcolm says that "my regular monthly visit to Mr. Muhammad was due the next day" (Malcolm X and Haley, *Autobiography*, 301). Most other sources, however, state that Elijah Muhammad specially requested that Malcolm come to Chicago.

5. On Malcolm's submission, the incrementally increasing scope of his silencing, his time in Florida, and the threats upon his life, see Malcolm X and Haley, *Autobiography*, 300–317; Goldman, *Death and Life*, 119–32; Branch, *Pillar of Fire*, 184–86, 200–203, 256–62; Perry, *Malcolm*, 241–50; Clegg, *Original Man*, 200–16. Perry makes the interesting point that Malcolm repeatedly talked with reporters to tell them that he had been silenced, thus submitting and rebelling at the same time. Clegg and Goldman note that Malcolm X had offered to prod Muhammad Ali into a public acknowledgment of his membership in the Nation of Islam in exchange for Malcolm's own reinstatement; and Clegg points out the irony in the fact that Muhammad Ali's public embrace of the Nation negated Elijah Muhammad's need for Malcolm X as a high-profile and articulate public spokesman.

6. Malcolm X, "A Declaration of Independence," in Breitman, *Malcolm X Speaks*, 18–22.

7. Goldman, *Death and Life*, 107. Malcolm lived a truly ascetic existence. The Nation provided him with a home in Queens, a blue Oldsmobile, and a wage barely enough to cover the costs of supporting himself, his wife, and, by 1963, their four daughters. Essien-Udom attempted to learn the salaries of Nation of Islam ministers—presented to them each week, in cash, in sealed envelopes labeled "charity"—but was unable to do so (*Black Nationalism*, 173–74). Benjamin Karim reports that in 1962 Malcolm was earning $175 a week (*Remembering Malcolm*, 122). Malcolm signed over all of his speaking fees to the Nation, including his advance for the publication of the *Autobiography*.

8. Perry, *Malcolm X: The Last Speeches*, 213–14.

9. Karim, *Remembering Malcolm*, 147–48. Evanzz notes that "the [financial] benefits of being in the Nation of Islam seemed to be limited primarily to Elijah and his family. The rank and file were better off health-wise, but were as poor or poorer (from extensive tithing) than before they became Muslims" (*Messenger*, 266). The FBI worked

feverishly to foment suspicion and discord within the Nation, fearing what might come should Malcolm indeed inherit the throne (Branch, *Pillar of Fire*, 19–20).

10. The quotations from Malcolm and from Elijah Muhammad are in Malcolm X and Haley, *Autobiography*, 294–99. See also Goldman, *Death and Life*, 112–16; Perry, *Malcolm X: The Last Speeches*, 230–36; Clegg, *Original Man*, 184–89.

11. Breitman, *Last Year of Malcolm X*, 15.

12. Lomax, *When the Word Is Given*, 179. Breitman also quotes this very similar passage in the *Autobiography:* "If I harbored any personal disappointment whatsoever, it was that privately I was convinced that our Nation of Islam could be an even greater force in the American black man's overall struggle—if we engaged in more *action*. By that, I mean I thought privately that we should have amended, or relaxed, our general non-engagement policy. I felt that, wherever black people committed themselves, in the Little Rocks and the Birminghams and the other places, militantly disciplined Muslims should also be there— for all the world to see, and respect, and discuss" (Malcolm X and Haley, *Autobiography*, 289).

13. Breitman, *Last Year of Malcolm X*, 19. Louis Lomax, writing in 1963, noted that "the Negro masses are beginning to indict the Black Muslims for impotence" and suggests that they need a "new policy" of *"active wait-and-see,"* a sort of middle ground between detached observation and active engagement (*When the Word Is Given*, 79, 83). Goldman details Malcolm's frustration at being forced to stand always on the sidelines of civil rights movement activities, "watching and photographing them from a distance" but never being able to participate (*Death and Life*, 94).

14. DeCaro, *On the Side of My People*, 162; Branch, *Pillar of Fire*, 16–18.

15. DeCaro, *One the Side of My People*, 167.

16. Karim, *Remembering Malcolm*, 147.

17. Peter Goldman makes a similar point regarding Malcolm's relationship to the press: "Malcolm understood the trap and fell into it anyway. He wanted a wider public; he couldn't reach it without the media; he couldn't crash the media without saying something excessive; all too often, he obliged" (*Death and Life*, 242). However, Goldman is arguing merely that Malcolm's relationship with the press may have contributed to the fact that his statements became increasingly radical. I am making a quite different argument—that Malcolm's

efforts to address broader audiences and more varied circumstances systematically propelled him out of the Nation.

18. Goldman, *Death and Life,* 100.
19. This short summary of the key civil rights events of 1963 relies upon multiple sources, including: Branch, *Parting the Waters,* 673–922; Branch, *Pillar of Fire,* 21–169; Sean Dennis Cashman, *African-Americans and the Quest for Civil Rights: 1900–1990* (New York: New York University Press, 1991), 157–71; Goldman, *Death and Life,* 101–7.
20. Two phone calls just before the 1960 election, one from John F. Kennedy to Coretta Scott King while Martin was in jail following lunch-counter sit-ins in Atlanta and one from Robert Kennedy to the presiding judge in order to secure King's release, had established a relationship between the Kennedys and King that always was somewhat distant but, for the most part, mutually beneficial. Taylor Branch, *Parting The Waters* (New York: Simon and Schuster, 1988), 351–378.
21. King drafted a second emancipation proclamation and sent it to Kennedy, who ignored it; the celebration of Lincoln's birthday was an affair studded with African American celebrities but staged so as to minimize its mention in the press (Branch, *Parting the Waters,* 589–90, 686–87).
22. Branch, *Pillar of Fire,* 411.
23. Garth E. Pauley, "John Lewis's 'Serious Revolution': Rhetoric, Resistance, and Revision at the March on Washington," *Quarterly Journal of Speech* 84 (1998): 320–40.
24. Malcolm X, "Message to the Grass Roots," 13–15.
25. Elijah Muhammad originally was scheduled to address the crowd but canceled, as he often did, for health reasons. Malcolm X agreed to speak in his place.
26. Goldman, *Death and Life,* 118; DeCaro, *On the Side of My People,* 191; Perry, *Malcolm X: The Last Speeches,* 240.
27. Malcolm X, "God's Judgment of White America (The Chickens Are Coming Home to Roost)," in Karim, *End of White World Supremacy,* 121. Karim gives the delivery date as December 4, 1963, but accounts from the *New York Times* confirm the date as December 1. It is not clear if this published version of the text is taken from a copy of Malcolm's typed manuscript or if it is a transcript from a tape recording of the speech; thus, it is not clear if the numerous parentheses in the text are present in Malcolm's written version or are attempts to capture Malcolm's habit of making verbal asides while speaking.

Subsequent references to this text will be by parenthetical page numbers, except when reference would not be clear.

28. A few of the many anthologies that contain "The Ballot or the Bullet" include: James R. Andrews, *A Choice of Worlds: The Practice and Criticism of Public Discourse* (New York: Harper and Row, 1973), 135–53; Philip S. Foner, *The Voice of Black America: Major Speeches by Negroes in the United States, 1797–1971* (New York: Simon and Schuster, 1972), 985–1001; Irving J. Rein, *The Relevant Rhetoric: Principles of Public Speaking through Case Studies* (Chicago: Free Press, 1969), 47–69. Interestingly, the Cory Methodist Church also had been the site of one of King's most important post-Birmingham speeches about a year earlier.

29. On "scene," as I am using the term, see Burke, *Grammar of Motives*, 3–15. "Circumference" is Burke's term for the breadth or scope of a scene (ibid., 77).

30. Malcolm X, "Ballot or the Bullet," 23–24. Subsequent references to this text will be by parenthetical page numbers, except when reference would not be clear.

31. Cone, *Martin & Malcolm & America*, 194. My reading of the possibilities for unity in the rhetoric of Malcolm X also is at odds with Condit and Lucaites, who argue that "it was . . . especially important during this phase of his dissent that [Malcolm X] stand for unity among Blacks" ("Limits of the Rhetoric of Revolutionary Dissent," 301). I am not denying that Malcolm X made repeated calls for unity throughout the last year of his life, but rather I am arguing that an audience constituted in and through his rhetoric would not be inclined toward such unity.

32. In Burkean terms, Malcolm is rejecting most sources of "consubstantiality" upon which he and these other leaders might experience some degree of "identification." See Burke, *Rhetoric of Motives*, 19–23.

33. Malcolm X, "Black Man's History," 40.

34. Malcolm recalls that he "was in Washington, D.C., a week ago Thursday, and when they were debating whether or not they should let the [civil rights] bill come onto the floor. And in the back of the room where the Senate meets, there's huge map of the United States, and on that map it shows the location of Negroes throughout the country" (29). Malcolm uses the map to note that the senators from the states with the most African Americans were the ones leading the filibuster. But this itself is a subtle ironic reversal, for the map that Malcolm is referring to was being used by Georgia senator Richard Russell as a

visual aid for his proposal that federal funds be used to forcefully re-
locate African Americans so that they were evenly distributed
throughout the nation. It was also during this visit to the Senate that
Malcolm and King met for the first, and only, time (Branch, *Parting
the Waters*, 258, 267–68).

35. For a discussion of some of the animal imagery in Malcolm's rhetoric,
    see Hank Flick and Lawrence Powell, "Animal Imagery in the
    Rhetoric of Malcolm X," *Journal of Black Studies* 18 (1988): 435–51.

36. DeCaro notes that while this attitude toward violence may be anath-
    ema to liberal thinking in the West, Malcolm found support for it in
    Islam (*On the Side of My People*, 248–49). In "God's Judgment of White
    America," Malcolm defines what he means by "'responsible' Negro
    leadership": "*Negro leaders who were responsible to the government*, and
    who could therefore be controlled by the government, and be used by
    that same government to control their impatient people" (140).

37. By making this distinction, Malcolm X is self-consciously challenging
    the Anglo-American tradition that aligns "human" and "civil" rights
    as near synonyms. As Shawna Maglangbayan suggests, the "differ-
    ence that Malcolm X made between *human* rights and *civil* rights was
    not a play on words. Nor was he launching a 'humanitarian' slogan.
    When he said that 'Civil rights is domestic. Human rights is interna-
    tional,' he was clearly rejecting the term 'civil rights' because of its ex-
    clusively *domestic* orientation. . . . In Malcolm X's thinking 'human
    rights' and ultimate *independent Black nationhood* were one and the
    same thing" (*Garvey, Lumumba and Malcolm: National-separatists*
    [Chicago: Third World Press, 1972], 99–100).

38. W. E. B. Du Bois advocated a similar U.N. plan in 1946 ("An Appeal
    to the World," in *The Oxford W. E. B. Du Bois Reader*, ed. Eric J.
    Sundquist [New York: Oxford University Press, 1996], 454–61). Mal-
    colm X makes this argument many times during his last year, and it is
    difficult to know to what extent he understood the limitations of the
    project. Goldman suggests that Malcolm "never quite abandoned the
    dream of a formal human rights case against the United States. But
    the people he had working on the petition never finished it—only a
    rough outline ever got on paper—and Malcolm had begun to despair
    of bringing it before the UN anyway. . . . Privately, among the broth-
    ers, he admitted his discouragement—conceded that the support was-
    n't there and wasn't likely to be as long as the Africans depended on
    American aid and American investments" (*Death and Life*, 241).

39. Probably this is a subtle refutation of Martin Luther King Jr.'s declaration in his "I Have a Dream" speech that "we refuse to believe that the bank of justice is bankrupt. We refuse to believe that there are insufficient funds in the great vaults of opportunity of this nation" (*I Have a Dream: Writings and Speeches that Changed the World*, ed. J. M. Washington [San Francisco: HarperSanFrancisco, 1992], 102). For Malcolm, that vault is empty.

40. Breitman, *Last Year of Malcolm X*, 76.

41. Malcolm X and Haley, *Autobiography*, 319–44; DeCaro, *On the Side of My People*, 199–210; Goldman, *Death and Life*, 160–72.

42. See Goldman, *Death and Life*, 172–73; Maya Angelou, *All God's Children Need Traveling Shoes* (New York: Random House, 1986).

43. Philbert X, "Malcolm: Exposed by His Brother," *Muhammad Speaks*, April 10, 1964, 3–4. This issue of *Muhammad Speaks* also carried a notice concerning the civil rights actions being organized in St. Augustine by Dr. Robert B. Hayling, head of the local SCLC chapter. See also Branch, *Pillar of Fire*, 268–69. Interestingly, Philbert's press conference occurred on the same day as the only meeting between Malcolm and King, when both were attracted at the same time by the spectacle of the Senate civil rights filibuster.

44. Minister Lewis [*sic*], "Minister Who Knew Him Best—Part I: Rips Malcolm's Treachery, Defection," *Muhammad Speaks*, May 6, 1964, 13; Minister Louis, "The Truth About: Fall of a Minister," *Muhammad Speaks*, June 5, 1964, 8.

45. Goldman, *Death and Life*, 90.

46. Maglangbayan, *Garvey, Lumumba and Malcolm*, 72.

47. DeCaro, *On the Side of My People*, 211–17.

48. Quoted in Goldman, *Death and Life*, 170.

49. Perry, *Malcolm X: The Last Speeches*, 260.

50. Malcolm X and Haley, *Autobiography*, 338–39.

51. M. S. Handler, "Malcolm X Pleased by Whites' Attitude on Trip to Mecca," *New York Times*, May 8, 1964; Malcolm X, "Letters from Abroad: Jedda, Saudi Arabia," in Breitman, *Malcolm X Speaks*, 59–60.

52. Malcolm X and Haley, *Autobiography*, 339–42. This version probably follows closely the letter that Malcolm sent to Alex Haley, perhaps modified somewhat through Haley's interviews with Malcolm. Subsequent references to this text within this section will be by parenthetical page numbers.

53. Goldman, *Death and Life*, 166.

54. Garvey, *Philosophy and Opinion*, 2:126

55. Malcolm X, "Speech at Militant Labor Forum, Jan. 7, 1965, on 'Prospects for Freedom in 1965,'" in *Two Speeches by Malcolm X*, 22.

56. Malcolm X, "Harlem 'Hate-Gang,'" 65, 66, 67.

57. Ibid., 70, 69.

58. Goldman, *Death and Life*, 189–90.

59. A. Peter Bailey, "I Remember Malcolm X," *Black Collegian*, January/February 1989, 66–67, 112–14.

60. Malcolm X, "Founding Rally of the OAAU," in *By Any Means Necessary: Speeches, Interviews, and a Letter by Malcolm X*, ed. G. Breitman (New York: Pathfinder Press, 1970), 33–67. The "Statement of Basic Aims," without the interspersed commentary by Malcolm, is reprinted as "Appendix A" in Breitman's *The Last Year of Malcolm X*, 105–11. The quotations that follow are from Malcolm's running commentary (and thus from "Founding Rally") rather than from the "Statement" itself. Subsequent references to this text will be by parenthetical page numbers, except when reference would not be clear.

61. Malcolm X, "The Second Rally of the OAAU," in Breitman, *By Any Means Necessary*, 90, 103.

62. John Shabazz, "Open Letter: Muslim Minister Writes to Malcolm," *Muhammad Speaks*, July 3, 1964, 9.

63. Malcolm X, "Appeal to African Heads of State," in Breitman, *Malcolm X Speaks*, 72–77.

64. M. S. Handler, "Malcolm X Seeks U.N. Negro Debate: He Asks African States to Cite U.S. Over Rights," *New York Times*, August 13, 1964.

65. Accounts of Malcolm's visits to Africa can be found in Goldman, *Death and Life*, 206–20; Perry, *Malcolm X: The Last Speeches*, 314–20; Leslie A. Lacy, "African Responses to Malcolm X," in *Black Fire: An Anthology of Afro-American Writing*, ed. A. I. Baraka and L. Neal (New York: Morrow, 1968), 19–38; Lacy, "Malcolm X in Ghana," in Clarke, *Malcolm X: The Man and His Times*, 217–25; Lacy, *The Rise and Fall of a Proper Negro: An Autobiography* (New York: Macmillan, 1970), 196–216.

66. Elijah Muhammad, "Beware of False Prophets," *Muhammad Speaks*, July 31, 1964, 1; Minister Louis X, "The Truth and Travails of a Righteous Prophet," *Muhammad Speaks*, July 31, 1964, 11. See also Elijah Muhammad, "Memo: From Desk of Muhammad; To: The Original Black People!" *Muhammad Speaks*, September 11, 1964, 5–10.

67. M. S. Handler, "Malcolm Rejects Racist Doctrine: Also Denounces Elijah as a Religious 'Faker,'" *New York Times*, October 4, 1964.

68. Goldman, *Death and Life*, 206; Branch, *Pillar of Fire*, 424.

69. See Goldman, *Death and Life*, 230–56; Branch, *Pillar of Fire*, 578–79; Perry, *Malcolm X: The Last Speeches*, 351–56. One of the most sensational claims in Perry's book is that Malcolm may have intentionally have set his own house on fire.

70. Malcolm X, "A Letter from Cairo," in Breitman, *By Any Means Necessary*, 108–12. Breitman provides a dateline for this letter of August 29, 1964, but says it "was originally printed in a mimeographed Harlem publication, *Black Force*, undated but issued around early 1967" (109).

71. Malcolm X, "At the Audubon," in *Malcolm X Speaks*, 115–36.

72. Malcolm X, "See for Yourself, Listen for Yourself, Think for Yourself," in Clark, *Malcolm X Talks to Young People*, 48–82. Malcolm reiterates these statements nearly word for word in Detroit, the morning after his house was firebombed: "Also, I am very pleased to see so many who have come out to always see for yourself, where you can hear for yourself, and then think for yourself. Then you'll be in a better position to make an intelligent judgment for yourself. But if you form the habit of listening to what others say about something or someone or reading what someone else has written about someone, somebody can confuse you and misuse you." See Malcolm X, "Educate Our People in the Science of Politics," in *February 1965: The Final Speeches*, ed. S. Clark (New York: Pathfinder Press, 1992), 82. This speech also is available in Breitman, *Malcolm X Speaks* (157–77), where it is titled "After the Bombing."

73. Malcolm X, "The Homecoming Rally of the OAAU," in Breitman, *By Any Means Necessary*, 137, 145.

74. Malcolm X, "At the Audubon," 117.

75. Malcolm X, "Any Means Necessary to Bring About Freedom," in Clark, *Malcolm X Talks to Young People*, 25.

76. Malcolm X, "Communication and Reality," in Clarke, *Malcolm X: The Man and His Times*, 312–13.

77. Malcolm X, "At the Audubon," 116–17.

78. Malcolm X, "See for Yourself," 67. It is possible that Malcolm was being ironic in saying that he did not advocate anything illegal. But it also is true that nowhere in Malcolm's rhetoric did he explicitly advocate that his listeners should break the law.

79. The Bandung Conference was held April 18–24, 1955, and was attended by representatives of twenty-nine either newly independent or soon to be independent Asian and African nations. It is generally acknowledged as the cradle of the "nonaligned" movement, which consisted of nations resistant (to varying and often contested degrees)

to forced Cold War alignment with either the United States or the Soviet Union. See L. Láng, *Bandung, Thirty Years Later: Proceedings of the Commemoration of the Thirtieth Anniversary of the Bandung Conference* (Budapest: Hungarian Peace, 1985); A. W. Singham and S. Hune, *Non-Alignment in an Age of Alignments* (Westport, Conn.: Lawrence Hill, 1986). Malcolm develops a position in this speech at Rochester that bears much resemblance to nonalignment, even to the potential importance of the United Nations. See K. Gopal, *Non-Alignment and Power Politics: A Documentary Survey* (New Delhi: V.I. Publications, 1983), 36–39.

80. Malcolm X, "At the Audubon," 132.

81. As was most often the case, Malcolm did not give this speech a title; the editors of both anthologies in which it appears call it "Not Just an American Problem, But a World Problem." The two versions differ only slightly, and I rely on the version published in 1992, edited by Steve Clark. See Malcolm X, "Not Just an American Problem," in Perry, *Malcolm X: The Last Speeches*, 151–81; Malcolm X, "Not Just an American Problem," in Clark, *February 1965*, 143–70. Subsequent references to this text will be by parenthetical page numbers, except when reference would not be clear. Photographs of Malcolm delivering the speech show a racially mixed audience in the first few rows (Perry, *Malcolm X: The Last Speeches*, plates facing p. 97). This is the last speech Malcolm delivered that survives in print, but the last one he delivered was at Barnard College, in New York, on February 18, 1965. No recording of that speech was made, and no text is available, but Steve Clark has collected excerpts reported in the press (*February 1965*, 176–78).

82. Malcolm X, "I'm Not an American, I'm a Victim of Americanism," in Clark, *Malcolm X Talks to Young People*, 13.

83. Martin Luther King Jr., "Time to Break Silence," in Washington, *I Have a Dream*, 135–52.

84. Malcolm discussed the situation in the Congo often throughout the last months of his life, perhaps because it provided a particularly vivid example of the sort of international racist conspiracy that he saw developing. Usually, the discussion of the Congo was implicated in a discussion of the way the white press manipulates images of Africa, just as it is in this speech at Rochester. His discussion of the situation in the Congo is especially well developed in his speech at Rochester. For comparison, see Malcolm X, "At the Audubon," 93–96; Malcolm X,

"Communication and Reality," 309; Malcolm X, "See for Yourself," 79.

85. Victor Turner, *Dramas, Fields, and Metaphors; Symbolic Action in Human Society* (Ithaca, N.Y.: Cornell University Press, 1974), 232; Turner, *From Ritual to Theatre: The Human Seriousness of Play* (New York: Performing Arts Journal Publications, 1982), 26–27, 42.

86. bell hooks, "marginality as a site of resistance," in *Out There: Marginalization and Contemporary Culture,* ed. R. Ferguson, M. Gever, T. T. Minh-ha, and C. West (New York: New Museum of Contemporary Art, 1990), 341–43.

87. Arthur L. Smith (Molefi Asante), *Rhetoric of Black Revolution* (Boston: Allyn and Bacon, 1969), 21. See also Molefi Asante, *The Afrocentric Idea* (Philadelphia: Temple University Press, 1987), 11.

88. "Chiasmus" takes its name from the Greek letter *chi,* or "X." Using John F. Kennedy's famous chiasmus from his inaugural address:

> ask not what your country can do for you,
> but what you can do for your country.

If one were to draw a line from "you" in the first line to "you" in the second and another from "country" in the first line to "country" in the second, the two lines would cross to form an "X." Using Malcolm's chiasmus from the speech at Rochester yields the same results:

> [It seems] like the victim is the criminal,
> and the criminal is the victim.

See Richard A. Lanham, *A Handlist of Rhetorical Terms* (Berkeley: University of California Press, 1991), 33–34.

89. Malcolm X, "Second Rally of the OAAU," 103.

Chapter 5

1. See *New York Times,* February 22, 1965. See also Goldman, *Death and Life,* 273–78; Perry, *Malcolm,* 357–67; George Breitman, *The Assassination of Malcolm X,* 2nd ed. (New York: Pathfinder Press, 1988); Karl Evanzz, *The Judas Factor: The Plot to Kill Malcolm X* (New York: Thunder's Mouth, 1992); Michael Friedly, *Malcolm X: The Assassination* (New York: Carroll and Graf/Richard Gallen, 1992). The assassination was recorded on audiotape, because Malcolm's speech was to be recorded, and Louis A. DeCaro Jr. provides a verbatim transcript of the event (*On the Side of My People,* 274).

2. Quoted in Goldman, *Death and Life,* 417.

3. Steven Barboza, "A Divided Legacy," *Emerge,* April 1992, 26–27, 30, 32.

4. Martha F. Lee, *The Nation of Islam: An American Millenarian Movement* (Lewiston, N.Y.: Edwin Mellen, 1988), 78–79.

5. Fareed Z. Munir, "Islam in America: An African American Pilgrimage toward Coherence" (Ph.D. diss., Temple University, 1993), 127–28. Munir provides an exceptionally thorough historical study of the Nation of Islam after the death of Malcolm X.

6. Evanzz, *Messenger,* 425; Clegg, *Original Man,* 274.

7. Goldman, *Death and Life,* 434. See also Lincoln, *Black Muslims,* 264–65; Mattias Gardell, *In the Name of Elijah Muhammad: Louis Farrakhan and the Nation of Islam* (Durham, N.C.: Duke University Press, 1996), 111–12; Lee, *Nation of Islam,* 86, 91–92. Clegg suggests that some of these changes, such as the divestiture of many Nation of Islam business holdings, may have been prompted not for ideological reasons as much as by the need to balance the Nation of Islam's books (*Original Man,* 278).

8. Gardell, *In the Name of Elijah Muhammad,* 105–6. Gardell quotes Wallace Muhammad on the dissolution of the remaining vestiges of Elijah Muhammad's Nation of Islam: "It's just the final step in the process of bringing our membership into the international Muslim community and to conform to where there's a normal Islamic life—just normal, practical Islamic life. The hangover from yesterday of 'Black Nationalist' influence is something that we have to get rid of, because it was in conflict with the open society and democratic order of an Islamic community" (113–14).

9. Ibid., 121, 137; Lincoln, *Black Muslims,* 258; Lee, *Nation of Islam,* 87, 94–95; Munir, *Nation of Islam,* 139–43.

10. Lee, *Nation of Islam,* 104. Gardell provides a thorough summary of the theology of Farrakhan's Nation of Islam, which illustrates its continuity with Elijah Muhammad's doctrines (*In the Name of Elijah Muhammad,* 144–86).

11. Gardell, *In the Name of Elijah Muhammad,* 135.

12. Munir, *Nation of Islam,* 160.

13. See John Arthos Jr., "The Shaman-Trickster's Art of Misdirection: The Rhetoric of Farrakhan and the Million Men," *Quarterly Journal of Speech* 87 (2001): 41–60. The text of Farrakhan's speech is widely available online: "Text of Louis Farrakhan's Speech at the 'Million Man March,'"

<http://www-cgi.cnn.com/US/9510/megamarch/10–16/transcript
/index.html> (1 June 2001). Originally presented October 17, 1995.

14. Perhaps Malcolm's discourse would be better understood as the foundation of something like a "New Social Movement," which Alberto Melucci, for example, describes as enacting "the end of a distinction between instrumental and expressive [consummatory] dimensions of action" and as such as being characterized by "mobile, reticulating, and apparently atomized demands" ("The Symbolic Challenge of Contemporary Movements," *Social Research* 52 [1985]: 812; Melucci, *Nomads of the Present: Social Movements and Individual Needs in Contemporary Society* [Philadelphia: Temple University Press, 1989], 72). Understanding Malcolm's rhetoric in this way may address the apparent disjunction between the inspiring power of his post–Nation of Islam discourse and the flaccid existence of the organizations he attempted to found, and it may help to reiterate my point from the first chapter than Malcolm's discourse cannot profitably be judged according to instrumental rhetorical expectations. Ultimately, however, as I argue below, I think it is misleading to frame Malcolm's project within as a "social movement."

15. Malcolm X, "Founding Rally of the OAAU," 33–67.

16. William W. Sales, *From Civil Rights to Black Liberation: Malcolm X and the Organization of Afro-American Unity* (Boston: South End Press, 1994), 109. DeCaro provides a brief overview of the specific challenges faced by the MMI (*On the Side of My People*, 230–34).

17. Sales, *From Civil Rights to Black Liberation*, 152.

18. DeCaro, *On the Side of My People*, 234; Perry, *Malcolm*, 318–19.

19. Malcolm's half-sister, Ella Collins, asserted leadership of the OAAU after his death, and many of the original members drifted away. Collins remade the organization into primarily a vehicle for the commemoration of Malcolm's memory. See Sales, *From Civil Rights to Black Liberation*, 160.

20. Goldman, *Death and Life*, 393.

21. Richard B. Gregg, "The Ego-Function of the Rhetoric of Protest," *Philosophy & Rhetoric* 4 (1971): 74. Aaron D. Gresson provides a promising emendation of Gregg's ego-function, suggesting that "it is not *merely* rewarding to the psyches of those who adhere to it" but is a "search for a new epistemological base" that will serve both speaker and audience as "*socially functional*" ("Minority Epistemology," 249).

22. Randall A. Lake, "Enacting Red Power: The Consummatory Function in Native American Protest Rhetoric," *Quarterly Journal of Speech* 69 (1983): 140.

23. Randall A. Lake, "Between Myth and History: Enacting Time in Native American Protest Rhetoric," *Quarterly Journal of Speech* 77 (1991): 140.

24. Edwin Black, "The Second Persona," in *Contemporary Rhetorical Theory: A Reader,* ed. J. L. Lucaites, C. M. Condit, and S. Caudill (New York: Guilford Press, 1999), 333–34. Black's essay originally appeared in *Quarterly Journal of Speech* 56 (1970): 109–19.

25. Michael Calvin McGee, "In Search of 'the People': A Rhetorical Alternative," in Lucaites, Condit, and Caudill, *Contemporary Rhetorical Theory,* 345–47. McGee's essay originally appeared in *Quarterly Journal of Speech* 61 (1975): 235–49.

26. Maurice Charland, "Constitutive Rhetoric: The Case of the *Peuple Québécois,*" in *Landmark Essays on Rhetorical Criticism,* ed. T. W. Benson (Davis, Calif.: Hermagoras Press, 1993), 220. Charland's essay originally appeared in *Quarterly Journal of Speech* 73 (1987): 133–50.

27. Charland, "Constitutive Rhetoric," 222.

28. Malcolm X, "Black Man's History," 24; Charland, "Constitutive Rhetoric," 222.

29. Charland, "Constitutive Rhetoric," 223.

30. Malcolm X, "Black Man's History," 26.

31. Charland, "Constitutive Rhetoric," 223.

32. Malcolm X, "Black Man's History," 40; Malcolm X and Haley, *Autobiography,* 205.

33. Malcolm X, "Ballot or the Bullet," 24.

34. Malcolm X and Haley, *Autobiography,* 340.

35. Malcolm X, "See for Yourself," 48–49. This story, with similar follow-up warnings to think for oneself, also appears in Malcolm X, "Communication and Reality," 308–9; Malcolm X, "At the Audubon," in *Malcolm X Speaks,* 91–92; and Malcolm X, "Harvard Law School Forum of December 16, 1964," in Epps, *Malcolm X: Speeches at Harvard,* 162–63.

36. Malcolm does sometimes collapse time in these speeches, referring to his present audiences as though they were consubstantial with past figures. For example, in "The Ballot or the Bullet," he briefly addresses his audience as though they *are* slaves: "Three hundred and ten years we worked in this country without a dime in return" (32). But such instances are rare in his post–Nation of Islam rhetoric, and

these do not present the sustained historical narrative of "Black Man's History."

37. Malcolm X, "Not Just an American Problem," in Clark, *February 1965,* 143–44.

38. Charland, "Constitutive Rhetoric," 225.

39. Ibid., 228.

40. Malcolm X, "At the Audubon," 133.

41. Kent A. Ono and John M. Sloop describe a contingent and flexible notion of critical telos that is similar to what I am ascribing to Malcolm's discourse ("Commitment to *Telos*—A Sustained Critical Rhetoric," *Communication Monographs* 59 [1992]: 48–60).

42. Black, "Second Persona," 334; McGee, "In Search of 'the People,'" 346.

43. Malcolm X, "Ballot or the Bullet," 28.

44. Karim, *Remembering Malcolm,* 97–98.

45. Gloria Anzaldúa, *Borderlands/La Frontera: The New Mestiza* (San Francisco: Spinsters/Aunt Lute, 1987), 73.

46. For a description of the relationship between symbolic borderlands and liminality, see Mae Henderson, "Introduction: Borders, Boundaries, and Frame(work)s," in *Borders, Boundaries, and Frames: Cultural Criticism and Cultural Studies,* ed. M. G. Henderson (New York: Routledge, 1995), 5; Turner, *From Ritual to Theatre,* 23–25, 33.

47. Turner, *From Ritual to Theatre,* 44–45.

48. Ibid., 45, 27.

49. Lewis Hyde, *Trickster Makes This World: Mischief, Myth, and Art* (New York: North Point Press, 1998), 39.

50. Ibid., 208, 222–25. See also Suzanne Evertsen Lundquist, *The Trickster: A Transformation Archetype* (San Francisco: Mellen Research University Press, 1991), 91.

51. Lawrence W. Levine, *Black Culture and Black Consciousness: Afro-American Folk Thought from Slavery to Freedom* (New York: Oxford University Press, 1977), 105, 115, 104.

52. Hyde, *Trickster Makes This World,* 256.

53. See, for example, Lucaites and Condit, "Reconstructing <Equality>," 11. Lewis Hyde analyzes the trickster qualities of Frederick Douglass, and Henry Louis Gates Jr. discusses Zora Neale Hurston, Ishmael Reed, and Alice Walker as trickster figures. See Gates, *The Signifying Monkey: A Theory of Afro-American Literary Criticism* (New York: Oxford University Press, 1988).

54. Gates, *Signifying Monkey,* 128. "The ironic reversal of a received racist image in the Western imagination of the black as simianlike, the Signifying Monkey—he who dwells at the margins of discourse, ever punning, ever troping, ever embodying the ambiguities of language—is our trope for repetition and revision, indeed our trope of chiasmus itself, repeating and reversing simultaneously as he does in one deft discursive act" (Henry Louis Gates Jr., *Figures in Black: Words, Signs, and the "Racial" Self* [New York: Oxford University Press, 1987], 236).

55. Hyde, *Trickster Makes This World,* 278.

56. Gates, *Figures in Black,* 238.

57. Gates, *Signifying Monkey,* 23, 35; Gates, *Figures in Black,* 49.

58. Leff, "Idea of Rhetoric," 97.

59. Among classical sources, Quintilian provides perhaps the fullest account of *imitatio,* in the first two books of his *Institutio Oratoria.* Quintilian, of course, is following Cicero's lead in this matter, particularly as it is articulated in Cicero's *Orator.* It is perhaps important to point out that I certainly do not mean to say that Malcolm is training his audiences to imitate white culture. Rather, my point is that he is using something like the classical mode of *imitatio* as a pedagogical device through which to demonstrate to his audiences strategies of critiquing—and triumphing over—white culture. See Gates, *Signifying Monkey,* 66.

60. Levine, *Black Culture,* 113–15. See also Lundquist, *Trickster,* 63; Hyde, *Trickster Makes This World,* 18. Levine points out, importantly, that the trickster hero of some slave tales seems intended to represent the slave owner rather than the slave (*Black Culture,* 118–21). But the pedagogical uses of the tales remains consistent—these tales illustrate the arbitrary and irrational nature of the "rules" of human culture and teach the necessity for the doubled arts of emulation and critique. When Malcolm X explains to his audience that sometimes whites seem to be foxes and sometimes they seem to be wolves, he is illustrating for his audience the tricksterish nature of their adversary. See Malcolm X, "God's Judgment of White America," 121–48.

61. Hyde, *Trickster Makes This World,* 28–30; Levine, *Black Culture,* 111–12.

62. Malcolm X, "Ballot or the Bullet," 38.

63. Ibid., 38–39. Note also the pronoun shifts in Malcolm's description of black nationalism, from the individual "he" to the collective "we."

64. Malcolm X, "Twenty Million Black People," 164.

65. Malcolm X, "Black Man's History," 58.

66. Robert Hariman and Francis A. Beer, "What Would Be Prudent? Forms of Reasoning in World Politics," *Rhetoric & Public Affairs* 3 (1998): 301.

67. Aristotle, *Nicomachean Ethics*, 2nd ed., trans. T. Irwin (Indianapolis, Ind.: Hackett, 1999), 1140a25–28. Subsequent references to this work are by Bekker numbers inserted parenthetically in the text.

68. Robert Hariman, "Theory without Modernity," in *Prudence: Classical Virtue, Postmodern Practice*, ed. R. Hariman (University Park: Pennsylvania State University Press, 2003), 5.

69. Victoria Kahn, *Rhetoric, Prudence, and Skepticism in the Renaissance* (Ithaca, N.Y.: Cornell University Press, 1985), 39.

70. Ronald Beiner, *Political Judgment* (Chicago: University of Chicago Press, 1983), 164, 87.

71. This quotation is from H. Rackham's translation of the *Nicomachean Ethics*, VI.v.5 (Cambridge: Harvard University Press, 1939), because it seems more forcefully to articulate prudence as a faculty of discernment. The Rackham translation lacks the standard Bekker numbers; the relevant passage is at 1140b9–11 in the Irwin translation, which I use elsewhere, where this passage is rendered: "This is why Pericles and such people are the ones whom we regard as prudent, because they are able to study what is good for themselves and for human beings; we think that household managers and politicians are such people."

72. Beiner, *Political Judgment*, 132.

73. Malcolm X, "At the Audubon,"132.

74. Hariman and Beer, "What Would Be Prudent?" 305.

75. Robert Hariman, "Prudence/Performance," *Rhetoric Society Quarterly* 21 (1991): 33.

76. Michael Leff, "The Habitation of Rhetoric," in *Argument and Critical Practices: Proceedings of the Fifth SCA/AFA Conference on Argumentation*, ed. Joseph W. Wenzel (Annandale, Va.: Speech Communication Association, 1987), 2.

77. Robert Hariman, "Decorum," in *Encyclopedia of Rhetoric*, ed. Thomas O. Sloane (Oxford: Oxford University Press, 2001), 199–209.

78. Cicero, *Orator*, trans. H. M. Hubbell (Cambridge: Harvard University Press, 1988), 71.

79. Michael Leff has thoroughly explicated these senses of Ciceronian decorum in "Decorum and Rhetorical Interpretation: The Latin Humanistic Tradition and Contemporary Critical Theory," *Vichiana, 3a serie* (1990): 107–26.

80. These two senses of decorum correspond most fully to the modes that Hariman describes as *sophistic* and *organic,* two of the modes he understands as subsumed within the Ciceronian or *humanist* mode. The alignment is not absolute, however; my focus here is on coming to terms with the particular innovations of prudence that Malcolm is crafting through his managing of decorum, rather than on aligning these modes of decorum with any particular definitions, however elegant such definitions may be.

81. Erving Goffman, "Performances," in *The Presentation of Self in Everyday Life* (New York: Anchor/Doubleday, 1959), 30.

82. Eugene Garver, *Machiavelli and the History of Prudence* (Madison: University of Wisconsin Press, 1987), 50; Beiner, *Political Judgment,* 162.

83. I am arguing that Malcolm's rhetoric functions differently, in this regard, than that of the anarchist Voltairine de Cleyre, as described by Thomas Rosteck and Michael Leff. They illustrate that "radical discourse becomes radical as it reconstructs rather than adjusts itself to the standards of propriety accepted by an audience" ("Piety, Propriety, and Perspective: An Interpretation and Application of Key Terms in Kenneth Burke's *Permanence and Change,*" *Western Journal of Speech Communication* 53 [1989]: 338). Malcolm's rhetoric, instead, resists establishing a new or competing set of standards. It may, in fact, finally construct such standards—but it is explicitly resistant to the process.

84. Michael Leff, "Rhetorical Timing in Lincoln's 'House Divided' Speech," Van Zelst Lecture in Communication (Evanston, Ill.: Northwestern University School of Speech, 1983), 18.

85. Respectively: Malcolm X, "Ballot or the Bullet," 28, 36, 33; Malcolm X and Haley, *Autobiography,* 341; Malcolm X, "Twenty Million Black People," 163, 162.

86. Malcolm X, "Ballot or the Bullet," 31, 34.

87. Eugene Garver, *Aristotle's Rhetoric: An Art of Character* (Chicago: University of Chicago Press, 1994), 233.

88. Robert W. Cape Jr., "Prudence," in Sloane, *Encyclopedia of Rhetoric,* 640.

89. Beiner, *Political Judgment,* 153.

90. One of the anonymous reviewers of this book asked a provocative question that I would like to address here rather than in the body of the text. The question was "whether imitating Malcolm would indeed make one more likely to act wisely." This probe is provocative because it is a sharper version of the question that, in part, has motivated this book: Was Malcolm X a success? By at least one measure, of course,

the answer would have to be "no," imitating Malcolm X would not ensure wise action. Malcolm was assassinated, and while this is the fate of any number of revolutionaries, it certainly is not an ideal outcome of prudential action. If the virtue of prudence involves balancing the needs of the individual and the group, then the successful preservation of one's own life would seem to be a prerequisite. But Malcolm's most significant legacy is his words, not his deeds; he would have his audience fashion their lives as he fashioned his *speeches* and not as he lived his own life. To live that way, as Malcolm spoke, would be to balance multiperspectival observation, communal commitment, and individualized judgment—it still might not protect one from getting shot, but it would encourage a finely grained analysis of the risks involved in particular situations. And Malcolm X, because of the prudential habits of mind revealed in his discourse and that he would pass on to his audiences, was well aware of the risks he faced. He got shot because he understood the threat and decided to act anyway. Prudential thought and action do not guarantee either individual or collective success; but neither Malcolm nor his audiences could walk blindly into harm's way.

91. See Edward Schiappa, *The Beginnings of Rhetorical Theory in Classical Greece* (New Haven, Conn.: Yale University Press, 1999), esp. chap. 4. In a sense, Schiappa's critique of Poulakos's position only makes that position more analogous to the rhetoric of Malcolm X: just as the Sophists were not generating a stable, codified, and coherent rhetorical theory, neither was Malcolm.

92. John Poulakos, "Toward a Sophistic Definition of Rhetoric," in Lucaites, Condit, and Caudill, *Contemporary Rhetorical Theory*, 26. Poulakos's essay originally appeared in *Philosophy and Rhetoric* 16 (1983): 35–48. Poulakos provides a fuller discussion in *Sophistical Rhetoric in Classical Greece* (Columbia: University of South Carolina Press, 1995).

93. Poulakos, "Sophist Definition," 30, 30–31.

94. This may be contrasted to the polysemic and multivocalic model of prophecy described in Margaret D. Zulick, "The Agon of Jeremiah: On the Dialogic Invention of Prophetic Ethos," *Quarterly Journal of Speech* 78 (1992): 125–48.

95. Aaron David Gresson III, *The Dialectics of Betrayal: Sacrifice, Violation, and the Oppressed* (Norwood, N.J.: Ablex, 1982), 13–14; Burke, *Rhetoric of Motives*, 193.

96. W. E. B. Du Bois, *The Souls of Black Folk* (New York: Penguin Books, 1989), 5.

97. Historically, the rhetoric of complicity has contributed to a number of problematic coalitions between black nationalists and white racists. Marcus Garvey, for example, did not reject the enthusiastic support of such white racists as Major Earnest Sevier Cox, author of *White America*, and John Powell, organizer of the Anglo-Saxon Clubs of America. In 1922, when Garvey traveled to Atlanta to meet with Edward Young Clark, Imperial Giant of the Ku Klux Klan, to seek financial and political support for the Back to Africa program of his UNIA, the meeting provoked general condemnation among other African American leaders. But Garvey wrote: "give me the Klan for their honesty of purpose toward the Negro." In 1996, Louis Farrakhan invited white supremacist Lyndon LaRouche to address a gathering of black nationalists in St. Louis. See Cronon, *Black Moses*, 188–90; Marcus Garvey, *Philosophy and Opinions* 2:71; Manning Marable, "Black Fundamentalism: Farrakhan and Conservative Black Nationalism," *Race & Class* 39 (1998): 4–5.

98. Mark McPhail, "The Complicity of Essentializing Difference: (Re)constructing the Color Line: Complicity and Black Conservatism," *Communication Theory* 7 (1997): 163.

99. Ibid., 164. See also Terrill and Leff, "Polemicist as Artist."

100. Mark McPhail, "Passionate Intensity: Louis Farrakhan and the Fallacies of Racial Reasoning," *Quarterly Journal of Speech* 84 (1998): 416–29.

101. Mark McPhail, "From Complicity to Coherence: Rereading the Rhetoric of Afrocentricity," *Western Journal of Communication* 62 (1998): 114–40; McPhail, *The Rhetoric of Racism* (New York: University Press of America, 1994); West, *Race Matters*, 35–49.

102. Kenneth Burke offers "transcendence" as a rhetorical strategy for escaping the paradox of liberation. This would entail positing, for example, a new set of ultimate terms that includes both the individual and group motives inherent in the paradox. Burke suggests that a Marxist rhetoric could perform this function: "It permits the member of a minority to place his problem in a graded series that keeps transcendence of individual status from seeming like disloyalty to one's group status, and keeps the sufferance of one's group status from assuming some form of mere 'vengeance'" (*Rhetoric of Motives*, 195). Malcolm offers a different and more radical strategy, one that does not depend on transcendence but instead on a perpetual suspicion of ultimate terms,

including but not limited to the ultimate terms that underlie the oppressive rhetoric of the dominant culture.

103. Gresson, *Recovery of Race,* 13–14, 16, 14.

104. Among the precursors of this strand of African American discourse, perhaps the most influential would be Booker T. Washington. He seemed willing to tolerate—or at least to seem to be willing to tolerate—racist exclusions while he went about the business of producing black shopkeepers and skilled laborers upon whose individual success the fortunes of the black race would depend. In literature, the most influential work in this vein is Ralph Ellison's *Invisible Man.* See Andrew A. King, "Booker T. Washington and the Myth of Heroic Materialism," *Quarterly Journal of Speech* 60 (1974): 323–27; S. Jay Walker, "Booker T. Washington: 'Separatist' in Golden Chains," in *Black Separatism and Social Reality: Rhetoric and Reason,* ed. Raymond L. Hall (New York: Pergamon Press, 1977), 56–62; J. P. Flynn, "Booker T. Washington: Uncle Tom or Wooden Horse," *Journal of Negro History* 54 (1969): 262–74; Andrew Hoberek, "Race Man, Organization Man, *Invisible Man,*" *Modern Language Quarterly* 59 (1998): 99–119.

105. Robert L. Ivie, "Rhetorical Deliberation and Democratic Politics in the Here and Now," *Rhetoric & Public Affairs* 5 (2002): 280.

106. The foundational text for such descriptions is, perhaps, Jean-François Lyotard, *The Postmodern Condition: A Report on Knowledge,* trans. G. Bennington and B. Massumi (1979; reprint, Minneapolis: University of Minnesota Press, 1984). For arguments that are equally well known and that in some ways are similar, but which approach contemporary fragmentation from more ethnographic and sociological perspectives, respectively, see Robert N. Bellah, Richard Madsen, William M. Sullivan, Ann Swidler, and Steven M. Tipton, *Habits of the Heart: Individualism and Commitment in American Life* (New York: Harper and Row, 1985); Robert D. Putnam, *Bowling Alone: The Collapse and Revival of American Community* (New York: Simon and Schuster, 2000).

107. Michael Calvin McGee, "Text, Context, and the Fragmentation of Contemporary Culture," in Lucaites, Condit, and Caudill, *Contemporary Rhetorical Theory,* 69. McGee's essay originally appeared in *Western Journal of Speech Communication* 54 (1990): 274–89. McGee, of course, is referring to academic rhetorical critics, and as such there is some slippage between the critical practice that he describes and Malcolm's critical practice. Malcolm is not an academic. But Malcolm is a rhetorician, in both the productive and critical senses of the word, and McGee's diagnosis of the fragmentation of contemporary culture,

together with his prescription for a revitalization of a neo-sophistic view of rhetoric as a fitting response, helps us to understand Malcolm's rhetorical practice as especially well suited to contemporary life.

108. Ibid., 76.
109. Ibid.
110. In this way, Malcolm X may help to expose a productive paradox in McGee's hypothesis—the way to learn to assemble fragments in a rhetorically effective manner is to engage in the close textual analysis of (temporarily) coherent public address.

Selected Bibliography

Andrews, James R. *A Choice of Worlds: The Practice and Criticism of Public Discourse*. New York: Harper and Row, 1973.

Angelou, Maya. *All God's Children Need Traveling Shoes*. New York: Random House, 1986.

Anzaldúa, Gloria. *Borderlands/La Frontera: The New Mestiza*. San Francisco: Spinsters/Aunt Lute, 1987.

Appiah, Anthony. "The Uncompleted Argument: Du Bois and the Illusion of Race." *Critical Inquiry* 12 (1985): 21–37.

Aptheker, Herbert. *American Negro Slave Revolts*. New York: Columbia University Press, 1943.

Aristotle. *Nicomachean Ethics*. 2nd ed. Translated by Terence Irwin. Indianapolis, Ind.: Hackett, 1999.

_____. *Nicomachean Ethics*. Translated by H. Rackham. Cambridge: Harvard University Press, 1939.

Arthos, John, Jr. "The Shaman-Trickster's Art of Misdirection: The Rhetoric of Farrakhan and the Million Men." *Quarterly Journal of Speech* 87 (2001): 41–60.

Asante, Molefi. *The Afrocentric Idea*. Philadelphia: Temple University Press, 1987.

Baraka, Imamu Amiri, and Larry Neal. *Black Fire: An Anthology of Afro-American Writing*. New York: Morrow, 1968.

Beiner, Ronald. *Political Judgment*. Chicago: University of Chicago Press, 1983.

Bell, Bernard W., Emily Grosholz, and James B. Stewart, eds. *W. E. B. Du Bois on Race and Culture: Philosophy, Politics, and Poetics*. New York: Routledge, 1996.

Benson, Thomas W. "Malcolm X." In *American Orators of the Twentieth Century: Critical Studies and Sources*, edited by Bernard K. Duffy and Halford R. Ryan, 317–22. Westport, Conn.: Greenwood Press, 1987.

_____. "Rhetoric and Autobiography: The Case of Malcolm X." *Quarterly Journal of Speech* 60 (1974): 1–13.

_____, ed. *Rhetoric and Political Culture in Nineteenth-Century America*. East Lansing: Michigan State University Press, 1997.

Bercovitch, Sacvan. *The American Jeremiad*. Madison: University of Wisconsin Press, 1978.

Beynon, Erdmann Doane. "The Voodoo Cult among Negro Migrants in Detroit." *American Journal of Sociology* 43 (1938): 894–907.

Black, Edwin. *Rhetorical Criticism: A Study in Method.* 1965. Reprint, Madison: University of Wisconsin Press, 1978.

———. "The Second Persona." *Quarterly Journal of Speech* 56 (1970): 109–19.

Bontemps, Arna, and Jack Conroy. *They Seek a City.* Garden City, N.Y.: Doubleday, Doran, 1945.

Boulware, Marcus H. "Minister Malcolm: Orator Profundo." *Negro History Bulletin* 30 (1967): 12–14.

Branch, Taylor. *Parting the Waters: America in the King Years, 1954–63.* New York: Simon and Schuster, 1988.

———. *Pillar of Fire: America in the King Years, 1963–1965.* New York: Simon and Schuster, 1998.

Breitman, George. *The Assassination of Malcolm X.* 2nd ed. New York: Pathfinder Press, 1988.

———. *The Last Year of Malcolm X: The Evolution of a Revolutionary.* New York: Pathfinder Press, 1967.

———, ed. *By Any Means Necessary: Speeches, Interviews, and a Letter by Malcolm X.* New York: Pathfinder Press, 1970.

———. *Malcolm X Speaks.* New York: Pathfinder Press, 1965.

Browne, Stephen H. "'The Unparalleled and Inhuman Massacre': The Gothic, the Sacred, and the Meaning of Nat Turner." *Rhetoric & Public Affairs* 3 (2000): 309–31.

Brummett, Barry. *Contemporary Apocalyptic Rhetoric.* New York: Praeger, 1991.

Burke, Kenneth. *A Grammar of Motives.* Berkeley: University of California Press, 1969.

———. *The Philosophy of Literary Form.* Berkeley: University of California Press, 1967.

———. *A Rhetoric of Motives.* Berkeley: University of California Press, 1969.

Campbell, Finley C. "Voices of Thunder, Voices of Rage: A Symbolic Analysis of a Selection from Malcolm X's Speech, 'Message to the Grass Roots.'" *Speech Teacher* 19 (1970): 101–10.

Campbell, Karlyn Kohrs. "The Rhetoric of Radical Black Nationalism: A Case Study in Self-Conscious Criticism." *Central States Speech Journal* 22 (1971): 150.

Campbell, Karlyn Kohrs, and Kathleen Hall Jamieson, eds. *Form and Genre: Shaping Rhetorical Action.* Falls Church, Va.: Speech Communication Association, 1978.

Cape, Robert W., Jr. "Prudence." In *Encyclopedia of Rhetoric*, edited by Thomas O. Sloane, 637–40. Oxford: Oxford University Press, 2001.

Cashman, Sean Dennis. *African-Americans and the Quest for Civil Rights, 1900–1990*. New York: New York University Press, 1991.

Castronovo, Russ. *Fathering the Nation: American Genealogies of Slavery and Freedom*. Berkeley: University of California Press, 1995.

Charland, Maurice. "Constitutive Rhetoric: The Case of the *Peuple Québécois*." *Quarterly Journal of Speech* 73 (1987): 133–50.

Chesebrough, David B. *Frederick Douglass: Oratory from Slavery*. Westport, Conn.: Greenwood Press, 1998.

Cicero. *Orator*. Translated by H. M. Hubbell. Cambridge: Harvard University Press, 1988.

Clark, Steve, ed. *February 1965: The Final Speeches*. New York: Pathfinder Press, 1992.

———. *Malcolm X Talks to Young People*. New York: Pathfinder Press, 1991.

Clarke, John H., ed. *Malcolm X: The Man and His Times*. New York: Macmillan, 1969.

Clegg, Claude Andrew III. *An Original Man: The Life and Times of Elijah Muhammad*. New York: St. Martin's Press, 1997.

Condit, Celeste Michelle, and John Louis Lucaites. "Malcolm X and the Limits of the Rhetoric of Revolutionary Dissent." *Journal of Black Studies* 23 (1993): 291–313.

———. *Crafting Equality: America's Anglo-African Word*. Chicago: Chicago University Press, 1993.

Cone, John H. *Martin & Malcolm & America: A Dream or a Nightmare*. Maryknoll, N.Y.: Orbis Books, 1991.

Cronon, E. David. *Black Moses: The Story of Marcus Garvey and the Universal Negro Improvement Association*. Madison: University of Wisconsin Press, 1955.

Crowley, Sharon. *The Methodical Memory: Invention in Current-Traditional Rhetoric*. Carbondale: Southern Illinois University Press, 1990.

Cruse, Harold. *Rebellion or Revolution?* New York: Morrow, 1968.

Darsey, James. *The Prophetic Tradition and Radical Rhetoric in America*. New York: New York University Press, 1997.

DeCaro, Louis A., Jr. *Malcolm and the Cross: The Nation of Islam, Malcolm X, and Christianity*. New York: New York University Press, 1998.

———. *On the Side of My People: A Religious Life of Malcolm X*. New York: New York University Press, 1996.

Douglass, Frederick. "What to the Slave Is the Fourth of July?: An Address Delivered in Rochester, New York, on 5 July 1852." In *The Frederick*

Douglass Papers. Vol. 2, edited by John W. Blassingame, 359–88. New Haven, Conn.: Yale University Press, 1982.

Du Bois, W. E. B. *The Conservation of Races*. Washington, D.C.: American Negro Academy, 1897.

———. *The Souls of Black Folk*. New York: Penguin Books, 1989.

———. *Writings by W. E. B. Du Bois in Periodicals Edited by Others*. Vol. 2, collated and edited by Herbert Aptheker. Millwood, N.Y.: Kraus-Thomson, 1982.

———. *Writings in Periodicals Edited by W. E. B. Du Bois: Selections from the Crisis*. Vol. 1, collated and edited by Herbert Aptheker. Millwood, N.Y.: Kraus-Thomson, 1983.

Dyson, Michael Eric. *Making Malcolm: The Myth and Meaning of Malcolm X*. Oxford: Oxford University Press, 1995.

Epps, Archie, ed. *Malcolm X and the American Negro Revolution: The Speeches of Malcolm X*. London: Peter Owen, 1968.

———. *The Speeches of Malcolm X at Harvard*. New York: William Morrow, 1969.

Essien-Udom, E. U. *Black Nationalism: A Search for an Identity in America*. Chicago: University of Chicago Press, 1962.

Essien-Udom, E. U., and Ruby Essien-Udom. "Malcolm X: An International Man." In *Malcolm X: The Man and His Times*, edited by John H. Clarke, 235–67. New York: Macmillan, 1969.

Evanzz, Karl. *The Judas Factor: The Plot to Kill Malcolm X*. New York: Thunder's Mouth, 1992.

———. *The Messenger: The Rise and Fall of Elijah Muhammad*. New York: Pantheon Books, 1999.

Fauset, Arthur H. "Moorish Science Temple of America." In *Religion, Society, and the Individual: An Introduction to the Sociology of Religion*, edited by John M. Yinger, 498–507. New York: Macmillan, 1957.

Flick, Hank, and Lawrence Powell. "Animal Imagery in the Rhetoric of Malcolm X." *Journal of Black Studies* 18 (1988): 435–51.

Foner, Philip S. *The Voice of Black America: Major Speeches by Negroes in the United States, 1797–1971*. New York: Simon and Schuster, 1972.

———, ed. *W. E. B. Du Bois Speaks: Speeches and Addresses*. New York: Pathfinder Press, 1970.

———. *W. E. B. Du Bois Speaks: Speeches and Addresses, 1890–1919*. New York: Pathfinder Press, 1966.

Friedly, Michael. *Malcolm X: The Assassination*. New York: Carroll and Graf/Richard Gallen, 1992.

Gardell, Mattias. *In the Name of Elijah Muhammad: Louis Farrakhan and the Nation of Islam*. Durham, N.C.: Duke University Press, 1996.

Garver, Eugene. *Aristotle's Rhetoric: An Art of Character*. Chicago: University of Chicago Press, 1994.

_____. *Machiavelli and the History of Prudence*. Madison: University of Wisconsin Press, 1987.

Garvey, Marcus M. *Philosophy and Opinions of Marcus Garvey*. 3rd ed., edited by Amy Jacques Garvey. Totowa, N.J.: Frank Cass, 1989.

Gates, Henry Louis. *Figures in Black: Words, Signs, and the "Racial" Self*. New York: Oxford University Press, 1987.

_____. *The Signifying Monkey: A Theory of Afro-American Literary Criticism*. New York: Oxford University Press, 1988.

Goetsch, Paul, and Gerd Hurm, eds. *The Fourth of July: Political Oratory and Literary Reactions, 1776–1876*. Tübingen, Germany: Gunter Narr Verlag, 1992.

Golden, John L., and Richard D. Rieke. *The Rhetoric of Black Americans*. Columbus, Ohio: Charles E. Merrill, 1971.

Goldman, Peter. *The Death and Life of Malcolm X*. Urbana: University of Illinois Press, 1979.

_____. "Malcolm X: Witness for the Prosecution." In *Black Leaders of the Twentieth Century*, edited by John Hope Franklin and August Meier, 305–30. Urbana: University of Illinois Press, 1982.

Gopal, Krishan. *Non-Alignment and Power Politics: A Documentary Survey*. New Delhi: V.I. Publications, 1983.

Gregg, Richard B. "The Ego-Function of the Rhetoric of Protest." *Philosophy & Rhetoric* 4 (1971): 71–91.

Gresson, Aaron D. "Minority Epistemology and the Rhetoric of Creation." *Philosophy & Rhetoric* 10 (1977): 244–62.

Gresson, Aaron David III. *The Dialectics of Betrayal: Sacrifice, Violation, and the Oppressed*. Norwood, NJ: Ablex, 1982.

Hall, Raymond. *Black Separatism in the United States*. Hanover, N.H.: University Press of New England, 1978.

Harding, Vincent. *There Is a River: The Black Struggle for Freedom in America*. New York: Vintage Books, 1983.

Hariman, Robert. "Decorum." In *Encyclopedia of Rhetoric*, edited by Thomas O. Sloane, 199–209. Oxford: Oxford University Press, 2001.

_____. "Prudence/Performance." *Rhetoric Society Quarterly* 21 (1991): 26–35.

_____, ed. *Prudence: Classical Virtue, Postmodern Practice*. University Park: Pennsylvania State University Press, 2003.

Hariman, Robert, and Francis A. Beer. "What Would Be Prudent? Forms of Reasoning in World Politics." *Rhetoric & Public Affairs* 1 (1998): 299–330.

Heath, Robert L. "Dialectical Confrontation: A Strategy of Black Radicalism," *Central States Speech Journal* 24 (1973): 168–77.

Henderson, Mae, ed. *Borders, Boundaries, and Frames: Cultural Criticism and Cultural Studies*. New York: Routledge, 1995.

Hinks, Peter B. *To Awaken My Afflicted Brethren: David Walker and the Problem of Antebellum Slave Resistance*. University Park: Pennsylvania State University Press, 1997.

hooks, bell. "marginality as a site of resistance." In *Out There: Marginalization and Contemporary Culture*, edited by Russell Ferguson, Martha Gever, Trinh T. Minh-ha, and Cornel West, 341–43. New York: New Museum of Contemporary Art, 1990.

Howard-Pitney, David. *The Afro-American Jeremiad: Appeals for Justice in America*. Philadelphia: Temple University Press, 1990.

Hutcheon, Linda. *Irony's Edge: The Theory and Politics of Irony*. New York: Routledge, 1994.

Hyde, Lewis. *Trickster Makes This World: Mischief, Myth, and Art*. New York: North Point Press, 1998.

Illo, John. "The Rhetoric of Malcolm X." *Columbia University Forum* 9 (1966): 5–12.

Jamal, Hakim A. *From the Dead Level: Malcolm X and Me*. New York: Random House, 1971.

Jasinski, James. *Sourcebook on Rhetoric*. Thousand Oaks, Calif.: Sage, 2001.

Kahn, Victoria. *Rhetoric, Prudence, and Skepticism in the Renaissance*. Ithaca, N.Y.: Cornell University Press, 1985.

Karim, Benjamin. *Remembering Malcolm*. New York: Carroll and Graf, 1992.

———, ed. *The End of White World Supremacy: Four Speeches by Malcolm X*. New York: Little, Brown, 1971.

Lacy, Leslie A. *The Rise and Fall of a Proper Negro: An Autobiography*. New York: Macmillan, 1970.

Lake, Randall A. "Between Myth and History: Enacting Time in Native American Protest Rhetoric." *Quarterly Journal of Speech* 77 (1991): 123–51.

———. "Enacting Red Power: The Consummatory Function in Native American Protest Rhetoric," *Quarterly Journal of Speech* 69 (1983): 127–42.

Láng, László. *Bandung, Thirty Years Later: Proceedings of the Commemoration of the Thirtieth Anniversary of the Bandung Conference*. Budapest: Hungarian Peace, 1985.

Lanham, Richard A. *The Electronic Word: Democracy, Technology, and the Arts*. Chicago: University of Chicago Press, 1993.

_____. *A Handlist of Rhetorical Terms*. Berkeley: University of California Press, 1991.

Lee, Martha F. *The Nation of Islam: An American Millenarian Movement*. Lewiston, N.Y.: Edwin Mellen, 1988.

Lee, Spike, and Ralph Wiley. *By Any Means Necessary: The Trials and Tribulations of the Making of* Malcolm X. New York: Hyperion, 1992.

Leeman, Richard W., ed. *African-American Orators: A Bio-Critical Sourcebook*. Westport, Conn.: Greenwood Press, 1996.

LeFevre, Karen B. *Invention as a Social Act*. Carbondale: Southern Illinois University Press, 1987.

Leff, Michael. "Cicero's *Pro Murena* and the Strong Case for Rhetoric." *Rhetoric & Public Affairs* 1 (1998): 61–88.

_____. "Decorum and Rhetorical Interpretation: The Latin Humanistic Tradition and Contemporary Critical Theory." *Vichiana, 3a serie* (1990): 107–26.

_____. "The Idea of Rhetoric as Interpretive Practice: A Humanist's Response to Gaonkar." In *Rhetorical Hermeneutics: Invention and Interpretation in the Age of Science*, edited by Alan G. Gross and William M. Keith, 89–100. Albany: State University of New York Press, 1997.

_____. "Rhetorical Timing in Lincoln's 'House Divided' Speech." Van Zelst Lecture in Communication. Evanston, Ill.: Northwestern University School of Speech, 1983.

_____. "Things Made by Words: Reflections on Textual Criticism." *Quarterly Journal of Speech* 78 (1992): 223–31.

Leroux, Neil. "Frederick Douglass and the Attention Shift." *Rhetoric Society Quarterly* 21 (1991): 36–46.

Levine, Lawrence W. *Black Culture and Black Consciousness: Afro-American Folk Thought from Slavery to Freedom*. New York: Oxford University Press, 1977.

Lewis, David Levering. *W. E. B. Du Bois, Biography of a Race*. New York: Henry Holt, 1993.

Lincoln, C. Eric. *The Black Muslims in America*. 3rd ed. Grand Rapids, Mich.: William B. Eerdmans, 1994.

Lomax, Louis E. *When the Word Is Given: A Report on Elijah Muhammad, Malcolm X, and the Black Muslim World*. New York: Signet Books, 1964.

Lucaites, John Louis, and Celeste Michelle Condit. "Reconstructing Equality: Culturetypal and Counter-Cultural Rhetorics in the Martyred Black Vision." *Communication Monographs* 57 (1990): 5–24.

Lundquist, Suzanne Evertsen. *The Trickster: A Transformation Archetype*. San Francisco: Mellen Research University Press, 1991.

Lyotard, Jean-François. *The Postmodern Condition: A Report on Knowledge*. Translated by Geoff Bennington and Brian Massumi. Minneapolis: University of Minnesota Press, 1984.

Maglangbayan, Shawna. *Garvey, Lumumba and Malcolm: National-Separatists*. Chicago: Third World Press, 1972.

Malcolm X. *Two Speeches by Malcolm X*. New York: Pathfinder Press, 1965.

Malcolm X and Alex Haley. *The Autobiography of Malcolm X*. New York: Grove Press, 1965.

Marable, Manning. *Through the Prism of Race and Class: Modern Black Nationalism in the U.S.* Dayton, Ohio: Black Research Associates, 1980.

———. *W. E. B. Du Bois: Black Radical Democrat*. Boston: Twayne, 1986.

McFeely, William S. *Frederick Douglass*. New York: W. W. Norton, 1991.

McGee, Michael C. "In Search of 'The People': A Rhetorical Alternative." *Quarterly Journal of Speech* 61 (1975): 235–49.

———. "Text, Context, and the Fragmentation of Contemporary Culture." *Western Journal of Speech Communication* 54 (1990): 274–89.

Melucci, Alberto. *Nomads of the Present: Social Movements and Individual Needs in Contemporary Society*. Philadelphia: Temple University Press, 1989.

Miller, Perry. *Errand into the Wilderness*. Cambridge: Harvard University Press, 1984.

Mohrmann, G. P., Charles J. Stewart, and Donovan J. Ochs, eds. *Explorations in Rhetorical Criticism*. University Park: Pennsylvania State University Press, 1973.

Moses, Wilson Jeremiah. *Black Messiahs and Uncle Toms: Social and Literary Manipulations of a Religious Myth*. University Park: Pennsylvania State University Press, 1982.

———. *The Golden Age of Black Nationalism, 1850–1925*. Hamden, Conn.: Archon Books, 1978.

Muhammad, Elijah. *Message to the Blackman in America*. Chicago: Muhammad's Temple No. 2, 1965.

Munir, Fareed Z. "Islam in America: An African American Pilgrimage toward Coherence." Ph.D. diss., Temple University, 1993.

Norman, Barbara Ann. "The Black Muslims: A Rhetorical Analysis." Ph.D. diss., University of Oklahoma, 1985.

Oates, Stephen B. *The Fires of Jubilee: Nat Turner's Fierce Rebellion*. New York: Harper and Row, 1975.

O'Leary, Stephen D. *Arguing the Apocalypse: A Theory of Millennial Rhetoric*. Oxford: Oxford University Press, 1994.

_____. "A Dramatistic Theory of Apocalyptic Rhetoric." *Quarterly Journal of Speech* 79 (1993): 385–426.

Ono, Kent A., and John Sloop. "Commitment to *Telos*—A Sustained Critical Rhetoric." *Communication Monographs* 59 (1992): 48–60.

Pauley, Garth E. "John Lewis's 'Serious Revolution': Rhetoric, Resistance, and Revision at the March on Washington." *Quarterly Journal of Speech* 84 (1998): 320–40.

Perry, Bruce. *Malcolm: A Life of the Man Who Changed Black America*. Barrytown, N.Y.: Station Hill Press, 1990.

_____, ed. *Malcolm X: The Last Speeches*. New York: Pathfinder Press, 1989.

Potter, David. *The Impending Crisis: 1848–1861*. New York: Harper and Row, 1976.

Poulakos, John. *Sophistical Rhetoric in Classical Greece*. Columbia: University of South Carolina Press, 1995.

_____. "Toward a Sophistic Definition of Rhetoric." *Philosophy and Rhetoric* 16 (1983): 35–48.

Rampersad, Arnold. *The Art and Imagination of W. E. B. Du Bois*. Cambridge: Harvard University Press, 1976.

Redkey, Edwin S. *Black Exodus: Black Nationalist and Back-to-Africa Movements, 1890–1910*. New Haven, Conn.: Yale University Press, 1969.

_____, ed. *Respect Black: The Writings and Speeches of Henry McNeal Turner*. New York: Arno Press, 1971.

Rein, Irving J. *The Relevant Rhetoric: Principles of Public Speaking through Case Studies*. Chicago: Free Press, 1969.

Rosteck, Thomas, and Michael Leff. "Piety, Propriety, and Perspective: An Interpretation and Application of Key Terms in Kenneth Burke's *Permanence and Change*." *Western Journal of Speech Communication* 53 (1989): 327–41.

Sales, William W. *From Civil Rights to Black Liberation: Malcolm X and the Organization of Afro-American Unity*. Boston: South End Press, 1994.

Schiappa, Edward. *The Beginnings of Rhetorical Theory in Classical Greece*. New Haven, Conn.: Yale University Press, 1999.

Scott, Robert L. "The Conservative Voice in Radical Rhetoric: A Common Response to Division." *Communication Monographs* 40 (1973): 123–35.

_____. "Justifying Violence—The Rhetoric of Militant Black Power." *Central States Speech Journal* 19 (1968): 96–104.

_____. "On Viewing Rhetoric as Epistemic." *Central States Speech Journal* 18 (1967): 9–17.

Simons, Herbert W., and Trevor Melia, eds. *The Legacy of Kenneth Burke*. Madison: University of Wisconsin Press, 1989.

Singham, A. W., and Shirley Hune. *Non-Alignment in an Age of Alignments.* Westport, Conn.: Lawrence Hill, 1986.

Skinner, Elliot P. *African Americans and U.S. Policy toward Africa, 1850–1924: In Defense of Black Nationality.* Washington, D.C.: Howard University Press, 1992.

Smith, Arthur L. (Molefi Asante). *Rhetoric of Black Revolution.* Boston: Allyn and Bacon, 1969.

Smith, Arthur L. (Molefi Asante), and Stephen Robb, eds. *The Voice of Black Rhetoric: Selections.* Boston: Allyn and Bacon, 1971.

Stephens, Gregory. *On Racial Frontiers: The New Culture of Frederick Douglass, Ralph Ellison, and Bob Marley.* Cambridge: Cambridge University Press, 1999.

Sundquist, Eric J., ed. *The Oxford W. E. B. Du Bois Reader.* New York: Oxford University Press, 1996.

Todorov, Tzvetan. *Theories of the Symbol.* Translated by Catherine Porter. Ithaca, N.Y.: Cornell University Press, 1982.

Travers, Len. *Celebrating the Fourth: Independence Day and the Rites of Nationalism in the Early Republic.* Amherst: University of Massachusetts Press, 1997.

Turner, Nat. *The Confessions of Nat Turner.* Edited by Kenneth S. Greenburg. Boston: Bedford Books, 1996.

Turner, Victor. *Dramas, Fields, and Metaphors; Symbolic Action in Human Society.* Ithaca, N.Y.: Cornell University Press, 1974.

———. *From Ritual to Theatre: The Human Seriousness of Play.* New York: Performing Arts Journal Publications, 1982.

Umoja, Akinyele O. "The Ballot and the Bullet." *Journal of Black Studies* 29 (1999): 558–79.

Walker, David. *David Walker's Appeal, in Four Articles; Together with a Preamble, to the Coloured Citizens of the World, but in Particular, and Very Expressly, to Those of the United States of America.* Revised by Sean Wilentz. New York: Hill and Wang, 1995.

Walzer, Michael. *Exodus and Revolution.* New York: Basic Books, 1985.

Ware, B. L., and Wil A. Linkugel. "The Rhetorical *Persona:* Marcus Garvey as Black Moses." *Communication Monographs* 49 (1982): 50–62.

Washington, Booker T. "Cotton States Exposition Address." In *Three Centuries of American Rhetorical Discourse: An Anthology and a Review,* edited by Ronald F. Reid, 521–25. Prospect Heights, Ill.: Waveland Press, 1988.

Washington, James M., ed. *I Have a Dream: Writings and Speeches That Changed the World.* San Francisco: Harper SanFrancisco, 1992.

Watson, Elwood. "Marcus Garvey's Garveyism: Message from a Forefather." *Journal of Religious Thought* 51 (1995): 77–94.

Watson, Walter. "Invention." In *Encyclopedia of Rhetoric*, edited by Thomas O. Sloane, 389–404. Oxford: Oxford University Press, 2001.

West, Cornel. *Race Matters*. New York: Vintage Books, 1994.

White, John. *Black Leadership in America: From Booker T. Washington to Jesse Jackson*. 3rd ed. New York: Longman, 1990.

Wilson, Kirt H. "Towards a Discursive Theory of Racial Identity: *The Souls of Black Folk* as a Response to Nineteenth-Century Biological Determinism." *Western Journal of Communication* 63 (1999): 193–215.

Wintz, Cary D., ed. *African American Political Thought, 1890–1930: Washington, Du Bois, Garvey, and Randolph*. Armonk, N.Y.: M. E. Sharpe, 1996.

Wojcik, Daniel. *The End of the World As We Know it: Faith, Fatalism, and Apocalypse in America*. New York: New York University Press, 1997.

Wolfenstein, Eugene Victor. *The Victims of Democracy: Malcolm X and the Black Revolution*. New York: Guilford, 1993.

Wood, Joe, ed. *Malcolm X: In Our Own Image*. New York: Anchor Books, 1992.

Zulick, Margaret D. "The Agon of Jeremiah: On the Dialogic Invention of Prophetic Ethos." *Quarterly Journal of Speech* 78 (1992): 125–48.

Index

Michigan State University Press is committed to preserving ancient forests and natural resources. We have elected to print this title on 55# Roland Enviro, which is 100% recycled (100% post-consumer waste) and processed chlorine free. As a result of our paper choice, Michigan State University Press has saved the following natural resources*:

18	Trees (40 feet in height)
7,605	Gallons of Water
3,059	Kilowatt-hours of Electricity
1,647	Pounds of Air Pollution
838	Pounds of Solid Waste

Both Michigan State University Press and our printer, Thomson-Shore, Inc., are members of the Green Press Initiative—a nonprofit program dedicated to supporting book publishers, authors, and suppliers in maximizing their use of fiber that is not sourced from ancient or endangered forests. For more information about the Green Press Initiative and the use of recycled paper in book publishing, please visit *www.greenpressinitiative.org.*

* Environmental benefits were calculated based on research provided by Conservatree and Californians Against Waste.